Raising Our Children to Be Resilient

A Guide to Helping Children
Cope with Trauma in Today's World

LINDA GOLDMAN

 Brunner-Routledge
Taylor & Francis Group

NEW YORK AND HOVE

Anecdotes that appear throughout this book contain names and particular incidents that have been modified to maintain privacy. The children, teens, adults, animals, and places in the photographs may not necessarily relate to the material on the page on which they appear.

Published in 2005 by
Brunner-Routledge
270 Madison Avenue
New York, NY 10016
www.brunner-routledge.com

Published in Great Britain by
Brunner-Routledge
27 Church Road
Hove, East Sussex
BN3 2FA
www.brunner-routledge.co.uk

10 9 8 7 6 5 4 3 2 1

Library of Congress Cataloging-in-Publication Data

Goldman, Linda, 1946–
    Raising our children to be resilient: a guide to helping children cope with trauma in today's world / Linda Goldman.
        p. cm.
    Includes bibliographical references and index.
    ISBN 0-415-94906-8 (pbk. : alk. paper)
    1. Post-traumatic stress disorder in children—Treatment.   2. Traumatic grief in children—Treatment.   3. Stress in children—Treatment.   4. Bullying in schools—Prevention.
5. School violence—Prevention.   6. School children—Mental health services. 7. Counseling in elementary education.   8. Resilience (Personality trait) in children.   9. Adjustment (Psychology) in children.
    [DNLM: 1. Stress Disorders, Post-Traumatic--prevention & control—Child.
2. Adaptation, Psychological—Child. 3. Counseling. 4. Grief—Child. 5. Violence.
 WS 350 G619r 2004]   I. Title.

RJ502.P55G654 2004
618.92'8521--dc22

                                                                                    2004011603

Raising Our Children to Be Resilient

This book is dedicated to my dad, Jerry.

He taught me by example the power of positive thinking,

the satisfaction of accomplishing a goal,

and the joy of a loving heart.

(Painting by Jon Goldman, his grandson)

Table of Contents

Foreword xvii
Acknowledgments xix
Introduction xxi

PART I
Grief and Trauma: The Impact on Children

C H A P T E R   1

Children Living in a Complex World 3
Grief, Trauma, and Their Many Complications 5
  Grief Defined 5
Children's Developmental Understandings of Death 6
  Pre-Operational Stage (Usually 2 to 7) 6
  Concrete Operations Stage (Usually 7 to 12) 7
  Prepositional Operations, Implications, and Logic Stage
    (Age 13 and Older) 8
The Nature of Children's Grief 8
  Children's Connection with the Deceased 9
  Children and Magical Thinking 10
Children's Losses 10
Common Signs of Grieving Children 11
Trauma, Terrorism, and Fear 12
  The Nature of Trauma 13
Traumatic Loss 14
Signs of Trauma in Children 15
The Vulnerability of Children 17
  Predictors of Vulnerability 18
Conclusion: Research Supports Early Intervention 22

C H A P T E R   2

*Traumatic Events in a Complex World: Terrorism, War, SARS, Random
  Violence, and More* 25
Talking to Children About Complex Events 27
  Understanding Children's Reactions to Trauma 27
  Clarifying Young Children's Misconceptions: Terrorism and 9/11 27

Sharing Feelings: SARS, A Contagious Disease 29
Responding to Traumatized Children 30
   Creating Words to Use 30
   Establishing Dialogue 32
   Preparing Children for Dialogue 34
   Accepting Children's Reactions 35
   Asking Children Questions 36
   Children and Anticipatory Grief 37
Re-triggering the Trauma 38
   Re-triggering Trauma Through Media Exposure 39
   Re-triggering Trauma Through Daily Events .40
Children's Voices 41
   The Voices of Young Children 41
   Middle School Voices 42
   Teenage Voices 44
   Ways to Help Children During Trauma 45
Reassuring Children 45
Dialoging About Everyday Risks 46
Monitoring Media 46
Becoming Role Models 47
Conclusion 48

C H A P T E R   3

Bullying and Victimization: A Deadly Disease and Invisible Killer **49**

Bullying, Victimization, and Unresolved Grief in Children 51
   Adult Modeling 51
   Facts About Bullies and Victims 52
Taking Action Against Bullying 54
   Bullying, Power, and Control 54
   Kids and Popularity 55
   Adult Involvement 55
Bullying in Our Schools 56
Special Issues for Girls 57
   A Journal About Bullying: Margaret's Story .58
Victims' Voices 62
Bullys' Voices 63
Onlookers' Voices 63
Adults' Voices 64
Ways to Help Children with Bullying 64
   Define Bullying 65
Bullying Behaviors 66
Adult Guidelines 67
   Listen Carefully and Document 68

Create Strong Guidelines 68
Create Harassment and Violence Policies for Schools 69
Emphasize and Model Democratic Values 69
Teach Positive Conflict Resolution Ideas and Skills 69
Emphasize the Power of the Onlooker 70
Strategies for Helping Bullies 71
Ways Kids Can Help Themselves 76
Interventions for Victims, Bullies, and Onlookers 77
Adult Strategies for Bullying 82
Conclusion 83
Resources 84
Resources for Students on Bullying 84
Bullying Curriculums for Educators .85
Resources for Adults on Bullying 85

C H A P T E R   4

School Violence: No Place to Feel Safe .87

School Shootings: Bullying and Hidden Rage 89
Friends Knew and Didn't Tell 89
Adults Knew and Didn't Help 90
Bullying and Victimization: Youth Violence 90
Warning Signs of Violence in Children 91
Projective Techniques for Anger Management 92
Children, Teens, and Guns 93
Children Witnessing School Violence 94
The Effect of Witnessing Trauma on Development 95
Random Acts of Violence: A School Shooting 96
Teachable Moments 97
Class Meeting: Grade 2 98
Model for Class Meeting Surrounding Trauma 99
An Eighth-Grade Boys' Guidance Group: Reaction to Violence 104
Gangs and School Violence: A Special Issue 105
What Makes a Gang Attractive? 106
Diminishing Gang Power 106
Signs of Gang Membership 107
Why Join a Gang? 107
Tookie's Story 108
Preventing School Shootings: A Summary of the U.S. Secret Service
    Safe Schools Initiative Report, 2002 109
Findings of the Report 109
Recommendations in the Report 110
Conclusion 111
Resources 112
For Educators on School Violence 112
For Children and Teens on School Violence 113
On Gang Violence 113

PART II
Working With Kids and Trauma: Home, School, Community

CHAPTER 5

Trauma Resolution Techniques: Helping Our Kids Succeed 117

Children Feeling Safe in Today's World .119
Activities That Help Kids Tell and Retell Their Story 119
   Children Tell Stories Through Drawing 120
   Teens Tell Their Stories 121
   Projective Play 121
   Post-Traumatic Play 123
   Puppets, Music, and Dream Work .124
   Memory Work 125
   Memory Boxes 126
   Telling the Story 127
   Drawing Pictures 129
   Repetitive Thoughts, Jittery Feelings, Fears, and Scary Places 130
   Writing Letters 136
   Poetry and Creative Writing 137
Activities That Help Kids Feel Safe 137
Suggestions for Kids To Help Themselves 141
Help Children Deal with Trauma 145
Conclusion 145
Resources for Children on Trauma 146

CHAPTER 6

School Systems Respond to Crisis 149

Children and War 151
The School Responds 151
   Children's Voices About War 151
   Classroom Discussions 154
Deployment and Loss 156
   A School System Accommodates Deployment 156
Prejudice, Racism, and Power 158
   Class Discussions: a Lesson on Wisdom 159
   Helping Each Other During Trauma 160
Peer Mentors 161
Peer Groups 162
Studying Past Cultures and Trauma 163
Video Conferencing 164
Resources 164
   For Educators 164
   For Children on War, Prejudice, and History 165

PART III
Coming Together to Create Change

CHAPTER 7

Parenting Through a Crisis, Preparing for the Future 169

Providing a Strong Foundation 171
Children Are Survivors of Traumatic Events 171
Establish a Sense of Order 171
Establish Family Activities 172
Initiate Safe Places to Express Feelings 174
Reinforce Values 175
Maintain a Sense of Humor 176
Give Comfort: Hugs and Food 177
Practice Mature Modeling 177
Monitor Television 178
Discuss Daily Risks 179
Create Teachable Moments 180
Prepare a Family Disaster Plan 181
Stress to Children That They Are Survivors 182
Patriotism in a Global Community 183
Parents As Mentors 184
Parenting Immigrant Children 185
Involve Children in Solutions 185
Emphasize the Enormous Outreach 187
Conclusion 187
Resources 188
For Children 188
For Adults 188

CHAPTER 8

Educators at Work: Meeting the Challenge of Traumatic Events 189

School Involvement with Trauma 191
Responding to 9/11: a Student Grieves 191
The Impact of Images 192
Daily Counseling Sessions 192
Sharing Feelings 192
Finding Out the Facts 193
Parent Involvement 194
Memory Work 195
School Systems Cope with Trauma 196
A Wall of Thoughts 196
Class Discussions on Bravery, Honor, Prejudice, and War 197
Poster Contest 198

Fundraising 199
School Activities for Helping and Healing 202
   Homework Assignments: Emergency Planning 202
   Personal Tributes 202
   Student Involvement 202
   School Book Ventures 203
   Memorial Projects 204
Schools Provide Child Trauma Information to Community 205
   Suggestions to Help Traumatized Students 206
   School Systems and Emergency Planning 207
   Research on Student and Teacher Reactions to 9/11 208
   Research Conclusions 209
At-Risk Children 210
   Identifying Children at Risk 211
Conclusion: The Responsibility of Educators 213
Resources 214
   For Children on 9/11 214
   For Educators 214

CHAPTER 9

Community Action: From Fear to Freedom *215*
Responsibility of a Community-Based Outreach Program 217
Tragedy Assistance Program for the Military 219
   Children's Outreach 219
   Grief Support Camp 219
   Honor Guards As Mentors 220
   Peer Mentors 221
   Memory Activities 222
   The Umbrella Project 223
   Balloon Release 225
   Children's Voices: Letters to TAPS 225
   Family Community Outreach 229
Activities To Help Children Participate in World Events 231
Archiving Children's Artifacts After 9/11 234
Resources for Adults About Community Tragedy 237

CHAPTER 10

Enhancing Resiliency in Children *239*
What Is Resilience? 241
Resilience and Youth 241
Adults As Models 243
Keys to Resilient Children 243
   Choice 244
   Optimism 245
   Courage 245

Realistic Goals 245
Humor 246
Self-Confidence 246
Appreciation of Self 247
Acceptance and Comfort 249
Processing Life Through Productive Action 249
Creativity 251
Spirituality 252
Service 254
Making a Difference: Mara's Story 256
Optimism 256
Perseverance 256
Parent Modeling 257
Insightfulness 257
Empathy 259
Sociability 259
Community Support 259
Models Promoting Resilience 261
Model Empathy 261
Offer Appreciation and Encouragement 261
Become an Advocate 262
Enhance Flexibility and Learning from Past Experience 263
Promote Self-Discipline 263
Support Opportunities to Become Responsible 263
Offer Inspiring Resources 264
Create Generational Family Role Models 265
Activities to Promote Resiliency 266
Signs of a Resilient Child 269
Conclusion 271
Resources 274
For Children on Resiliency 274

PART IV
Resources and Information

C H A P T E R   1 1

Oases of Safety: National Resources That Help 277
Organizations 278
For Grief and Trauma 278
For Children's Issues 279
For Disaster 280
For Schools 280
For Parenting 281
For Mentoring 281
For Resilience 282

For the Military 282
For Trauma and Violent Death 282
For Gangs 283
For Suicide 284
Support Groups 285
Hotlines 286
Crisis Lines 286
Internet Resources 287
On Death and Trauma for Children and Teens 287
On Education 288
On Bullying 288
On Gangs 288
On Resilience 288
On Grief 289
On Service 289
Book Services 289

C H A P T E R 1 2

Topics, Trends, and Timely Information: Annotated Bibliography 291

Resources for Adults 292
On Trauma 292
On Death and Dying 293
On Suicide 295
On Homicide and Violent Death 296
On Bullying 297
On Aggression 297
On Resilience 297
On Education 298
On Parenting 299
On Counseling and Therapy 299
On Philosophy 300
CD-ROMS 301
Curricula 301
On Bullying 301
On Violence 302
On Suicide 302
On Therapeutic Techniques 302
On Divorce 303
On Death and Crisis in the Schools 303
On Peace in the Classroom 303
On Anger and Stress Management 304
On Resilience 304
Guides for Grief Support Groups 304
Videos 305
Tapes 306
Resources for Children and Teens 307
On Death for Children 307

On Death for Teens 308
On Trauma 309
On a Parent Dying 309
On Hospice 309
On the Death of a Parent 310
On Sibling Death 311
On a Friend's Death 312
On the Death of a Grandparent 313
On Pet Death 313
On Cremation 313
On Funerals and Memorial Services 314
Workbooks About Death 315
On Life Cycles and Spirituality 315
On Depressed Parents 316
On Suicide 316
On Violence and Murder 317
On Bullying 318
On War 319
On 9/11 319
On the Holocaust 319
On Drugs 320
On Media Input 320
On Prejudice 320
On Weight Disorders and Eating Problems 321
On Foster Homes and Abandonment 321
On Homelessness 321
On Sexual Abuse 322
On Sexual Issues 322
On Violence in the Home 323
On Gangs 323
On Immigration 324
On Moving 324
On Divorce 324
On Natural Disaster 325
On Magical Thinking 325
On Feelings 326
On Perfectionism 327
On Stress 327
On Nightmares 327
On Family 328
On Resilience 328
On Service 328
On Affirmations and Meditations 329
On Empowerment 329
On Hope and Optimism 330
On Peace 330
References 331
About the Author 337
Index 339

Foreword

Robert Kastenbaum (1972) in an influential essay in *Saturday Review of Literature* once described childhood as a "Kingdom Where Nobody Dies." Kastenbaum's thesis was that adults attempt to protect children from death and other difficulties. We perceive the child's world as one of innocence, enchantment, and safety. Kastenbaum, of course, notes how naïve this perspective is. Children have always experienced the specter of death. It is evident in their fairy tales, stories, songs, and even prayers. Classic children's stories such as *Bambi* or *The Lion King* warn that even strong parents are mortal and that loss can be both sudden and devastating. Remember how each night we would pray, "If I die before I wake . . . "

Yet we still try to protect children from loss and death. We still pretend that these most human experiences have some sort of "R" rating—one that shelters children from them. This perspective is not only foolish; it is dangerous. It leaves children to face these experiences alone. It leaves adults unready to prepare, educate, and support children as they face loss and difficulty.

This is one of the great strengths of Linda Goldman's work. She fully appreciates Kastenbaum's lesson that there is no such "kingdom where nobody dies." Goldman recognizes that children live in a scary world. She understands that children daily face small terrors, whether it is the corrosive nature of gossip or rumor or the aggressive behaviors of bullies. Goldman empathizes with their loss experiences such as the death of friends or family members or other losses such as divorce or separation. She recognizes that even children are affected by the presence of terrorism and the increased sense of vulnerability that is now part of our world.

More than that, Goldman offers tools to help empower children. Her book is a collage of activities for parents, educators, mental health professionals and other caring adults. She presents more than theory. Goldman offers solid, tangible exercises to do for and with children. These positive, proactive activities prepare children.

For example, she suggests that families prepare a "disaster plan." A protective approach would suggest that this might trouble children, introducing ideas that would merely serve to frighten the child. In fact, most children are well aware of the potential for disaster. They have heard these ideas discussed in school, seen them on the news, perhaps even viewed them in movies. A plan offers a tangible way to cope with these fears. It allows discussion. It empowers children with knowledge. It can be hoped that the plan will never be implemented, but the mere existence of the plan opens dialogue and reinforces the concept that both they and their families can deal with even disaster.

A number of years ago, I was preparing to edit a book entitled *Living with Grief: Children, Adolescents and Loss* (2000). One of the things I wanted was to ensure that the book included the voices of children. My godson, then 14 years of age, had faced the death of his father the day before his fourth birthday. I asked his mother if she would mind if I approached Keith about writing a brief piece on the book. She gave permission freely. She was, however, skeptical. "He was so young," his mother noted. "What could he possibly remember from the experience," she wondered.

Keith's piece was amazing. In an essay entitled "I never knew my father," he talked about that early loss. He noted that barely a day went by in which he did not think of his dad. He struggled with his own fragmentary memories of his dad's illness and death. Happily, the essay opened a healing dialogue between mother and son and a shared appreciation of their collective loss. As she reviewed the experience, Keith's mother said to me, "I suspect that I never took that loss as seriously as I ought."

That is the greatest gift of Linda Goldman's work. It takes the losses of children seriously. It acknowledges that their world can sometimes be scary, even terrifying. Most important, it offers tools, techniques, activities, and advice so that parents, teachers, mental health professionals and other caring adults can build resilience in children so that they can adapt to that scary world.

Kenneth J. Doka, Ph.D.
Professor, The College of New Rochelle
Senior Consultant, The Hospice Foundation of America

Acknowledgments

To my husband Michael and my son Jon, who have given me their love, patience, advice, editing, and important computer expertise, and become my treasured support system.

To Greg N., Jacqueline Martin-Hutman, Carol Feikin, and Molly Sheehan for their beloved friendship.

To Carol Connor for her consistent guidance, wisdom, and love.

My deepest thanks go to the following participants who offered time, resources, personal disclosure, information, and editing to help make this book possible.

To Sandra Burt (author of *Parents as Mentors*), Linda Goldstein Loewinger, (pediatrician), and Judy Madden (supervisor of guidance, Montgomery County, Maryland) for their invaluable editing and wise input.

To Bonnie Carroll, Dan Druen, Brian Bauman, Joyce Harvey, and Judith Mathewson for sharing the story and photos of TAPS and their important work with grieving children involved with the military.

To the family of Joseph Oliver Reed III in loving memory of their husband and father.

To Jaime Brinkman and Michelle Brown, past students and innovative educators, for sharing their sensitive work in schools during public tragedy.

To Montgomery County Schools for creating models of how school systems remain flexible and caring during a public tragedy.

To Carla Sofka and Craig Williams, New York State Museum, for their work in saving and restoring children's artifacts from 9/11.

To Reverend Honeygam for caring about children and sharing their voices about the terrorist attack.

To Stanley Tookie Williams, Barbara Cottman Becknell, and Michael Evans for their dedication to educate children about gangs.

To Mara Mattis and her family for their courage in sharing their beloved Chris's death and for their resilience in living with this personal tragedy.

To Matte and Jeni Stephanik for their courage and inspiration during difficult times.

To Glenon Butler and Dana Ward Bliss for their superior editing and supervision of this project.

And to all of the resilient children and adults who shared their photographs, drawings, and writings to help others.

Introduction

Terrorism, Trauma, and Children: What Can We Do?

Although many children may appear unaffected by their outer world, more and more of our children are showing signs of stress. It is the goal of *Raising Our Children to Be Resilient* to provide effective ways for adults to safely help our youth transform fear, sadness, worry, and anger into stronger emotional, intellectual, and spiritual growth and development. This book is a guide to develop in our youth expanded minds to work in new ways with the complexities of the human condition in which they are living.

Children can not only survive; they can thrive by enlarging their capacity for empathy, understanding, and resilience after a trauma. "Trauma exposure refers to the degree to which an individual experiences, witnesses, or is confronted with actual or threatened death or serious injury to self or others" (Pfefferbaum et al., p. 9). Children and adults experience this exposure daily throughout our planet. This exposure demands of parents, educators, mental health professionals, and other caring adults the creation of new ways of processing these challenging events.

Today's youth are dealing with many issues that were not spoken of in the past. These issues include death-related tragedies involving suicide, homicide, and disease. Other challenges in their environment include safety concerns involving war, terrorism, and social traumas such as extreme bullying and victimization, rampant divorce and separation, foster care and abandonment, violence and abuse, drugs and alcohol, sexuality and gender issues. Too many children are left unsuccessfully trying to deal with their trauma, and becoming increasingly overwhelmed with feelings and distracted by thoughts.

As our children struggled with these complicated factors, September 11 heightened their fears with the new paradigm of terrorism, war, and biological and nuclear threat. The adult world that children look to for security and comfort has become a world of fear, panic, and jitteriness. Our girls and boys had too many questions with no clear-cut answers about their future. Our task was, and is, to re-instill safety, comfort, and hope for the future.

On September 11, 2001, our young people, either directly or vicariously, witnessed the terrorist assault upon our nation. They watched over and over again as fanatics crashed American planes into the World Trade Centers, the Pentagon, and the fields of Pennsylvania. They witnessed adults running frantically out of control, jumping helplessly out of windows, screaming, crying, and bewildered. Through black smoke-filled skies and burning buildings an insidious and hidden enemy emerged to wreak pandemonium and panic on their lives. The media that acted as a surrogate parent and extended family *before* this horrific event, shared visually, auditorally, and viscerally with our children *during* this event sounds and images that were so graphic that they will be forever imprinted on our children's and on our psyches.

Worldwide terrorism and pockets of warring factions throughout the globe either impact our girls and boys directly or beseech them indirectly through television and other mass media, presenting proof throughout the day that this world is not a safe place. Their internal structures at school and home threaten as unprotected environments with bullying at school, drugs, alcohol, and sexuality in the community, and too often violence or apathy in their homes.

Identifying factors of trauma are many and varied. Sometimes children and teens avoid any reminders of the disaster and show little observable conscious interest. They may also reexperience the event through play reenactment, nightmares, flashbacks, and disturbing thoughts and feelings. *Raising Our Children to Be Resilient* informs the reader of the indicators of trauma in order to identify, normalize, and intervene for those young people exhibiting signs of stress.

Although there is much sadness to see, we can, if we look more closely, recognize much that is encouraging and positive. Properly focused, these observations can give us clues to stimulate new attitudes and strengths in our children and help them create a conceptual shift before, during, and after these unavoidable traumas. After witnessing public violence, children may feel anxious and distracted. This guide provides information and techniques of reassurance that adults are working hard to keep them safe and reinforces that much of what they are feeling is normal under these circumstances. Following a tragedy, young people can be encouraged to contribute and feel a part of a community team. By becoming proactive and involved they can create goals and make choices that strengthen their development as well as help others. Dialogues, interventions, and broadened understandings are presented throughout these chapters to allow girls and boys to express thoughts and feelings and create constructive communication and optimistic outlooks.

Too often parents and professionals try to "fix" problems and situations that really have not been broken. Taking reactions to hard life issues as personality deficits rather than focusing on supporting resilient attributes has often impeded progress in working through complex situations. Our ultimate responsibility is to enhance young people's ability to cope with and overcome adversity during dramatically challenging times. By identifying and encouraging resilient qualities in our children we *can* make a positive difference.

Raising Our Children to Be Resilient shares the vision of creating responsible human beings that have the inner strength not just to make it through an uncomfortable event, but also to have the capacity for transforming themselves and their world during difficult times. Our challenge is to recognize and understand the new situations and stresses our children are facing and then come together as a community to protect, support, and nurture them as future world citizens.

PART I

Grief and Trauma:
The Impact on Children

CHAPTER 1
Children Living In a Complex World

TRAUMA • TERRORISM • CHILDREN'S GRIEF • FEAR
DEVELOPMENTAL UNDERSTANDINGS • MAGICAL
THINKING • TRAUMA REACTIONS • CHILDREN'S
VULNERABILITY • STRATEGIES • RESEARCH

From the moment of birth every human being wants happiness and wants to avoid suffering. In this we are all the same.

The Dalai Lama

Grief, Trauma, and Their Many Complications

We often ask ourselves "What can we do to help our children in today's world?" It becomes clear our mission is to provide a sense of safety, protection, hope and optimism amidst adversity. We have created a very complex world for children, often leaving them with its fear, its confusion, and its uncertainty. Our youth live in a world that broadcasts sniper attacks, terrorists' threats, violent school shootings, sexuality, war, and gun-related issues as quickly as it takes to click the remote on their TVs or touch the mouse on their computers. The possibility of war, the risk of violence, the danger of biological harm, and the threat of nuclear destruction have become all too common. Our goal is to hold the vision for our children that they will not only make it through difficult times, but can actually become stronger and more resilient.

GRIEF DEFINED

Grief is not just about death. "Grief is defined as a normal, internalized reaction to the loss of a person, thing, or idea. It is our emotional response to loss" (Goldman 2000, Life and Loss, p. 25). Childhood losses range from the death of a loved one to divorce or abandonment; loss in the environment due to moving or change in family structure; loss of self-esteem from physical, emotional or sexual abuse, neglect or deprivation; or family separation from Dad being sent to military service or Mom being imprisoned.

Children often have secondary losses during a grief experience that may include the loss of their daily routine, the loss of skills and abilities in school and other activities, the loss of the protection of the adult world, and the loss of their perceived future. Everything that existed in the past and present and had been hoped for in the future may suddenly and dramatically have been changed. If not directly, then vicariously, most of our children have experienced many of these losses through an intimate media view of traumatic public events.

Grief work can be messy, and children can be inundated with waves of feelings when they least expect them. Listening to a song on the radio, talking to a friend, or reading a story can evoke sudden thoughts and feelings that may engulf the grieving child. These "grief bullets" can result in a sudden release of tears, anxiety, regression, or withdrawal, with many children unable or unwilling to express their experience.

Children's Developmental Understandings of Death

Children's understanding of death changes as they develop, as explained by Piaget's cognitive stages of development (Ginsberg and Opper, 1969). Gaining insight into children's developmental stages allows predictability and knowledge of age-appropriate responses.

PRE-OPERATIONAL STAGE (USUALLY 2 TO 7)

At this stage, the child conceptualizes death with magical thinking, egocentricity, reversibility, and causality.

Young children developmentally live in an *egocentric* world, filled with the notion that they have caused and are responsible for everything. Children's *magical thinking* causes them to feel their words and thoughts can magically cause an event. Five-year-old Sam screamed at his older brother, "I hate you and I wish you were dead!" He was haunted with the idea that his words created his brother's murder the following day. Sam's egocentric perception sees him at the center of the universe, capable of creating and destroying the world around him at will.

Alice, at age four, displayed her egocentricity when she relayed to me that she killed her mother. When I asked how she did that she responded, "My mom picked me up on the night she had her heart attack. If she hadn't picked me up she wouldn't have died, so I killed her." She felt she was the central cause of the death. Talking about the medical facts of how Mom died—her heart condition, smoking, and failure to take proper medicine—helped reduce the common mindset of a young child that she magically caused the death to happen.

Angela, a six-year-old first grader, was very sad after her dad died in a plane crash. She age-appropriately perceived death as reversible and told her friends and family her dad was coming back. She even wrote him a letter and waited patiently for the mailman to bring back a response. Angela's mom explained to her the following definition of death for young children: "Death is when a person's body stops working. Usually someone dies when they are very, very old, or very, very, very sick, or their bodies are so injured that the doctors and nurses can't make their bodies work again" (Goldman, 2000).

CONCRETE OPERATIONS STAGE (USUALLY 7 TO 12)

During this stage the child is very curious about the concept of death, and he or she seeks realistic new information.

Ten-year-old Mary wanted to know everything about her mother's death. She said she had heard so many stories about her mom's fatal car crash and she wanted to look up the story in the newspaper to find out the facts. Eleven-year-old Margaret wondered about her friend who got killed in a sudden plane crash: "What was she thinking before the crash, was she scared, and did she suffer?" Tom age-appropriately wondered if there was an afterlife and exactly where his dad was.

At this stage of development kids commonly express logical thoughts and fears about death, can conceptualize that all body functions stop, and begin to internalize the universality and permanence of death. They may ponder the facts about how the terrorists got the plane to crash, wanting to know every detail. When working with this age group, it is important to ask, "What are the facts you would like to know?" and help to find answers through family, friends, media, and experts.

PREPOSITIONAL OPERATIONS, IMPLICATIONS, AND LOGIC STAGE (AGE 13 AND OLDER)

This stage is usually characterized by the adolescent's concept of death.

Many are self-absorbed at this age, seeing mortality and death as a natural process that is very remote from their day-to-day life and something they can't control. Teens are often absorbed with shaping their own lives and denying the possibility of their own deaths.

Sixteen-year-old Malcolm expressed the following age-appropriate thoughts when he proclaimed, "I won't let those terrorists control my life. I'll visit the mall in Washington, D.C. whenever I want. They can't hurt me!" One of the best techniques for adolescents is peer support and discussion groups, because they are much more comfortable at this age talking with peers about death and trauma than with adults. Many teen survivors of trauma feel comforted and free to share their thoughts when they are placed in support groups only for other teens who are survivors of similar experiences. Their fear of judgement is reduced and self disclosure increased with a connecting bond to others with comparable experiences to similar events.

The Nature of Children's Grief

The bereaved child reconstructs the person who died through an ongoing cognitive process of establishing memories, feelings, and actions connected to the child's development level. This inner representation leads to a continuing bond to the loved one, creating a relationship that changes as the child matures and his or her grief lessens. Silverman, Nickman, and Worden (1992) maintain in their research article, "Detachment Revisited: The Child's Reconstruction of a Dead Parent," that it is normal for children "to maintain a presence and connection with the deceased and that this presence is not static" (p. 495). They provide the following categories of connection with a loved one.

CHILDREN'S CONNECTION WITH THE DECEASED

- Making an effort to locate the deceased
- Actually experiencing the deceased in some way
- Reaching out to initiate a connection
- Remembering
- Keeping something that belonged to the deceased.

Roger was 14 years old when he experienced the death of his dad in the World Trade Center. Grief stricken and angry, he suffered over the shocking death of a parent he loved so much. He longed to know exactly what happened to his father, and found the concept of not knowing all the facts and having no remains of his dad extremely difficult. As time went by, Roger realized he needed to visit ground zero and be where the tragedy occurred. He traveled alone and spent an hour there, feeling for the first time that he was in some way with his dad again. As he went to leave, Roger noticed a guitar pick in the rubble. It reminded him of one his dad used to play his own guitar. He picked it up, wiped it off, and placed it in his wallet, as a sacred keepsake he felt was a message from his dad. Roger said it was the first time he felt at peace after the terrorist attack. He needed to go to the place where his dad died, feel his presence, remember precious times, and discover a cherished keepsake.

Identifying connections to loved ones enables children to normalize their patterns of grief and reduce anxiety about experiencing them. Parents, educators, and mental health professionals working with the grieving child "may need to focus on how to transform connections and place the relationship in a new perspective, rather than on how to separate from the deceased" (Silverman, Nickman, & Worden, 1992, p. 503).

CHILDREN AND MAGICAL THINKING

Young children employ magical thinking during traumatic events. Their world is usually one filled with egocentricity, causality, and the magical notion that they have created or are responsible for everything that happens around them. Five-year-old Andrew's dad was in the World Trade Center when the plane hit. He managed to survive, but lost his place of work and was greatly distressed. Andrew asked his mom, "What did I do that was so bad that the terrorists had to smash his building? Did I do anything wrong? What did we do to make them so angry?"

Seven-year-old Sally confessed, "It's my fault my mom got killed in the World Trade Center. She hated her job and I should have made her quit." Children believe that they somehow caused the problem, whether it is the death of a goldfish or an assault on the United States. Adults can reassure them that there was nothing they could have done to cause or prevent terrorism. Terrorism is an act of violence and should be punished. People are not allowed to do this to other people. There is a law against this kind of violence. Some kids may also feel survival guilt. "Why am I living when so many others have died?" Adults can reframe guilt and magical thinking from "What could I have done?" to "What can I do now?"

Children's Losses

Children processing their grief and trauma may not necessarily progress in a linear way through typical grief phases. The four tasks of grief are: "understanding, grieving, commemorating, and going on" (Goldman, 2000, p. 21; Fox, 1988). These tasks may surface and resurface in varying order, intensity, and duration. Grief and trauma reactions can unsuspectingly hit with "grief and trauma bullets" while listening to the news, seeing or hearing an airplane overhead, or watching the video of the New York devastation or the Pentagon crash. A fireman's siren, a jet fighter, a soldier in uniform, a postal letter, or a balloon bursting can trigger sudden intense feelings without any warning, and often without any conscious connection to their trauma and loss.

Tom, a middle-school student, explained his recent loss of skills and abilities to his teacher, "I can't do my homework, and I just want to feel secure. I keep thinking it doesn't matter anyway." Amy, an eighth grader, also had difficulty with homework. "I can't concentrate anymore. I just keep seeing the airplane hit the World Trade Centers." Perhaps a caring teacher could have Tom and Amy write about their feelings as a classroom or homework activity. The guidance counselor could begin a support group for kids affected by the terrorist attack, because children this age respond well to sharing with peers.

Common Signs of Grieving Children

Learning to recognize the signs of grieving children is essential to normalizing their experience of grief and trauma. Children may experience the following physical, emotional, cognitive, and behavioral symptoms common in the grieving process.

- Child continually re-tells events about his or her loved one's life and death
- Child feels the loved one is present and speaks of him or her in the present tense
- Child dreams about loved one and longs to be with him or her
- Child experiences nightmares and sleeplessness
- Child cannot concentrate on schoolwork
- Child appears at times to feel nothing
- Child is preoccupied with death and worried excessively about health issues
- Child is afraid to be left alone
- Child often cries at unexpected times
- Child wets the bed or loses appetite
- Child idealizes loved one and assumes his or her mannerisms
- Child becomes "class bully" or "class clown"

- Child has headaches and stomach aches
- Child rejects old friends, withdraws or acts out (Goldman, 2000)

Young children may be clingy, regress, and bed-wet or suck their thumbs. Teenagers may become involved with drugs, alcohol, sexuality, or crime, and show a disinterest in school.

Trauma, Terrorism, and Fear

Children living in the United States and many other nations witnessed an event so horrific and unconscionable on September 11, 2001, that the world they knew and their perception of this world have been forever changed. The visual impact of terrorists crashing planes into the World Trade Center, the Pentagon, and the fields of Pennsylvania will live on in the hearts and minds of today's young people. The media served as eyes and ears for the world as it witnessed and relayed to our children the horror that was unfolding. Our kids watched graphic images of people falling from windows, buildings bursting with flames, and mounds of rubble replacing human beings and treasured places. They worried who was next and whether it could be them.

Today's children are living with fear, and caring adults must develop new paradigms of working with terrorism, trauma, war, and threats of mass destruction. The children of the twenty-first century have been faced with extraordinary life issues that were hidden or ignored in earlier times. These issues range from death-related tragedies involving suicide, homicide, and AIDS, to life traumas such as bullying and victimization, divorce and separation, foster care and abandonment, violence and abuse, and gender issues and sexuality. For many of our children the unprecedented tragedy of September 11 acts as a traumatic overlay for all of the preexisting life issues they faced before that tragic day.

Adults may wonder if the vivid images of September 11 will disappear as time passes or if they will remain somewhere for children to revisit. They may question whether children can forget this horrific event and move forward. Somewhere the trauma has been stored, and access or availability is possible. Amplified by the continuing threat of war, biological destruction, and nuclear annihilation, our children are now living in a world that didn't exist for them before. This world is filled with new fears, new worries, new questions, and few resolutions. In the adult world that our children looked toward for security and comfort, they now see or sense a world of fear, panic, and anxiety, with too many questions and too few answers about their future.

THE NATURE OF TRAUMA

Exposure to trauma refers to the extent a child reacts to the experiencing, witnessing, or confronting of actual or life-threatening events. One of those reactions is fear. Children living with this fear is a concept that has strongly emerged since the terrorist attacks of September 11, 2001. Childhood's ordinary fears are a normal part of developmental growth, and children create internal and external mechanisms to cope. Moms and dads can soothe nightmares and fears of the dark with saying "everything will be alright."

The assault on the United States has transformed ordinary childhood fear into very real survival fear as a natural consequence of a dangerous real-life event. This real survival fear is based on an actual life experience that is not imagined or misinterpreted, but is displayed over and over again for them by the media, and on the worry and uncertainty of the adult's around them. Adults and children agonizingly wondered if everything would be all right again.

These extraordinary circumstances affect today's children by bombarding them with input that creates panic, stress, and extreme anxiety. These feelings of danger are heightened and retriggered as the media reminds them daily of new threats and concerns in our nation and the world. Our children's instinctual reaction to past and present terrifying and ongoing circumstances is tension, fear, and uncertainty about real physical or psychological trauma and real threats of impending loss.

Traumatic Loss

When speaking of children experiencing a traumatic death, it is important to recognize the factors that can create complications. "Although virtually any death may be perceived by the mourner as personally traumatic because of the internal subjective feeling involved . . . circumstances that are objectively traumatic are associated with five factors known to increase complications for mourners" (Webb, 2002, p. 368). These factors that may increase complications for the grief process include suddenness and lack of anticipation, violence, mutilation and destruction, multiple deaths, and the child's personal encounter such as a threat or shocking confrontation.

Children who had a loved one die because of a violent public death such as terrorism, natural disaster, war, or rampage shootings could well fit into all of these categories. This sudden, public, brutal devastation presents concrete reasons for the traumatic expression of grief and mourning. Children affected by public tragedy have witnessed directly people killed in indescribable ways, and often this is relentlessly repeated by the media for them to review over and over again. They become concerned with the impending threat of more violence and the huge losses that have occurred in their lives.

One little girl had faced multiple losses before the September tragedy. She lived with her mom before the attack in a single-parent home since her parents' divorce. She had experienced the loss of her family unit, her family home, and the loss of her day-to-day routine prior to her mom's death. Mom was killed while working at the World Trade Center. Within one week this little girl experienced multiple new losses because of her mom's sudden, traumatic, and publicized death, and her immediate move to New Jersey to live with her dad. These tragedies compounded her previous grief over divorce and moving. In the blink of an eye, she lost her home, her friends, her school, her neighborhood, and her daily routine with Mom forever.

Traumatized kids feel:

- **POWERLESS**: to change what happens to them.
- **HOPELESS**: to see a future. They feel that things will never be the same.
- **HELPLESS**: to stop their feelings. They can't seem to stop the bad, sad, and scary feelings. (Sheppard, 1998)

Signs of Trauma in Children

Children usually respond to a traumatic event with common identifying factors such as reexperiencing the event through play reenactment, nightmares, recurring waking memories, and disturbing thoughts and feelings. Some children may exhibit posttraumatic play by compulsively repeating some aspect of the trauma.

After the death of his Aunt Joan in the World Trade Center, five-year-old Tommy continually created the Twin Towers with blocks, and then knocked them down. Young children often use play as a grief therapy technique to reenact a situation. Ten-year-old Alice's mom died in the Pentagon crash. She repeatedly blames herself. Her mom had felt sick that morning: "If only I made her stay home she still would be alive."

Children may magically believe they are capable of recognizing warning signs to predict a future trauma. Jane imagines that if she can only stay hyper-alert, listening through the night for airplanes in the sky, she can prevent another terrorist trauma from happening at her house.

Traumatized children may feel unable to change the event, unable to stop the scary and sad feelings, and unable to see that life can be different. Sometimes kids avoid reminders of the traumatic event and show little conscious interest. Many withdraw and isolate themselves or become anxious and fearful. Traumatized boys and girls may exhibit hyperarousal, extreme sensitivity, and reactivity to stimuli. This manifests in increased sleep problems, irritability, inability to concentrate, startle reactions, and regressive behaviors.

Traumatized kids often:

1. Reexperience the traumatic event through play reenactment, nightmares, flashbacks, and disturbing thoughts and feelings about the event

2. Sometimes avoid any reminders of the disaster, showing little conscious interest

3. Exhibit generalized fears that manifest through stranger or separation anxiety, avoidance of situations that may or may not appear to be related to the trauma, sleep disturbances, and preoccupation with words or symbols that may be directly or indirectly related to the trauma

An Everyday Trauma

Susie was terrorized while on a walk with her dad when a dog suddenly attacked her. She had twenty-seven stitches on her face and several operations after the incident. Her dad asked for some guidance, saying he was flooded with feelings about the dog and its owner but that Susie appeared fine and didn't even talk about what happened. Asking Dad if the family had a dog, he explained they had no dog but had just gotten a kitten for Susie. "What did Susie name the kitten?" I asked. Dad responded, "Stitches."

Traumatized children often have difficulty putting their behaviors into any context of safety as the harsh and overwhelming feelings engulf them when they least expect it. Many withdraw and isolate themselves, regress and appear anxious, distance themselves from the incident, or create sleep and eating disorders as a mask for their deep interpretations of their trauma. *Children often respond to a traumatic event with fear, terror, and extreme vulnerability.*

Children's Trauma Reactions

- Trauma can create distorted perceptions of self in children: "I know I'm ugly now."

- Trauma creates guilt: "It's my fault my mom died. I should have made her stay home that day."

- Trauma reactions may override grief responses. Fear may override sadness; "I'm so sad my mom died in the fire. But I'm too scared to cry."

- Trauma creates nightmares of dying or being hurt: "Last night I dreamed I was in a car crash. I was so frightened."

- Trauma usually creates the overriding feeling of terror: "I can't concentrate on homework. I worry a plane will crash into my house. I'm afraid I'll die."

- Trauma commonly produces angry, sometimes combative reactions: "If I ever found the guy that murdered my brother, I'd kill him!!!!"

Adults can use their understanding of these reactions to identify traumatized children and teens and normalize their feelings of vulnerability. Developing avenues of expression and modeling behaviors provides comfort and support. Reading books such as *Brave Bart* initiates discussion about trauma for young children. Creating support groups for teens experiencing trauma provides meaningful age-appropriate peer support. Using concrete measures such as installing a family alarm system, talking to police about neighborhood protection, and creating conversations about daily risk can all be helpful in bringing feelings of security and protection back into their lives.

The Vulnerability of Children

In considering children's reactions to public tragedy such as terrorist assaults, predictors of their vulnerability help in our understanding of their experience of shock, pain, and terror, and they speed our abilities to help. Physical proximity to the disaster, psychological proximity to the disaster, and age are significant indicators of vulnerability in children (Rosenfeld, 2001). Which children will experience the greatest impact relates to their direct experience of the trauma and their previous life circumstances and history of loss and trauma.

PREDICTORS OF VULNERABILITY

Physical Proximity to the Disaster

Children are most vulnerable to a trauma if they are victims and have direct exposure to the trauma (Rosenfeld, 2001). The second level of vulnerability is the proximity of those children that almost were victims and still were witnesses. The next levels of vulnerability are those children who were within hearing or sight of the event but did not witness it. The least level of vulnerability includes those children outside of the disaster area, although they may still witness the event through newspapers and television.

Ten-year-old Willy's uncle died in the World Trade Center. Willy was at a school nearby at the time of the event. Willy doesn't sleep well and when he does he has nightmares. Willy sleeps on the floor because he says that way "he will be ready if the terrorists come." Dwayne also goes to school near the Twin Towers in New York. His picture about September 11 includes the warning, "Run for your life."

Psychological Proximity to the Disaster

Social vulnerability is highest in those girls and boys who were close to the victims, such as family members; is next highest in those who knew victims socially but were not close; and then in those who can identify with the victims but didn't know them. Age will affect their reactions and their perceptions of trauma and death. Alice is a first grader who went to school near the Twin Towers and heard the sounds and smelled the smells of their destruction. Her friend's mom was killed that day. Soon after September 11 she attended a birthday party. When a balloon burst she ran out of the room screaming, "The terrorists are coming, the terrorists are coming."

Responses Related with Children's Age

Children's response reactions may appear directly after the trauma or may not appear until several weeks or months later. Persistence of responses is an indicator that outside help may be needed.

Young Children (Birth to 5)

Young children may regress and become clingy. "The extent to which the family is disrupted—which includes the degree to which the parents are anxious or excessively distraught—is a good predictor of how upset the child will be" (Rosenfeld, 2001, p. 3). If their routines are disrupted, and the adults around them are distraught, their lack of cognitive understanding forces them to integrate the cues in their environment. The adults around them may be so absorbed with their own trauma responses that they are not available for the child.

Young children may also cry, regress, thumb suck, bed wet, and have sleep disturbances as their response to a traumatic event. Some appear hypervigilant, and stay up all night protecting the family. Others have excessive startle reactions, and appear aggressive or sad. Still others reenact the event over and over again. Five-year-old Susie was terrified by the events of September 11. She knew some "bad people had killed lots of Americans." She cried every time she left her mom and wanted to sleep in her mom's bed at night. Six months later her play in kindergarten showed she was still frightened. She played that the terrorists were coming and she hid under her rest mat.

Older Children (6 to 11)

In this age group, children have a more realistic concept of what is happening in the world around them. Eight-year-old Sam asked his teacher, "Can the terrorists come to our school?" Ten-year-old Nancy wanted to know "what we did wrong to make the terrorists destroy so many people and buildings." Children at this level experience anxiety and fear as they realize there is real danger and they could possibly be hurt. Nightmares, fear of the dark, physical symptoms of headaches and stomachaches, or a desire to stay home may manifest. Darlene was in third grade in a Virginia school close to the Pentagon and heard the crash. She begged her mom to let her stay home from school and sleep in her mom's bed at night. She was afraid the terrorists were coming to her home next.

Teenagers (12 to 19)

Preadolescents and adolescents may withdraw, bully, or resort to drugs and violence as a reaction to a trauma around them. Teens often have a sense of bravado and a feeling that nothing can harm them. Their world may suddenly feel unpredictable and unsafe, and they may become anxious, angry, or depressed as a reaction.

Fifteen-year-old Carlos said he didn't care about the terrorist attack. He wasn't afraid. He got a gun for protection and carried it wherever he went. He also had a typical teen reaction; he began to drink alcohol, experiment with drugs, and show a disinterest in schoolwork.

The article "Assessment of Posttraumatic Symptoms in Children: Development and Preliminary Validation of Parent and Child Scales" (Greenwald & Rubin, 1999) presents the following common symptoms of posttraumatic stress disorder for children between the ages of eight and thirteen. The researchers warn that a few of the symptoms may be common for many children, but the presence of many of them in a child can be an indicator of a more serious problem.

- Difficulty concentrating
- Mood swings
- Involvment in trouble
- Worry
- Fearfulness
- Bad memories
- Spacing out
- Feelings of guilt
- Withdrawal
- Anxiety
- Strong startle response

- Irritability
- Repetitive acts
- Nightmares
- Fights
- Irrational fears
- Secretivness
- Clinging to adults
- Hyperalertness
- Lethargy
- Avoidance of former interests
- Headaches
- Sadness or depression
- Stomachaches
- Argumentativeness
- Difficulty sleeping
- Bossiness
- Feeling picked on

Previous Life Circumstances

The last predictor of children's vulnerability may be their experience of previous traumas. An event like September 11 is likely to retrigger and cause the child to reexperience stress-related feelings and thoughts. If Tony's dad was killed in a plane crash or Josh's dad murdered as a soldier by terrorists in Iraq, they may feel extremely vulnerable after September 11. Suzanne's mom was killed in a car crash. Watching images of the demolished plane and destroyed Twin Towers brought screams of horror from her as she realized again, "That's what my mom went through."

Conclusion: Research Supports Early Intervention

Certain mental health outcomes are more likely to evolve for the grieving child in the absence of intervention. Research suggests (Lutzke, Ayers, Sandler, & Barr, 1997) that bereaved children may show more depression, withdrawal, and anxiety than nonbereaved children. Bereaved children developmentally show lower self-esteem and less hope of the future than nonbereaved children. Vedantam (2004) revealed that the number of depressed American children being treated with antidepressants has soared over the past decade from threefold to tenfold, with the "spike in prescriptions over the past five years especially sharp among children younger than 6" (p. 1). Adults who were bereaved children tend to exhibit higher degrees of suicide ideation, and depression, and are more at risk for panic disorders and anxiety. Support for bereaved children is essential in helping to reduce negative outcomes from grief left unresolved or unexplored during childhood. Research findings suggest that although trauma associated with death-related situations can not always predict later symptom formation, therapeutic intervention at the time of the trauma may help to reduce or extinguish future anxiety that would be more likely to escalate without intervention.

A key debilitating factor creating ongoing trauma for grieving children often is a sense of loss of control in their lives. Early interventions through counseling and grief support groups can help boys and girls regain their sense of control and reduce the stress and anxiety that is so often associated with the death of a loved one. An extensive FBI report, "Preventing School Shootings: A Summary of U.S. Secret Service Safety School Initiative" (2002), stresses "the importance of giving attention to students who are having difficulty coping with major losses . . . particularly when feelings of desperation and hopelessness are involved" (p. 14).

Early interventions may provide another factor for supporting children in their grief: a meaningful relationship with at least one caring adult. This relationship can involve a teacher, a counselor, a coach, or the school nurse. Research indicates that children with strong social supports have a reduced presence of suicidal ideation (Rigby and Slee, 1999). The report suggests that an important aspect in prevention may be in providing adult support and encouraging young people to talk and connect with caring adults.

Many children will show signs of stress during difficult times. Some may have a hard time concentrating or doing their homework. Others may feel sick, scared, worried, or depressed. Still others may become hyperactive, want to act out in a revengeful way, or choose not to talk at all. Awareness of the common signs of stress in young people and implementation of appropriate interventions are initial steps in helping them cope with and participate in their complex new world.

C H A P T E R   2

Traumatic Events in a Complex World: Terrorism, War, SARS, Random Violence, and More

SNIPERS • SARS • ANTHRAX • TERRORISM
U.N. RESOLUTIONS • IRAQ • WAR • SPACE SHUTTLE
DISASTER • MILITARY • DRUGS • PATRIOTISM
HOMELAND SECURITY • RETRIBUTION • REVENGE
SURVIVORS • VICTIMS • AFGHANISTAN

Once you know that catastrophe dwells next door and can strike anyone at any time, you interpret reality differently.

Ronnie Janoff-Bulman

Talking to Children About Complex Events

One question weighing heavily on the minds of parents, educators, and mental health professionals is "How do we talk to our children about war, terrorism, conflict, biochemical attack, and nuclear destruction?" Our kids seem to know the world events that have become a new piece of their everyday existence. Girls and boys are plagued by questions. "Is anthrax in my mail?" "Was the plane destroyed by terrorists?" "What is smallpox?" "When is the next attack?" "Will I catch SARS on the plane?" and "Should I eat a hamburger?" One four-year-old asked his mom "What is a *swiper*?" after the sniper rampage in Washington, D.C.

UNDERSTANDING CHILDREN'S REACTIONS TO TRAUMA

Many young people, who usually like to draw and write, seem reluctant to do so after a trauma. They appear shy and explain that this is too hard to do or that they are not ready. Young children may not process information they see or hear accurately. We can ask, "What do you think happened?" and "How are you feeling now?" Then we can clarify any misinterpretations and ask them to repeat their understandings to be sure they are correct.

CLARIFYING YOUNG CHILDREN'S MISCONCEPTIONS: TERRORISM AND 9/11

It is important when dialoging with children to correct any misconceptions children may have perceived through their own magical thinking or incorrect processing from other children, adults, or the media. By questioning them about what they think the facts of the event are, we can gain a clearer understanding of their perceptions. Then, by asking them how they feel, we can begin to allow them to process their experience. Some children may want to talk; others find expression through writing or drawing.

Six-year-old Andrew thought the terrorists destroyed hundreds of buildings because he saw repeated broadcasts of videotapes of the planes crashing into the towers and thought every viewing was a new attack. Jose, a five-year-old living in El Salvador, began to cry to his grandmother as they talked on the telephone. After watching the plane crash on TV, he explained to her. "Grandma you live in New York. Now that the plane crashed I'll never be able to come and visit America!" He thought the plane he saw blow up was the only plane to take people to the United States. Grandmother explained that there are many more planes that go to America.

Still another pre-schooler, Carlos, was asked to draw a picture about the World Trade Center attack and responded, "I just can't. The towers are too big to draw. They are just too big." He may have taken literally, as so many young children do, the instruction to draw the towers in their actual size and become overwhelmed with such an impossible task.

Perhaps Carlos was innocently voicing the sentiments of our country and our world, shocked into realizing their own vulnerability and not yet able to process the scope of these national events. Normally, children can easily draw airplanes and buildings, but to many, this event is too big to draw, too big to understand.

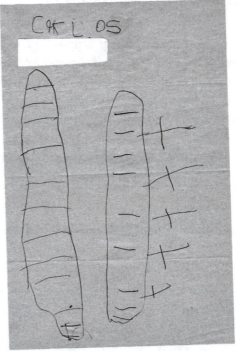

"I can't draw it. The towers are too big!" Age 4

Sharing Feelings: SARS, A Contagious Disease

Children throughout the world knew about a disease called SARS that people could catch like a cold and that could make them very sick or die. They heard they could get it on an airplane or from a person coming back from another country. Asian children were warned to wear masks. The universal fear of contagious disease spread into the lives of children throughout the planet as this new invisible threat emerged.

One twelve-year-old in China, Liuxinyu, presents an intimate view of her life and exposure to the virus. The following drawing depicts a child's life in China, with pedestrians and drivers masked, while huge germs loom overhead, making the clouds and sky very sad. Her picture allows her to share her life with SARS and her perceptions of those around working hard to live life with the disease looming overhead.

Six-year-old Jennifer lives in Beijing, and she and her friends worried about catching SARS. She shares the following drawing and explains, "The people are sad about SARS." By expressing the sadness of the people about SARS, she allows herself to release some of her own sadness about living with fear of the disease.

Responding to Traumatized Children

The complexities of working with children and trauma lead us to not only learn the signs of traumatized children, but also to develop ways to respond to their reactions. Creating words to use, appropriate definitions, and age-appropriate dialogue are useful tools for listening and responding.

CREATING WORDS TO USE

Sometimes it may help to ask children if they have been thinking about world events and if they are open to a dialogue. Some children don't want to talk about it. Some live in fear that they will be killed, and others say there is nothing to worry about. Some may want to know the facts, and for this we sometimes need to create words to use in these dialogues. Because so many of us feel "it's just too big," we need to be able to discuss each piece of this huge experience, a little at a time. To create discussions we need to provide appropriate language and meanings. The following are suggestions for definitions helpful for explaining these difficult concepts to children.

Children's Definitions About Traumatic Events in Today's World

Anthrax is a disease that usually only cattle or sheep can get. Scientists can change it into a different form that can make people sick and use it as a weapon. Most of the time medicines can cure anthrax in people. Using anthrax as a weapon is called *biological warfare*.

Biological Warfare is a conflict that spreads germs that can cause people to become sick or die.

A Bomb is an exploding device that can harm people and property.

A Criminal is a person who has committed a crime, like stealing something or murdering someone.

Deployment is calling troops in the army, navy, or marines to active military service if they are needed throughout the world.

Homeland is a word for one's own country.

Integrity is a characteristic of honesty that people have when we feel they can be trusted and keep their word.

A Nuclear Bomb is an explosive device that uses radioactive material.

Nuclear War is a conflict that uses atomic bombs to injure or destroy an enemy.

Patriotism is showing acts of love, honor, and bravery for your country. We can show patriotism for our country by waving a flag, singing the national anthem, joining the army, or helping others.

Revenge is a feeling of wanting to do something back to someone who has hurt you or someone you care about.

SARS stands for Severe Acute Respiratory Syndrome. It is a respiratory virus that can make people very sick and in some cases cause death.

Security means helping to keep us feeling safe and protected.

A Sniper is someone who shoots a gun randomly at people and scares, hurts, or kills them.

Terror is intense, overpowering fear.

Terrorism is an act or acts of violence, abuse, murder, or devastation against unsuspecting people and countries by a person or group of people who believe their cause is more important than human life or property. Their feeling of "being right" is more important to them (sometimes) than their own life. Terrorists can be big or small, black, white, or any color, American or foreign. Their goal is to create terror, disruption, and vulnerability.

Trauma is an experience that can be scary and difficult. It may create feelings of fear, anger, rage, and revenge. A trauma can be the death of someone close to us, caused by a car accident or a terrorist bombing. It can also be from knowing something that happened scary that we saw on TV, or to someone we know, or even to a stranger we see on a news video.

War is a state of armed conflict between people and countries where a struggle or attack has occurred. Soldiers fight with guns, missiles, and other weapons.

ESTABLISHING DIALOGUE

When creating dialogues with children, it is important to use accurate, real, and age-appropriate language, avoiding clichés or denial of their experience. Concentrate on giving the facts, keeping responses to questions simple and age appropriate. This helps adults follow the lead of children as to how much information they choose to take in. Especially with young children, ask them what they think happened, clarify the facts, and avoid overwhelming them with too much information.

Keeping explanations developmentally appropriate allows children to process this experience at their own level. Young elementary school children need simple information balanced with reassurance that trustworthy adults are bringing stability to their day-to-day life. Middle-school children may seek out more facts and want to know more about what is being done to keep them safe and healthy at home, at school, and in the community. High school students may more strongly voice opinions about what happened and why, and need to develop ways to combat terrorism, rationalize war, and prevent world annihilation.

Tell Children the Truth

Telling the truth, age appropriately, is very important for children. They often have a conscious or unconscious knowledge of events happening around them and can sense the impact of a trauma on the adult world. One mom relayed an experience in the car with her four-year-old son, Andy. Mom shared that she was "sneaking" a listen of the news on the day of the terrorist attack. As the reporter began talking about the destruction of the World Trade Center, she quickly turned it off so Andy couldn't hear. Andy immediately responded, indicating his level of awareness, "Mommy, they are talking about the plane crash that blew up buildings today."

He just knew about it. If Andy were then told his experience wasn't real, he might begin to doubt himself and/or the adult world and question their truthfulness. If Andy felt his mom was hiding the truth about what happened, he might worry more because something was so bad that mom was too afraid to tell him. Either way, Andy might experience another loss: the loss of the trust of his adult world. Teachable moments for all children can evolve with teachers and parents on subjects such as bullying, violence, prejudice, sexual discrimination, and conflict resolution.

Express Feelings Honestly

Let children know you are upset and worried too. It's often hard for them to reconcile messages of "Don't worry, everything is fine" with the enormity of anxiety they may feel coming from their adult world. Find out what they may know about the traumatic event, remembering that they may process what they see and hear inaccurately. Search for faulty perceptions and replace them with simple truths. Young children usually worry about their immediate environment, their family and friends and pets, and their ongoing day-to-day routine. The following page features a sample dialogue to use with children ages five to ten.

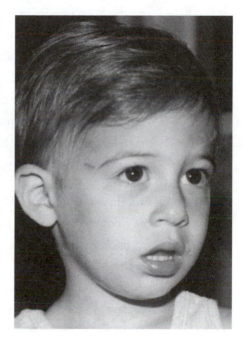

Sometimes when we watch violence on TV we can get scared. Watching the terrorists' acts, war, or violence on TV can be very scary. Some kids said they are afraid to go to sleep and have nightmares. They aren't hungry. They have stomachaches, and they can't concentrate on schoolwork. Children may say they don't want to talk about what they see or hear. Others may cry or just want to stay with their moms and dads. Kids may worry about safety for themselves and their family, and have fears about going to school, riding the bus, or going on an airplane.

Others are very angry. They don't like that their country was hurt and the people in it. They want to yell or scream or have some revenge to get back at the terrorists or even people that may look like the terrorists. All of these feelings are common after witnessing such awful violence and destruction. We need to think of ways of working with our anger that won't hurt ourselves or other people.

PREPARING CHILDREN FOR DIALOGUE

Children will see the imagery associated with disaster, if not at their own house or school, then at a neighbor's or friend's house. Prepare them for this by talking about the disaster, keeping in mind their age and level of awareness of the world around them. The images that they see later may retrigger their initial fears and children may experience their original reactions once again.

Sometimes we can ask kids what they think happened and begin to see if they are processing the event accurately. Children may choose to talk, write, or draw their interpretation of the disaster. Kiana is a seven-year-old child who attended a New York elementary school near the Twin Towers. The following is her response to that traumatic event. She shares her initial reaction to the event and tells what happened for her through writing and drawing.

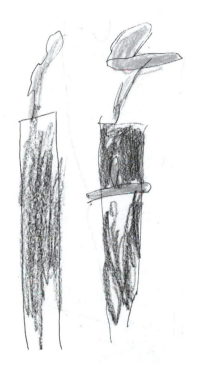

The World Trade Center

On September 11, 2002 I felt sad because the two airplanes crashed into 2 sky scrapers. The World Trade tower fell down and there was smoke all over New York City. My two aunties almost got killed by the tower. Many Fire fighters were trying to save people but they were killed by pieces of the tower. I am very unhappy and upset because Osama Bin Laden sent his soldiers to destroy the tower. I pray that all people will be safe from Osama Bun Loden.

By Kiana ̣̣̣ ̣ ̣ ̣

Age 7

January 19, 2002

ACCEPTING CHILDREN'S REACTIONS

Although there are several commonly seen reactions to trauma in children, these reactions range widely. Some children will listen to your explanation and then go out to play. Others will want to stay near you and talk about it for a length of time, or maybe ask you to drive them to school instead of taking the bus. Still others may be angry that adults can't immediately fix the problem. Reinforce to children that lots of other children feel the same way they do, and that whatever their thoughts and feelings are, they are OK.

Adults must watch for symptoms of heightened anxiety. This may include stomachaches, nightmares, and difficulty in carrying on the regular routine. This can happen to people of all ages, but children need special attention to help them through it. Secondary reactions may emerge, such as fear of riding on a plane or visiting downtown Washington, D.C. or New York City or going on the school bus. Parents, teachers, and therapists can anticipate these reactions and listening carefully to children and watch for signs of stress. Simple interventions such as allowing children to list worries and fears or make a safe and peaceful "feel good" box containing pictures, toys, and objects can help reduce some of their concerns.

Sometimes we need to help young children to find out the facts about a trauma, since they often misinterpret what they see and hear. After a dramatic traumatic event, many young children may think it is happening repeatedly as they watch replays on TV over and over again.

ASKING CHILDREN QUESTIONS

"What do you think happened?"

Young children use magical thinking for survival guilt and self-blame. We can ask them the following:

"Is there something you feel sorry for?

Is there some you think you did wrong? What could you have done?"

Children react very differently from each other when they are processing a tragedy, and that is okay. Reassure children that there is no "right" or "wrong" reaction. Kids can be encouraged to talk about their feelings, tell their story over and over again, or write or draw about how they feel.

Darian, a first grader, shared his feelings about September 11 with his teacher. "I saw the plane crash on TV into the big buildings. I saw all the people running and screaming and lots of smoke. I feel sad that the terrorists hurt nice people," he explained. "I'm scared they will hurt me too." The image above is Darian's picture showing how he felt about what he saw on TV.

This is a plane that hurt nice people. Darian. M

CHILDREN AND ANTICIPATORY GRIEF

Children also experience anticipatory grief because of trauma witnessed directly or indirectly. They fear future repetition in some way. For example, children and adults ask the unanswerable question, "Will the terrorist attacks happen again? Where and when?"

Seven-year old Victoria drew a picture of a large building with a plane crashing into it. She explained her drawing. "This is the terrorists crashing into the next building they were going to destroy." Another five-year-old, Tommy, drew a picture and explained it to his mom, "If the terrorists can crash into the World Trade Centers and the Pentagon, they can crash into a regular house like mine!"

"If the terrorists can crash into the World Trade Centers and the Pentagon, they can crash into a regular house like mine!"

Ten-year-old Sam expressed that his greatest fear is that "Anthrax will come through the mail. If it can come to our neighborhood post office it can come to my house too."

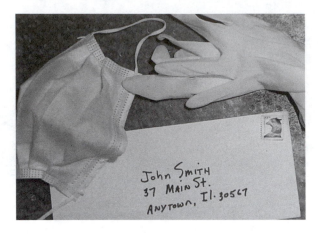

Re-triggering the Trauma

Children watching the news media and television programming that blast images of war, violence, terrorism, sexuality, and random violence often digest, assimilate, and absorb at all too young an age graphic pictures and sounds that they soak into their beings and store in conscious and unconscious ways. From borderline pornography in commercials during a family show, to language that could be found in a brothel as part of a sit-com, to images of war and violence played over and over again, our children are forced to become active witnesses held captive to the messages they innocently receive.

It is almost impossible for a four-year-old or fifteen-year-old to get though the day without being bombarded by negative images. The frequency of occurrence of these images so desensitizes children to their surroundings that in time they may not only lose their instinctual capacity to empathize, but these images may enhance a predisposition to act out, as they ponder whether these disturbing words and actions are not real or too real.

RE-TRIGGERING TRAUMA THROUGH MEDIA EXPOSURE

Watching the news media air visuals of the 9/11 terrorist attack over and over again re-triggered for too many children trauma they had previously experienced. Many young children misunderstood the frequently repeated videotape of the twin towers as separate attacks happening to many different buildings. Asking them what they thought happened can help adults to realize children's misinterpretations and clarify them. Middle-school and teenage students can also be greatly affected by cues that initiate stress responses, as exemplified by the following responses from every age group.

Ariel, a French six-year-old, had made an excellent transition from leaving her country to beginning a new life in the United States. She appeared to enjoy school and her American first-grade friendships. After watching the terrorist bombing she refused to go to school, crying and begging mom to take her back to her school in France.

Eight-year-old Andrew's mom was killed in a car crash. After seeing the wreckage of the Pentagon plane, he began to regress. He only wanted to be with his dad and was scared whenever Dad was out of sight. He became hysterical when he heard his dad had to fly for business. "I won't let you go!" he screamed. "I don't want you to die too."

Alex, age 12, had visited the World Trade Center two weeks before the terrorist attack. He had stayed overnight in the building. After he watched the video of the plane crash over and over, he began to regress, sleeping with his parents, and stuttering. He couldn't believe he had just slept in the building. He was terrified.

Sixteen-year-old Mary's dad died when she was seven. He had worked in the World Trade Center. As she watched the planes explode in the building she was transported to the exact time of her father's death. She gasped as she watched the buildings burn and disintegrate, screaming, "DADDY, DADDY!" as present reality and past trauma blurred in reliving her dad's death. She proceeded to have nightmares and anxiety for several weeks, re-grieving her dad. She also felt the huge loss of the World Trade Center, a great linking object to her dad. She had spent much time in his office with him as a child and now that was gone, too.

RE-TRIGGERING TRAUMA THROUGH DAILY EVENTS

Planes flying in the sky and videos replaying war and terrorism can re-trigger a trauma. Deep feelings of panic, fear, revenge, sadness, and anxiety may resurface for children at all age levels and at unexpected times. It is important to reassure them that these feelings are common and that many adults feel the same things.

Mrs. Jones' first graders had varied reactions to the attack on America. Brian told his friends, "Don't worry, everything will be fine." This was the same thing his dad had told him. Robert drew a picture of a plane crashing into a building, with the words "Run for your life or you'll die" in big letters. Mary had lots of fears before the terrorist attack. After the attack she became petrified. A fire drill created panic in her, and she was consumed with knowing where her teacher would be all of the time because she was afraid "the terrorists were going to get" her.

One six-year-old, Jeremy, saw a plane fly over his head at recess. He ran over to his teacher and explained "I hope that's not a terrorist flying to my house now. My dog Lucy is home alone and they could attack my house and hurt her. That scares me."

Sally, age 11, and her little sister Susan, age 6, were playing at home. They began to hear helicopters flying loudly overhead. They ran, closed the windows, locked the doors, and ran into the closet and stayed there until they heard their mom come into the room.

Twelve-year-old Tony lived in Washington, D.C., and began having headaches, nightmares, and difficulty concentrating after the terrorist attack. New sounds and sights like the constant roar of fighter jets and flying helicopters invaded his world. He explained wearily,

"Every time I look up at the sky I see the terrorist plane crash in my head. If I see an airplane, or hear one go by, I get nervous and think, Will it be us, are we next? I feel jittery all the time."

Children's Voices

Children's reactions to terrorism, war, anthrax, violence, and any perceived loss of safety and protection provide a window into their psyches and help suggest ways that the adults around them can help. Our ability to listen to questions, thoughts, and feelings is paramount in creating a safe zone for our children to process these life-changing times they are living through. Their ability to express their thoughts and feelings during traumatic times is a powerful intervention.

THE VOICES OF YOUNG CHILDREN

Five-year-old Tommy, after sitting and listening to his mom's careful explanation about the terrorist attack, explained that he was really upset about terrorism, "This is a real tragedy, because I kept searching and searching all day and couldn't find any of my cartoons on TV."

Rumors of a repeated terrorist attack on Halloween dampened this American tradition for many kids. Warnings were given for children not to trick-or-treat. Tommy questioned Mom over and over: "It's just not fair. Because of the terrorists I can't go trick-or-treating. I lost Halloween. It's just not fair!

MIDDLE SCHOOL VOICES

Thomas was twelve years old when the Pentagon crash took place. He lived nearby and knew people who died from that event. He expressed his worry about the future in the following way.

I think eventually the world will end. And it will be very scary!

Tiara, a middle-school child, expressed in the following essay her deep feelings about the terrorist attack. She continually expressed how unprotected she felt.

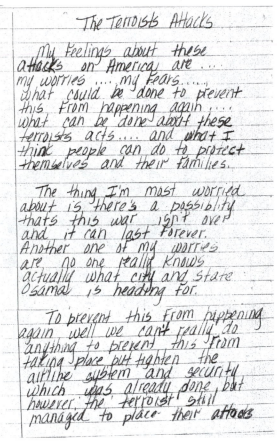

The Terrorists Attacks

My feelings about these attacks on America are ... my worries .... my fears....., what could be done to prevent this from happening again .... what can be done about these terrorists acts.... and what I think people can do to protect themselves and their families.

The thing I'm most worried about is there's a possibility thats this war isn't over and it can last forever. Another one of my worries are no one really knows actually what city and state Osama is heading for.

To prevent this from happening again well we can't really do anything to prevent this from taking place put tighten the airline system and security which was already done, but however, the terrorist still managed to place their attacks

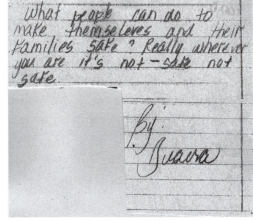

What people can do to make themseleves and their families safe? Really wherever you are it's not - safe not safe.

By: Tiara

She explained how difficult her picture was to draw as she said, "I just can't get it right." In the middle of one of the towers she drew the big letter "Y" below a clock. Although it may be arbitrary, perhaps she was asking the question people all over the world asked themselves that day, "Why [did this have to happen]?"

A Baghdad school child drew the following in her drawing when the Iraq war began. She, too, amidst the chaos, expresses the universal question, why?

San, a fifth grader, also wondered why the terrorist attack took place. "Could this have been our fault? What did we do wrong? How can I understand why this happened?" He expressed his unanswered questions in the following poem.

Permission by Puffin Foundation Ltd., Carl Rosenstein and Patrick Dillon.

Why Did This Happen
by San

Dust everywhere.
Smoke in the sky.
Buildings collapsing.
Why?

Why did this happen?
What did we do?
Did we do wrong?
Or is it just you?

People screaming, people running!
People suffocating!
Why did this happen?
Is something wrong?

Planes are bursting!
Cars are crashing!
People yelling.
Why?
Why did this happen?

What did we do?
Did we do wrong?
Or is it just you?

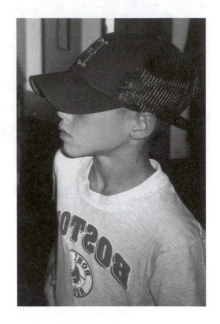

TEENAGE VOICES

One teen created a photo of blackness like the picture below. The following is her explanation of the loss of her assumptive world of safety and her projected future destruction (Washington Post, 2001).

"This is a picture of nothing because the president said we might have nuclear war and the world will look like this."

-*Washington Post (November 2, 2001)*

Sixteen-year-old Mark came home the day of the terrorist bombing and asked, "Does this mean I have to leave school and go into the army?" Many teens worried they would get drafted. Some teens fantasized about "kicking butt" in the army. Others said they were bored talking about the terrorist attack and wanted everyone to stop.

Fifteen-year-old Ari, a Palestinian, overheard a fellow student say, "I can't wait to go to war, get in the army, and kill a terrorist." He became fearful for his own life and stayed home from school the next day. Eleven-year-old Mara worried about going to the sixth-grade dance after the attack. She decided to stay home for fear her classmates would blame her for the bombings.

WAYS TO HELP CHILDREN DURING TRAUMA

Children may experience a trauma differently from adults. It is a sensory experience involving sights, smells, and sounds that re-trigger a visceral reaction. Their sense of vulnerability causes worry and feelings of being unprotected. Providing comfort through hugs, favorite foods, stuffed animals, and familiar routines helps them to feel safe again.

Reassuring Children

Reassure children that what they are feeling is very common. Adults may wonder why in the same way that a child might. Emphasize to them that adults feel a lot of the same things that they are feeling. Remind them that everyone has different ways of showing their feelings and that is all right. Restore confidence by reassuring them that problems are being handled, people who were hurt are being cared for, buildings are being cleared, and that things are getting a little better each day.

Carlos gets scared every time the mail comes to house. "Don't touch it without gloves and a mask," he screams at Dad. The threat of anthrax was very great where he lived in New York City. The visual imprint of mail arriving re-triggers past fear in Carlos. We can reframe some of that fear into a feeling of protection by saying gloves and masks protect the postal workers and other people while we check to make sure our post offices and mail are safe from anthrax.

Dialoging About Everyday Risks

Adults can also begin a dialogue about everyday risks we lived with before a traumatic event. Driving cars, flying in planes, crossing the street, and learning to ride a bike are all risks that are commonly around us. Creating teachable moments about everyday risks when a threatening occurrence is presented can help to reduce anxiety. Children can be reminded that although these incidents are newsworthy, the constant exposure to them can create a skewed perspective. Emphasizing to young people the small amount of actual cases in an incident like anthrax helps to reduce the effects of media bombardment. Creating awareness of a small number of incidences of highly publicized events can reduce fear and offer children a more reassuring outlook.

Monitoring Media

Monitoring media coverage for children is essential. Create "no TV times" or family time with teachable moments and parent monitoring. Carefully consider whether children should be watching the unfolding news coverage. It can be very frightening to children. Restrict the time to family viewing, allowing adults to be present to help children process and interpret their observations, thoughts, and feelings about what they see and hear. Adults can use this time as a teachable moment to discuss terrorism, prejudice, shootings, and other difficult topics.

Becoming Role Models

Adults are role models for children. After the assault on our nation, adults had many different reactions. One mom slept in her clothes with a packed suitcase next to her bed; another stayed in her pajamas and wouldn't leave the house for days; still another mom kept her child home from school all week. We can use mature modeling of responsible roles for our children during traumatic times, since they look to our reactions as a barometer of their own safety. Displaying calmness and an ability to serve help allows kids to do the same. We can be honest about feeling afraid and still model behaviors in a calming way.

Mature modeling guides children to create responsible ways to be helpful during the crisis. Emphasize ways that adults can help. Parents can volunteer blood, food, time, and money. Relief agencies such as the Red Cross issue appeals for help. Contributions of needed goods and family money can be taken to needed areas. Children can be included in planning ways families can help and in delivering food and clothing. Families and schools may want to join together in saying a prayer for the victims and their families, and for community or global leaders to bring about peace.

Conclusion

Children normally assume they live in a friendly, secure, and caring world. Terrorism, war, and violence amplify youngsters' preexisting insecurities that their world may be unprotected, scary, and uncertain. This deepened loss of assumptive protection creates a new set of voices all parents, educators, and health professionals must heed.

Understanding children's perceptions of an event, allowing dialogue to express thoughts and feelings, modeling mature coping mechanisms, and creating reassurances that there are resources available to maintain safety are helpful interventions for young people in navigating life during these times.

CHAPTER 3

Bullying and Victimization: A Deadly Disease and Invisible Killer

NAME CALLING • VERBAL THREATS • PUSHING
STEALING • CORNERING HATE IDEOLOGY • MEAN
JOKES • TEASING • SPREADING • RUMORS
MALICIOUS LIES AND GOSSIP • DOMINANCE
SHAKEDOWNS • HITTING • IGNORING SOMEONE
INTIMIDATION

No act of kindness, no matter how small, is ever wasted.

Aesop

Bullying, Victimization, and Unresolved Grief in Children

Bullying and victimization issues among our children have reached epidemic proportions in this new millennium. Over and over we have asked ourselves as grief educators and grief therapists, teachers, counselors, and parents, "How is the unresolved grief of today's children expressed?" The usual answer has been poor grades, detachment, learning problems, depression, and low self-esteem. The more extreme response may be violence, crime, drugs, sex, suicide, and homicide.

Thousands and thousands of boys and girls are sitting in their homes, schools, and communities with unresolved, unrecognized grief issues that all too often get projected out into the world in the form of bullying, abuse, violence, and homicide, or inwardly in the form of victimization and low self-esteem, depression, suicidal ideation, and suicide. "The continuum is ever growing, with suicide on the one extreme and homicide on the other" (Goldman, 2002). Too many of today's children are holding unresolved and unexpressed grief, loss, and pain.

Research by Rigby and Slee (1999), presented in the article "Suicidal Ideation Among Adolescent School Children, Involvement in Bully-Victim Problems, and Perceived Social Support," indicated that student "involvement in bully-victim problems at school, especially for students with little social support, was significantly related to the degree of suicidal ideation" (p. 119). Bullying is grossly misunderstood and largely invisible. The loss of self-esteem, safety, and protection so common to grieving children is magnified with bully-victimization issues. One boy who was continually harassed by classmates wondered aloud about his ongoing abuse as he asked, "Isn't bullying a lot like terrorism?"

ADULT MODELING

"Children learn what they live" is a useful phrase to emphasis the huge effect adult modeling has on our youth. Family systems that foster aggression and condone bullying only perpetuate the misconception that bullying toughens kids. School systems that allow "boys to be boys" and hold no strong boundaries and guidelines against bullying clearly reinforce the abuse. Communities that value winning at sport competitions or in business arenas at all cost only promote misconduct. The media teaches children through film after film, song after song, and video game after video game that violence and hurtful behaviors are an integral and valued part of our society.

Family Violence

We must examine our own behaviors that justify tolerance of bullying in others and in ourselves if we are to help our children. Research by Thormachien and Bass-Fled in the article "Children: The Secondary Victims of Domestic Violence" (1994) emphasizes that children who witness domestic violence are more likely to grow up exhibiting the same behaviors as their parents, with 30% of those who witness violence in their homes growing up to become the perpetrators of violence (as compared to 2% to 4% found in the general population). Children learn that violence and abusive behaviors are effective ways to control others, or they learn to become victims and be controlled. "Sons that witness their father's violence have a 100% greater rate of wife abuse then sons who do not" (p. 355).

What Can We Do About Violence: Solutions for Children (Moyers, 1995) is a film documenting the plight of children exposed to violence. Interventions for traumatized children are explored in a safe house in Michigan for victimized children. Interventions include removing children from a violent environment, creating support groups for children subjected to violence, educating both parents, and providing an empathic adult non-family member to listen to what happened to them. The ultimate goal was to model a vision of nonviolent adults and nonviolent families.

FACTS ABOUT BULLIES AND VICTIMS

The Maine Project against Bullying "Brave enough to be kind" (ed. 2004) offers the following facts about bullying:

- 80% of adolescents report being bullied during their school years..
- 90% of fourth through eighth graders report being victims.
- Up to 7% of eighth grade students stay home at least once a month because of bullies.

- Bullies identified by age eight and six times more likely to be convicted of a crime by age 24 and five times more likely than non-bullies to end up with serious criminal records by age 30.

- Students reported 71% of the teachers or other adults in the classroom ignored bullying incidents.

- Aggressive behavior is learned early and becomes resistant to change if it persists beyond age eight.

"The Study: Kids rate bullying and teasing as big problems" (Arce, march 8, 2001) shares the following statistics.

- 4% of 8-11 year olds say bulling occur in their school (more than smoking, drinking, drugs, and sex).

- 6% of 12-15 year olds say that bullying in school occurs.

- All age groups called teasing and bullying "big problems" that rank higher than racism, AIDS, and the pressure of having sex or try alcohol or drugs.

- Two million U.S. teenagers were having serious problems in school because they were taunted with anti-gay slurs. (Reported by Human Rights Watch in Stepp, L. Washington Post, *A Lesson in Cruelty: Anti-Gay Slurs Common at School, June 19, 2001).*

"Every day, some 160,000 American kids skip school out of fear of being harassed." (Boodman, S., Washington Post, July 8, 2001, P. A11). Bullying is a problem in every school in the country and throughout the world. Unfortunately, too many parents and educators refuse to take the problem seriously by offering sufficient support and action. In addition, homes, schools, and communities allow an environment where bullying is tolerated, modeled, or perpetuated. Strauss, in the Washington Post, May 8th 2001, shares a study showing two-thirds of student's ages 14-17 don't believe that bullies get in trouble. They therefore are more likely not to report bullying for fear the adults around them may make matters worse. The expectation of children handling this abuse alone must be replaced by a systematic program of awareness and adult intervention to insure our children's safety and well being.

Nicole was a fifth-grade-student who complained often to her teacher about being teased at school. Her teacher told her to tease back. One day she came home from school sobbing after a devastating experience on the bus. She explained that kids begain screaming Fatty! Piggy! and barked at her like a dog. Ashamed and embarrassed, she didn't look up until she left the bus. Her mom said she had to learn how to calm down, handle it, and be brave. Her grades dropped, her weight increased, and she began feeling too sick to go to school.

Taking Action Against Bullying

Educators, therapists, parents, and all caring professionals need to take action against the power structure inherent in bullying. Caring adults must become role models through language and action, creating strong boundaries of nontolerance of any verbal, physical, social, or sexual abuse of any kind.

BULLYING, POWER, AND CONTROL

Our kids are living in a world that rewards perceived strength and dominance. Many of our children and the adults around them admire those who can exhibit power over someone else. The sports arena, corporate culture, and media coverage consistently reward those who win at any cost, creating a society that views a bully as a kind of hero. Often traits of dominance, strength, and power over others are valued as masculine.

Our goal is to change thinking and consciousness to allow the adult world to see bullying-victimization encounters as dangerous to our children. Bullying is no longer an innocuous schoolyard activity or sibling interchange. Youths who engage in tormenting, teasing, and abusing others are beginning to be seen as criminals. Many schools not only implement a zero-tolerance policy for violent behavior, along with expulsion, but also are concurrently referring chargeable offenses to the criminal justice system.

KIDS AND POPULARITY

A middle-school poll of what makes a kid popular had some interesting results (Stossel, "The Incrowd and Social Cruelty," 2002). The characteristics associated with girls were looks first, then clothes, and charisma third. The boy's identifiable traits in order were sports, stature, and humor. Children reported that wealthy kids are more popular. They felt "it was how you were born." They explained that popular kids didn't have to be nice and could get away with anything.

ADULT INVOLVEMENT

In today's world, our children can't stop bullying or violence without the guidance, modeling, and absolute support of the adult world. A potentially powerful concept for children to integrate at a young age is that being a bully is anything but "cool." Zero tolerance of violent threats and actions is imperative. Parents, educators, and all community members must vigilantly create no-bullying policies and use no-bullying curricula to teach children from kindergarten through twelfth grade to recognize bullying behaviors in themselves and others. It is important to define bullying for children, explain the difference between telling and tattling, and instill the concept that we help people and save lives by speaking out. Children need a clear policy for strategies to deal with bullying and accessibility to adults that will take charge.

It is impossible for children to solve bullying issues alone.

Parents, educators, and other caring professionals are role models. Their behaviors and words can reflect nonviolent relationships and safe ways to express anger. Verbal abuse, physical threats, and sexual innuendoes cannot be tolerated. One six-year-old relayed a story of being picked on and called names for being overweight. She ran home to be comforted by her mom, tears streaming down her face. "Stop that crying," her mother demanded, as she slapped her daughter hard on the face. Third grader, Tony, was tormented on the playground by bullies. They constantly called him names and taunted him and his friends. Telling the teacher did him no good. The bullies and victims were punished together for creating a disturbance. In both instances the harassed kids were punished for telling adults. ("Breaking the silence" 2002, p. 94)

Rigby and Slee (1999) in their research indicate relationships between suicidal ideation, involvement in bully-victim problems at school, and perceived social support. Results obtained from self-reports and peer nomination procedures to identify bullies and victims reveal that such students who have good social support will significantly decrease the degree of suicidal ideation.

SCHOOL SUPPORT

School systems need to create and incorporate a comprehensive bullying program at multiple levels. Olweus suggests the following model:

School Wide Interventions that would include a survey of bullying at each school, increased supervision, school wide assemblies and teacher in-service training.

Classroom Interventions to establish classroom rules agaiinst bullying and parent meetings.

Individual-Level Interventions that create discussions between students identified as bullies, their victims, and onlookers.

Bullying in Our Schools

In 1998 *Weekly Reader* did a survey of 50,000 fourth, fifth, and sixth graders across the United States and reported that bullying was a tremendous problem. "Over

70% of the kids polled in this survey report they have been bullied, and the bullying takes place on the playground, in the halls, in the cafeteria, and on the busses of our schools" (Weekly Reader, 1998).

This survey helped to take bullying out of the closet of our school systems by substantiating the need for school-based victim/offender mediation programs or Peacemakers' Clubs, which teach student conflict resolution, and early and continuing education. Teaching curricula and social studies units on bullying, as well as sensitizing students to issues, understandings, respectful behaviors, and unacceptable behaviors creates a framework for children. We may want to have a dialogue with children by asking:

- Can teasing ever be innocent?
- When does name calling go too far?
- What are the school's guidelines?
- What actions are parts of school policy?
- When can someone retaliate in self-defense?
- If you could change school policy, what guidelines would you suggest?

Special Issues for Girls

Pipher (1994) explains in her best-selling novel *Reviving Ophelia* that more adolescent girls are prone to depression, eating disorders, addictions, suicidal ideation, and acts of rage than ever before. "We live in a look obsessed, media saturated, girl poisoning culture, with escalating levels of sexism and violence—from undervalued intelligence to sexual harassment in elementary school, destroying self esteem. Yet girls often blame themselves or their families for this 'problem with no name' instead of looking at the world around them (back cover)."

A JOURNAL ABOUT BULLYING: MARGARET'S STORY

Margaret is a high school student who experienced bullying for most of her school years. From elementary school through high school, she felt surrounded by aggression from girls and boys. This aggression presented itself in many forms. She decided to chronicle her bullying episodes in a journal of her childhood experiences, naming it *Bully Prey*. It became a timeline representing the overt and covert forms of bullying she felt she experienced throughout her childhood.

A TimeLine

Intimidation: 10 Years Old

"The hateful cycle of bullying first took its roots when I was in fifth grade. At the time the method was intimidation. Older sixth grade students appeared so utterly powerful, and I felt as though they 'ruled the school.' Never friendly or welcoming, the sixth grade girls would glare at me regularly, evoking fear and a deep sense of inferiority in me."

Verbal Attacks: 11 Years Old

"When I was in sixth grade I was an avid tennis player. A painful injury prevented me from playing, and I sank into depression and anorexia. I will never forget the pain that remarks and abusive comments [from others] caused me. The first hurtful remark came from my supposed best friend when she informed me in an astonished and appalled tone that my leg muscles were 'so huge.' As a sensitive girl, I unfortunately took what she said to heart."

A Cruel Internet Joke: 12 Years Old

"Friends played a cruel joke on me over the Internet, which involved pretending to be a popular eighth grader that I liked, and tricked me into confessing my feelings for him. After I did so, they signed offline and proceeded to make a laughing stock of me, pointing and cackling at my expense. I was completely humiliated."

Ridicule: 12 Years Old

"I decided to run for vice president of a club—and when I went to give my speech, I mentioned heartfelt reasons why I would make a good vice president. My best friend began to laugh hysterically at me. She ripped away any feeling of pride that I had and turned my running into a big joke. She belittled me in front of the club— I was so mortified that I was speechless. I became afraid to go to school and made excuses to stay home."

Physical Harassment by Girls: Sixth Grade

"Occasionally I would be tormented physically. One day in sixth grade my (so called) best friend tackled me in the middle of the playground and began to rip off my clothes. A fair-sized crowd came to watch as she attempted to tear the shirt off my back."

Physical Harassment by Boys: 14 Years Old

"Boys routinely started to pinch my stomach 'flab' and tell me that I had a fat abdomen. Their hands made me terribly uncomfortable, and directly reinforced my anorexic paranoia. Never mind the fact that I was actually extremely thin, their comments were hurtful and disrespectful just as much as they would be to an overweight person. I believed their accusation, and starved myself daily so I would lose weight and not be 'fat' anymore."

Racial Taunting: Ninth Grade

"A boy in my school harassed me daily by making fun of my race (I am white and he is black), belittling me on the way I dressed, and telling me that I had no rhythm and couldn't dance. He also threatened to have his boys come and get me. I was so fearful of him and his threats, I didn't attend the school dance."

Physical Harassment by a Group: 15 Years Old

"Seniors obtained a huge water balloon launcher, which was immense and took the strength of seven males to fire. A sophomore girl who had a spiteful grudge against me prompted the guys to fire the balloons at me, which pelted my body and left painful bruises. I was the only girl to be targeted, and the entire school witnessed my humiliation as the balloons hit me again and again. In many ways the act could be considered an assault with a weapon."

Sexual Harassment: 12 Years Old

"So many individuals have harassed me during the years that they almost blend into one enormous face of torment. A group of girls . . . began to call me a slut and a whore. One girl got her 14-year-old-brother involved in rumors—that I performed oral sex on him. I started to receive instant messages over the Internet from this fourteen-year-old and other boys, threatening they would 'ruin my high school career.'"

Rumors: 13 Years Old

"One of the most foul and devious lies was spread while I was out sick with mononucleosis. My friend told the guy I was interested in as well as others that I had the herpes virus, inciting a whole new fire of rumors. I felt helpless to the whim of the general pubic at my school, since it seemed like nothing I could do would put together my desecrated reputation."

Humor: 14 Years Old

"One boy constantly harassed me sexually—and his style was humor. He felt it was funny and entertaining to make sexually explicit jokes at my expense. He would belittle me with sexual innuendo that would refer to me as giving oral sex to many boys. The 'jokes' infuriated me, and often I would tell him to stop or 'Shut up.' He did not stop after I firmly told him to quit it. Shame surrounded me everywhere I went, since it seemed as though the whole school identified me as a dirty 'whore.' My life from day to day was an enormous struggle to get up in the morning, driven by the fear of learning what new scandal I would be 'involved' in next."

Exclusion: 15 Years Old

"Because my reputation was so desecrated, few people wanted to befriend or be involved with me. To this day I haven't figured out the reason I was the target, or why no one seemed to defend me. I had been excluded from football games and parties and had been recently 'dumped' after inviting people to come over to my house. I attempted one more invitation and made plans with my 'friends' to gather at my (near-by) house for a pregame football party on Friday night. At the end of the school day people who had agreed to come to my house started to inform me that they could not come over and had made other plans for that night. I was appalled and devastated, because once again I had been played for a fool when my supposed friends chose to exclude me. I left school that day and planned on never returning."

Margaret's Solutions: What Could Have Been Done

Margaret shared the following feelings about these bullying episodes. She gave explanations about what could have been done to help her.

"It took enormous courage to stand up for a student when they were being bullied, and I always hoped that someone would try to defend me. No one showed this type of bravery or strength, so I was left to fend for myself."

"People blindly believed the rumors spread about me, no matter how ridiculous they were. I wish that even just one person would have stopped and logically reasoned if there was any truth to the lies that went around the school about me."

"None of my close friends supported me. Merely having a show of empathy and concern would have been comforting."

"The students were the people who could have changed the course of the bullying, but instead they chose to be spectators at the arena of my persecution."

"I wish that the school had had a concrete policy against harassment, both sexual and other forms, which could have deterred my bullies from antagonizing me."

"When I mustered up the courage and reported bullying, instead of disciplining the bully, they talked to her. She received more ammunition and retaliated against me for speaking up."

"I wished my school would have held more educational assemblies and forums on bullying because the students might have been less likely to torment me if they had more information on the harm that bullying causes."

"Although I am now a much more brave and assertive individual than I was before being bullied, I will never say that I am glad that I went through it. The lessons I learned came at way too elevated a price to be considered beneficial. I do not wish onto anyone, even my worst enemy, the pain and suffering I have endured."

Margaret was one of the fortunate students able to change her environment and get help. Educating parents and professionals for signs of bullying and victimization issues, providing strong guidelines for children involved in these circumstances, and creating well-defined policies of nontolerance for abuse will allow adults to become the advocates our children must have to emerge safely from these incidents. Bullies, victims, and bystanders need interventions to change the unequal balance of power that prevails in bully-victim circumstances. Working with adults and children on all levels of these difficult problems can create a new paradigm to prevent the further mistreatment of children in our schools.

Victims' Voices

"I just snapped. I figured if I got lucky and took her [the bully] out, all the other 'Stuff' would stop."

"I took it for seven months. Then I couldn't stand it anymore."

"I felt a rush of power with a gun. It was the only way to get rid of the anger."

"I got spit stuff thrown at me, I got spit on, I got beat up. Sometimes I fought back but I wasn't that good at fighting."

"After a while they told me to just ignore everybody. But then you can't take it anymore."

"I'll show you one day."

"They would walk up to me and punch me in the face. I wouldn't do anything about it."

"I wanted to kill myself, but I killed them instead."

"I told them I would blow up the classroom. Nobody believed me."

"Why don't people get that it puts you over the edge?"

Bullys' Voices

"We abused him pretty much, I mean verbally."

"Idiot, dummy, fat, ugly, retard, faggot."

"Yeah, I'm a girl. If I am with friends and we see someone coming along we can beat up, we do it. It's like a natural high."

"We beat up a kid so badly—sticking his head in the toilet—the only thing I wished is that we could have hurt him worse before we got caught."

"I made fun of him. I am sorry now."

Onlookers' Voices

"It's the kids' code not to tell. If you do you will be called a snitch. You don't want to tell anyone and you are scared."

"I watched them kick Steve in the stomach and push him against the wall. It just broke him."

"Bullying is a part of growing up. All this attention to what is school tradition will only create a country of weaklings."

"A lot of times the more popular or athletic kids would make him a target."

"If I tell I'll get bullied too."

"I tried to tell, but they said to handle it myself."

Adults' Voices

"I watched a little kid be beat up and never did anything about it. I was eight. It plaques me today."

"I came to this country from Russia at 11. It was difficult for me to understand why I got pushed and shoved every day on the playground. I didn't speak the language. I still don't understand."

"I was knocked down and hit. I remember feeling scared and confused. I hadn't done anything wrong. When I told my mom she said I had to learn to stand up for myself. I still don't feel comfortable doing that as an adult."

"I called a girl fat and teased her all the time. Everybody did. She killed herself during our senior year. I am so angry that no teacher stopped us. They knew we were tormenting her."

Ways to Help Children with Bullying

- Identify bullying behaviors.

- Give the victim more power.
- Change the inherent social structure of bullying.
- Reduce the unequal balance of power.
- Diminish repeated negative experiences.
- Lessen the contrasting feelings of powerlessness and humiliation for the bully and victim.

"Go back to where you came from!" Sally shouted as she and Lisa shoved Maria to the ground. "Ouch!" cried Maria. "Don't do that! That hurts!" Maria was the new girl from El Salvador who had arrived at school two weeks earlier. She was smaller than most of the girls and stayed by herself a lot. Mary, Alice, and Cindy heard her cries and looked for the teacher on playground patrol. She was nowhere to be seen. Sally pulled Maria's hair and screamed "skinny ugly brat!" in her ear. The girls watched it all happen. They couldn't find an adult. They didn't know what to do.

Too often adults are confronted with helping children in a scenario like this. The following are some suggestions that may be helpful in branding bullying and giving the victim more power. In this way we can assist in changing the inherent social structure of bullying by reducing the unequal balance of power, reducing repeated and consistent negative actions, and diminishing the contrasting feelings of powerfulness and humiliation for the bully and victim.

DEFINE BULLYING

For Children and Teens

> BULLYING HAPPENS . . . when someone hurts someone else on purpose to make them look weak or bad or embarrassed and to make oneself look tough or cool or right. It is characterized by cowardly, aggressive behavior whether with fist, weapons, words, glances, or the hurtful spreading of rumors, damaging gossip, or lies.

> BULLYING HAPPENS . . . when someone with greater power unfairly hurts someone with lesser power over and over again. (No-Bullying Program. Johnson Institute, 1999, p. 17)

For Young Children

A bully is someone who is intentionally mean to other children a lot of the time. The bully uses power in a cruel or negative way. Sometimes he or she may be older, stronger or more "street smart" than the kids being picked on.

Both boys and girls can be bullies. Short or tall, fat or skinny, rich or poor, black or white—bullies come in all shapes, sizes, and colors. There is one thing they have in common—they all know how to be mean. Being a bully is not cool. It's cruel and cowardly! It is or should be against school rules and can even be against the law. Even though the bully might appear tough, his or her being unkind is a sign of weakness.

Bullies aren't born; bullies are made into bullies. Some bullies are very under-confidant and insecure, and pick on weaker people to make them feel stronger. They may appear strong, but inside they are always weak. Usually bullies have learned their behaviors from someone who has bullied them, like a brother or sister, a mom or dad, or a friend or classmate at school. Sometimes bullies are the popular kids and like to be in control and have power. Bullies may not even know why they are cruel. They just do to others what has been done to them. It's very sad and it's bad for everybody, both the bullies and the bullied.

Most of the time bullies harass other kids in secret, and teachers or other adults are not around to help. Although other kids may see or know of the bully and what he or she is doing, they often do not speak up because they are afraid too. Some kids say they don't feel safe on the bus, in the gym, in the halls, in the cafeteria, or even on the playground, because they are the places bullies can 'get you' when no one is watching. Remember that bullying happens when one kid hurts another kid over and over and over again. Since this behavior cannot be accepted from anyone who goes to school, we must work together to stop it. Together, we can stop bullying. (Goldman, 2001, p. 98)

Bullying Behaviors

- Bullies pick on other kids who are smaller than they are or on animals.
- Bullies tease or make fun of other kids.
- Bullies laugh at other people's mistakes.
- Bullies like to ruin other people's things.
- Bullies like to look tough and mean.
- Bullies stay angry a lot.

- Bullies like to have revenge if someone hurts them.
- Bullies blame other people when something goes wrong for them.
- Bullies have to win at a game or sport and it doesn't matter to them if they play fair or not.
- Bullies hate it when good things happen to other kids, and they say or do bad things to others because they are jealous.

For Middle and High School Students

Bullying is a form of aggressive and cowardly peer abuse. Bullying occurs when one or more students harm another by using power over them and appearing to enjoy it. Because it is an imbalance of power, it is an act of weakness. Bullying can be face to face or behind someone's back. Bullying can occur one time or many times. The behaviors can range from "a little" spreading of painful rumors about a classmate to beating up others who can't defend themselves.

- ***Physical Aggression:*** hitting, kicking, spitting, pushing, cornering
- ***Verbal Aggression:*** hate ideology (race, religion, sexual orientation), name calling, verbal threats, swearing, mean jokes
- ***Social Alienation:*** separating into cliques, ostracizing or ignoring someone, actively rejecting a peer, talking behind his/her back, gossiping and spreading rumors and malicious lies
- ***Intimidation:*** threatening to reveal personal information, playing a dirty trick, extortion, taking possessions, sexual or racial taunting, threatening harm

---

Adult Guidelines

So many bullying-victimization situations exist below the radar of adult awareness. Glances, threats, verbal harassment, and malicious gossip often are invisible to the most caring parents and professionals. Creating strong boundaries for our children and enforcing them are first steps in the long road to eliminating bullying behaviors. We can clarify situations in which these behaviors are unacceptable.

LISTEN CAREFULLY AND DOCUMENT

At home, in our schools, and throughout the community, adults need to set up structures for consequences when these behaviors appear, establishing firm guidelines for all to adhere to.

Stop Bullying Behavior When

- Victim says "stop" or "no"
- Victim cries
- Victim runs away
- Everyone is laughing except the victim
- Observer gets the feeling something cruel or mean is happening
- Observer can't put himself in the victim's place without feeling bad
- Everyone recognizes this behavior could be against the law

CREATE STRONG GUIDELINES

The responsibility lies with parents and educators to curtail the power of bullies. "When a bully abuses power it is hard for one person to be the determining factor in deflating the bully. . . . When the community makes it clear that bullying is not tolerated and that message is given by enough people to convince the bully that his/her actions are unacceptable, bullying can be stopped. Everyone in the community has to respond immediately and decisively" (Cleventer, pp. 140–141).

Parents and teachers must take quick action to listen and address student concerns and reports. Requesting an appointment with the principal of the school and documenting conversations and incidents can speed the process of distinguishing the bullying behaviors. If a parent finds the school system is uncooperative, that parent's advocacy is important and must be pursued through other channels such as the school board, law enforcement, or other community agencies.

Adults can also mentor students in creating their own committee on peer abuse and school policy against violence. This committee can serve as a liaison to faculty and parents, creating guidelines and procedures they feel are useful from the student point of view. Mentorship programs for bullies and victims can be established as well as guidance groups for bullies, victims, and onlookers.

CREATE HARASSMENT AND VIOLENCE POLICIES FOR SCHOOLS

School systems should adapt, enforce, and post their policy on harassment and violence in the school. This policy should contain specific racial, sexual, physical, and religious acts of violence or harassment and the reporting procedures for staff and students as well as the disciplinary policy for violations. This policy should be posted in schools, given to parents and others working with children, placed in student handbooks, and presented at assemblies and within classrooms.

EMPHASIZE AND MODEL DEMOCRATIC VALUES

Adults must emphasize the inherent rights of all citizens, including children, to feel free to attend to life without being harassed or abused. We should take a deeper look at our own values and those that society condones. Just as police intercede if violence occurs between adults, parents and educators can also model immediate intervention to stop bullying. By not interceding, adults are sending a strong message that this behavior is condoned. "Every individual should have the right to be spared oppression and repeated, intentional humiliation, in school as in society at large" (Olweus, 2000, p, 49). This is a part of our fundamental democratic principles and must be reinforced as important for our children.

TEACH POSITIVE CONFLICT RESOLUTION IDEAS AND SKILLS

For bullying to stop, bullies must learn new behaviors after understanding their underlying feelings. Bystanders, too, must be equipped to take action rather than stand as silent witnesses. Victims must be given protection, allies, and new ways of dealing with aggression. Caring adults must recognize, strategize, and intervene with all roles of the bully, victim, and onlooker in order to change the unequal balance of power.

Help children roleplay possible solutions and help children empathize with bullies, victims, and bystanders. Explain to children that conflicts can't be solved if:

- They want everything their own way.
- They always have to be right.

- They think they have no power.
- They are not willing to risk being honest about how they feel.
- They hit, name call, or use physical force to get their way instead of trying to work it out.
- They pretend the problem doesn't exist.

EMPHASIZE THE POWER OF THE ONLOOKER

Strategies for working with children who are bystanders range in a continuum of perceived risk for the child. Promoting advocacy for children who are onlookers must include a strong program within the school that enforces no tolerance for abusive behavior and provides channels for onlookers to safely explore interventions. Mary wanted to tell Susan to stop picking on Jane, but she was afraid she would get picked on too or get in trouble with the teacher for telling. Instead of getting help, she said nothing.

Children can dialogue about ways they can intervene in a bullying situation that incorporate the concept that telling is helping and tattling is not. Adults can reinforce to children the concept that joining or supporting the victim holds great power in changing the abuse. Creating discussions about victim feelings and possible dialogue to use when bullying occurs empowers onlookers to take an active stance. The following interventions are strategies for interventions for onlookers with varying degrees of risk levels for them (adapted from Garrity et al, 2000, p. 279).

Onlooker Strategies

Intervention I: Not Joining with the Bully

Children have the option of walking away from a difficult situation. They can also stay but not participate or clearly state they are not participating in unacceptable behaviors.

Intervention II: Getting Adult Help

Children who are onlookers can get help anonymously or go to an adult they trust. They can also declare during the bullying episode that they are going to get help, and then do that.

Intervention III: Mobilizing Peer Group

The strategy of getting adult help if a bystander sees bullying can include getting another friend to join with standing up to the bully. Children can also choose to become a leader and initiate gaining other peer support to stand up against the bully.

Intervention IV: Taking an Individual Stand

Children can take an individual stand at the time of bullying. This stand can range from taking the hand of the victim and walking him or her away to openly advocating to the bully to "Leave him alone," or saying "We don't treat people like that."

Intervention V: Befriending the Victim

The strategy of befriending the victim is powerful in bullying scenarios. Acknowledging to the victim that what happened was unfair can help him or her not feel so alone. Inviting the victim to join the peer group offsets the power structure inherent in the situation. Standing with the victim and publicly declaring that this is an unjust situation is a strong statement of friendship and help.

STRATEGIES FOR HELPING BULLIES

Create simple descriptions of unacceptable behavior and consequences. Children can rate their thinking process to see if they can identify with bullying thinking patterns. Responses such as "I don't care about other people's feelings" or "I always need to be right" can indicate thinking that can be destructive to others. Creating new thinking patterns by seeing that power is misused is an initial step. The goal would be to help a bully identify a thought pattern that tells him or her that it "is someone else's fault I do bad things" and to evolve that thought pattern into the recognition that "I am responsible for my behavior."

Give clear and unwavering guidelines about given boundaries. Adults must present clear guidelines that bullying will not be tolerated. It is important to list specific behaviors that are unacceptable and clear consequences of these behaviors that are not negotiable. Ultimately, these guidelines must be consistently enforced to be effective. Create an incident report for each bullying episode reported. Have children describe what happened, how they handled their feelings, what they could have done, how they think the other person felt, and what they could have done to handle the situation better. This report can be presented to parents, and both the parent and child read together and sign.

Teach identification of victim's feelings and develop underlying empathy*.*
Creating role-play scenarios where bullies are placed in victim or onlooker roles allows them to begin to understand what others may be going through. (See examples at the end of the chapter.)

***Identify the power of the bully and reframe this power in nondestructive
ways.*** An integral part of rechanneling power is to first help bullies recognize their
anger and how they work with this anger. Help bullies identify what makes them
angry and how they deal with this anger. Redirecting destructive force into positive energy can be done by developing physical abilities through sports, or leadership skills using inner strength. Create an anger contract whereby the bully
chooses three interventions he or she feels will be effective and signs the contract,
committing to adhere to the strategies. Another student and adult can sign as witnesses.

ANGER CONTRACT

I, _____ agree to use the following ways to work with my anger
for one week. Today's date is _____. I choose basketball, listening to
music, and calling a friend.

_____ Student signature

_____ Peer signature

_____ Adult signature

The identification of violent youth and presentation of activities to work with anger
will be expanded in chapter 4 on school shootings.

Create a school environment of consensus that bullying is wrong. A student concensus that bullying is unacceptable can be very effective in reducing the power of a bully. Creating a solidified stance against bullying includes school assemblies presenting the destructiveness of abuse and aggression against one another. Education for parents about bullying behavior and interventions for bullies, victims, and onlookers can enlarge the enforcement of eliminating bullying behaviors. Establishing firm guidelines for children of behaviors that are and are not acceptable, with accompanying consequences that are firmly enforced, is imperative. These guidelines and consequences must be presented to the entire student body, enforced by the total faculty, and reviewed with all parents.

"The silent majority in schools consists of the 85% of students who are neither bullies nor victims but who stand helplessly by as their classmates get beaten up emotionally or physically. By doing so, the bystander children are implicitly allowing this to happen" (Garrity et al., 2000, p. 269). The key to creating a climate of respect and safety is to empower this silent majority of children into a caring majority through reducing the fear of bullying.

Empowering children to intervene in bullying situations could be our most valuable strategy.

Dispel the Myths of Bullying

There are many myths of bullying that we have carried from childhood and are perpetuated today. These misconceptions thwart a change of consciousness in this area.

Myth I: Bullies Are Only Boys. "Boys Will Be Boys."

Usually boys bully more than girls and often boys will bully girls. Their behavior may be more physical: hitting, threatening, or physically intimidating by stealing lunch money or fistfights. However, in today's violent world, girls are becoming more violent and more physically abusive. Girls tend to be more "relational" bullies, spreading malicious gossip, excluding another girl, or trying to break up a friendship.

Myth II: Victims Are Taunted Only Because of Their Appearance.
"You're Fat, You're Skinny, and You're Ugly."

Bullies may torment kids who are short, wear glasses, or have a speech impediment. More often they seek out the children who appear overly anxious and insecure with classmates, have few friends, and are unassertive and withdrawn. These lonely kids are more likely to be singled out regardless of their appearance. They are easy targets because they rarely stand up for themselves.

Myth III: Victims Are Defective or "Less Than" in Some Way. "Popular Kids, Smart Students, and Star Athletes Never Get Bullied. It's Only the Stupid, Weak, and Unpopular Kids."

Bullies may pick on anybody when they feel they can get away with it. A bully might pick on a small kid with thick glasses the way a bully might abuse a helpless small pet. Or he or she might single out the most popular boy or girl in an effort to appear better than they are.

Myth IV: Children Should Solve the Bullying Problem on Their Own.
"Don't Tell Me. You Kids Solve It by Yourselves."

This attitude corresponds to the police telling a victim to go work it out with a stalker, or a child who was sexually abused to work it through with his or her abuser. Immediate intervention is required by adults with a clear and consistent rule of conduct and stated consequences. Failure of the adult world to appropriately intervene only sends kids the message that this behavior is approved of and acceptable and infractions are not serious enough to warrant adult attention.

Adults need to be role models to equalize the power imbalance inherent in bullying and victimization issues that make bullied children reluctant to speak up for themselves. Annie came home from school so angry after trying to tell her teacher that Mary and Alice called her names all day. "Settle it yourself," was the only feedback.

"I didn't know what to do!" she explained. "If I did, why would I have ever gone to my teacher for help?" Annie needed adult guidance and support, and not getting it created a loss of trust in her adult environment.

Myth V: Bullies Have Low Self-Esteem. "They Only Do That Because They Don't Like Themselves."

Dan Olweus, a professor at University of Bergen, stresses that bullies "had unusually little anxiety or insecurity." Often, especially for boys, bullying is associated with being popular. Usually bullies have a strong need to control others and an impaired sense of empathy. They may be the ones who are the strongest and most physical and most active in the sports arena. Admired by much of the student population, bullies are often viewed as the "in crowd," and their behaviors are reinforced by peers. Juvonen's study (2004) with 2,000 sixth graders in the Los Angeles area indicates that bullies were consistently among the most liked and respected students in the school and that their peer status was important in boosting their well-being; she emphasizes, "It is disturbing to think that bullies are feeling really good about themselves" (Svoboda, 2004, p. 20).

Myth VI: Bystanders Should Not Get Involved. "Stay Safe and Don't Speak Up."

Usually the students who stand by silently as uncomfortable witnesses are the very ones who can be the most effective in changing the power structure of bullying. By branding bullying behaviors, kids can help diminish them. When others refuse to reinforce bad behavior, the bully may get bored and stop.

Onlookers are the children who need to be involved. We need to change the behaviors of the children around the bully. These onlookers participate in the bullying by passively condoning and thereby giving energetic support to it. Their silent failure to take a stand against the (primary) bully creates onlookers as secondary extensions of bullying.

WAYS KIDS CAN HELP THEMSELVES

1. Learn to protect yourself. Children can learn self-defense such as karate or judo to encourage self-protection and enhance self-esteem.

2. Stay away from a bully. Tell kids to stay safe and away from a bully. If a bully is scaring a child, he or she can scream loudly, "Stop!" or "Get away from me!" and run away. If a bully threatens to hurt someone, a child shouldn't bring a weapon to school for protection. Instead, a child should get help.

3. Report loss of possessions and threats of violence to someone you trust. If the bully continues to harass a child, he or she needs to tell someone trustworthy. Explain to children that there is a difference between telling and tattling. Telling is helping to stop harm to them or someone they care about. Tattling is to hurt someone. When someone takes something away by force, it is stealing and it is illegal. If someone has a weapon or is threatening to harm someone, informing an adult can help save a life.

4. Take a look at yourself for signs of bullying behavior. Children need to recognize if they have any bullying behaviors, such as hurting or teasing someone. Hurting someone's body or things, hurting someone's feelings, or hurting someone's friendship is bullying. Help them see they need to stop it in themselves and recognize it in friends and classmates. Role playing with bully-victim scenarios can help develop compassion and empathy for victims. Remind children they have a choice in how they want to act and with whom they want to be friends.

5. Walk in groups on the playground, in the hall, and to and from school. Explain to children that walking with other friends helps prevent bullying. Bullies tend to pick on kids more if they are alone. Remind children who are alone to walk confidently, heads up. Standing tall helps children keep alert and it discourages anyone from bothering them.

6. Don't ignore bullying. Ignoring bullies will not make them go away. The problem won't go away until they know they have to stop. Keeping bullying a secret compounds the fear and humiliation of being bullied with the isolation of not sharing it. Children should tell at least three trusted friends and three trusted adults.

7. Defend classmates from bullying. When a bully is mistreating a classmate, boys and girls should not stand by and just watch or pretend they don't see. They can stay in groups and tell the bully they don't like how he or she is threatening their friend.

8. Children are more effective in speaking up against bullying in groups. These groups can increase their power and diminish that of the bully. They can write a note to the principal, guidance counselor, or teacher about any incident. If they are afraid to sign their names, they can leave the bully's name and ask for help.

9. Start a bully prevention program in school. Students can ask teachers, counselors, and administrators to create an educational program to prevent bullying and request open discussions about this issue. Kids can ask educators and parents to use their adult power to stop bullying.

10. Create a bully policy in school. Children can urge school personnel to set up rules and consequences for kids about any physical, emotional, or sexual abuse. Parents of bullies and victims should be called and told of the incident. Educators and kids should know and adhere to uniform rules and consequences of breaking the rules. Boys and girls can request strong playground, bus, and cafeteria supervision.

Interventions for Victims, Bullies, and Onlookers

1. Promote discussions on telling versus tattling. Define telling and tattling: "Tattling is telling on someone to get them into trouble. Telling is reporting something to prevent trouble."

2. Create bully-victim role plays: Farhad was from Iran and was Muslim. Ralph taunted him and called him names. "Hey, Osama, where did you park your camel!" taunted Ralph as he tripped Farhad in the hall and spilled his books on the floor. "Leave me alone!" yelled Farhad. "I'm an American just like you!" Farhad was a new student at this school and a recently naturalized U.S. citizen. He still had a thick accent and looked different from the other kids. Christina and Matt heard Farhad shouting and saw him get tripped and fall. If you were Farhad what would you do? What should Christina and Matt do?

Allow children to feel what a bully and victim may feel by acting out short scenarios. Have each child play the bully and victim role. Underscore empathy and compassion for the victim and identifying traits of a bully. Suggest telling a trusted adult, asking friends for help, and practicing conflict resolution through peer mediation.

3. Create dialogue about bullying: Ask questions like, "What did you think when you saw your friend be teased?" and "If a friend told you he was going to do something scary, what would you do?"

4. Confide your experiences of bullying to share with children: "I had a friend in high

school who got hit and teased so much at school he had to leave," or "I was a bully in second grade."

5. Insert teachable moments when school violence appears in the media: Give opportunities for students to express concerns, talk about violence, and participate as members of a global community to help one another. Discussion questions could include: "How did you feel when you saw the school shootings on TV? What do you worry about? Would you like to do anything to help?" Children can write letters, draw pictures, collect money, and send these items to the troubled school.

6. Suggest letter writing: Invite a child to write a letter to a bully. He or she can choose whether to send it or not. Amy decided to write the following letter and not send it. Writing allowed her to release some of her feelings safely (and share it with others).

A Letter to a Bully by Amy, Age 8

Dear Sally,

Many people could enjoy your company. I would like to be your friend, but I don't like some of the behaviors you have. You push people onto the pavement. You also talk down to people as if they were your slaves. I feel that if you didn't do all these atrocious actions, many people would be your friend.

You have much to offer the world such as your quick tongue. Who else do I know who can speak and think at the same time? You also have immense physical strength. If you use your talents for good and not evil, the world would be a happier place for us and for you to live.

Your classmate,

Amy

---

7. Brainstorm channels of communication to report bullying: What is the school policy? What kinds of issues would you report? What might stop you from reporting something scary? Who are the people you would go to? If they didn't listen, what would you do?

8. Create a group play about teasing, taunting, or tormenting. Within the skit, kids should be as authentic as they can. Then conclude with ways each person involved—the bully, the victim, and the onlookers—can take responsibility for his or her part in the scene.

9. Write a bullying story: Create a story where each character tells his or her point of view (bully-victim, mom of bully-victim, teacher, onlookers, etc.) or a story from a personal experience with bullying.

10. Compose bullying essays: Kids can write their own definition of bullying. Then they can design their own school policy for bullying or write a letter to the principal stating their ideas and implementation procedures.

11. Give children a bully inventory: Help them identify thoughts and feelings.

1. Were you ever bullied? _____

2. Were you ever a bully? _____

3. Were you ever an onlooker?_____

4. Draw or write about what happened.

5. Did you tell anyone? _____ Who? _____

   What did they say? _____

   _____

6. How did the adults around you handle the bullying?

   _____

   _____

7. How did the kids around you handle the bullying?

   _____

   _____

8. Is there anything that still sticks with you?

   _____

   _____

12. Provide children with an open-ended process: The following is twelve-year-old Barbara's response to the question "Do You Ever Have Jittery Feelings? What do you do?" Her class was asked to respond to jittery feelings during an episode of school violence in their community. The ongoing violence appeared secondary to a past trauma involving bullying.

What makes you feel jittery?

I have only felt jittery once, but, I do know what it is like. I was in school and these girl were slaping me, and I really felt scared and shaky.

What do you do?

I will just go somewhere I can be alone and write something.

Barbara Age 12

Adult Strategies for Bullying

1. Provide support and modeling: Children cannot solve the problem of bullying without the firm support of their adult world. Educators and students must join together to eradicate bullying behaviors from their school environment. The old advice of ignoring tormentors doesn't work in today's world. Adults can no longer give children the message that they are capable of solving the bullying on their own. Teachers, counselors, administrators, and parents need to step in, stop the bullying, recognize the victim's feelings, and teach alternative behaviors to bullying.

2. Maintain a no-bullying policy: Educators and students need to create and adhere to a no-bullying policy at school. This policy does not allow physical, verbal, or sexual abuse inside or outside of school and is modeled by school staff. Mean-spirited behaviors are unacceptable by everyone and will be reported immediately with appropriate repercussions. This reporting policy must be clear and relayed effectively to the entire student body through assemblies, class meetings, and letters to parents about these guidelines. A sensible and rational code must be developed that clearly brands unacceptable behaviors in ways children understand.

3. Teach the difference between telling and tattling: Children need to understand that telling is a way to help friends, not get them into trouble. Help them discover ways to break "a code of silence" that exists around bullying by

emphasizing adult protection. Becoming tough with bullying behaviors can help all children feel more powerful and less victimized. Create a bully telephone hotline number to give kids.

4. Find supportive research on bullying: Involvement in bully-victim problems at school, especially for students with relatively little social support, is significantly related to suicide ideation (Rigby and Slee, 1999). These findings emphasize the importance of adult intervention, peer intervention, and onlooker intervention in deterring or eliminating the isolation of many victimized children and teens.

5. Use resources and curricula on bullying: Bullying resources and curricula can create safe schools. Educators need to use lessons and classroom discussion branding bullying behaviors, defining bullying, creating compassion for victims through role playing, exploring feelings of bullies and victims, and presenting other ways to solve problems.

Adults can spontaneously create teachable moments about bullying when watching news with kids, teaching current events in the classroom, or even witnessing mistreatment at a shopping mall. Talk with children about what is acceptable and appropriate behavior. Teach children guidelines to report threats safely. Guide them to see any bullying behaviors in themselves and identify boundaries to help them eliminate these behaviors.

Conclusion

Bullying and victimization issues have reached epidemic proportions in our country and the world. American schools harbor "2.1 million bullies and 2.7 million of their victims" (Fried, 1996, p.x.). The complex issues involved in bullying include the powerlessness of the victims, the cruelty of the bully, the abstinence of the onlookers, and the obliviousness of adults to recognize and to stop this insidious cycle of violence.

Research presented by Simon Hunter, James Boyle, and David Warden in the *British Journal of Educational Psychology,* in the article "Help Seeking Amongst Child and Adolescent Victims of Peer-Aggression and Bullying: The Influence of

School-stage, Gender, Victimization, Appraisal, and Emotion" (in press, 2004), indicate that pupils are more willing to seek help when they see the situation as one in which something can be achieved, and that this needs to be emphasized to teachers. This study shows that an extremely small percentage of victimized students felt endorsed by teachers, but felt freer telling friends and family members who proved to be valuable allies in tackling the problem. These findings suggest the need for more teacher involvement in identifying bullying incidents and teacher support for protection. Telling a trusted ally indicates that the peer support initiatives can be used as a powerful intervention.

Too often we see victims of prolonged bulling eventually become withdrawn or isolated, or, in extreme cases, aggressive and violent, ultimately resulting in a quick resolution for a prolonged painful problem in the form of suicide or violent rampage. Ronald Stevens, executive director of the National School Safety Center, said, "As we look at the profile of perpetrators, the majority were victims first" (Walls, p. 1). This subject of victims of bullying turning to violence will be addressed in Chapter 4 on school shootings.

It seems all too apparent that one of the answers to social violence may be the prevention of bullying behavior. Part of the prevention is education, for adults and children. When a community is educated in recognizing hurtful behaviors, they are more likely to intervene and eliminate them.

Resources

RESOURCES FOR STUDENTS ON BULLYING

Bullies Are a Pain in the Brain (1997) by Trevor Romain is an easy-to-read book that talks to kids about bullies and ways to stop them.

Getting Equipped to Stop Bullying (1998) by Becki Boatwright, Teresa Mathis, and Susan Smith is a kid's survival kit for understanding and coping with violence in the schools.

How to Handle Bullies, Teasers and Other Meanies: A Book That Takes the Nuisance Out of Name Calling and Other Nonsense (1995) by Kate Cohen-Posey is a book that gives ideas and healthy ways to respond to meanness such as name calling and insults.

"How to Make Yourself Bully-Proof" (*Current Health,* Oct., 1998) by Linda Goldman is an article written for middle-school children about bullying and practical ways to work with the problem.

BULLYING CURRICULA FOR EDUCATORS

No-Bullying Curriculum (1998) is a curriculum on bullying that provides classroom teachers with tools to deal with bullying and that involves all school personnel, students, and parents.

No Putdowns Character-Building Violence Prevention Curriculum (1998) is a school-based curriculum dealing with violence prevention and character building for educators.

The Peaceful Classroom by Charles Smith (1993) is a curriculum with many activities to teach preschoolers compassion and cooperation.

RESOURCES FOR ADULTS ON BULLYING

Olweus, Dan. *Bullying at School.* (2000). Maiden, MA: Blackwell. This book provides understandings about bullying at school and what can be done about it.

Ross, Dorothea. *Childhood Bullying and Teasing.* (1996). Alexandria, VA: ACA. Suggestions about what school personnel and other caring adults can do about bullying.

*(Please refer to Chapter 12 for additional resources for Curricula for Educators and Adults on Bullying.)

C H A P T E R 4

School Violence: No Place to Feel Safe

SCHOOL SHOOTINGS • YOUTH VIOLENCE
WARNING SIGNS • TECHNIQUES FOR ANGER
THE SNIPER • CODE BLUE • WITNESSING
A TRAUMA • SPONTANEOUS LEARNING
CLASS MEETINGS • GUNS • GANGS
SECRET SERVICE REPORT

An eye for an eye ends up making the whole world blind.

Mahatma Ghandi

School Shootings: Bullying and Hidden Rage

We need to see the unmistakable relationship between juvenile homicide and suicide and repressed rage from years and years of bullying, taunting, intimidation, isolation, and abuse by classmates taking place within our schools in this country. Bullying has become a national disease, an epidemic reaching record proportions with kids, from preschoolers to teens. Thousands and thousands of children stay home from school each day, terrified of humiliation or worse at the hands of bullies or violent crimes within our schools.

"160,000 children miss school every day due to fear of attack or intimidation by other students"

(Fried & Fried, 1996).

School shootings affect kids, parents, educators, communities, and nations. The violence in our youth terrifies their peers and the surrounding adults. The shooting at Santana High in San Diego, California, is one of the many horrific examples with bullying and victimization at its core. The gunman was a fifteen-year-old boy whose rampage killed two of his classmates and injured thirteen others. It was reported that he had suffered verbal abuse and was constantly subjected to ridicule at school. He was called "gay," "skinny," and "a country boy."

FRIENDS KNEW AND DIDN'T TELL

Friends of this enraged boy have been ostracized and told not to come back to their schools for their own safety at school. Classmates were enraged at their failure to take the warning signs of the young gunman's boastings of future killings seriously. They did not tell authorities.

These friends experienced many secondary losses. Some include the death of classmates, the incarceration of a friend, being ostracized by classmates and faculty, the loss of their school, and the guilt of knowing perhaps they could have done something to stop the violence and did not. Media that sometimes exploit young people when they are most vulnerable compounds this. Student witnesses and survivors of violence may be exposed immediately after an incident on national TV. In interviews sharing their raw emotions, they may continually be displayed for the country and the world to see over and over again (Goldman 2001, 93).

ADULTS KNEW AND DIDN'T HELP

Like the shooter's friends who heard plans to kill classmates and kept silent, the adult who was told also did not tell. This adult said the troubled teen was just kidding about his threats and explained, "I never thought he would do that. I knew he was teased and taunted. I saw it happen myself."

Again and again we hear of students who resort to violent rampages after being themselves victims of continuing harassment at school over long periods of time. No adult or peer stood up to stop the abuse. Victimized youth disown their confusion, sadness, and rage, and all too often project these attributes onto the world through guns, drugs, and shooting sprees. These are kids living in isolated, hate-filled worlds, with no moral compass to help them navigate through their destructive feelings and thoughts (Goldman 2001, 93).

Bullying and Victimization: Youth Violence

So often repeated bullying through taunting, teasing, hitting, and isolating leads children into uncharted territories, whereby nice kids feel enraged and don't know what to do with new feelings of hatred and revenge. The American Academy of Child and Adolescent Psychiatry warns, "Violent behavior in a child at any age always needs to be taken seriously," and should "not be dismissed as a phase they are going through."

Elizabeth was a fourteen-year-old who had been continually bullied at her middle school. She was taunted, teased, and alienated from her peers at school. Sometimes she was called "fat" and "stupid," other times she was barked at like a dog. The harassment became so frequent and intense that Elizabeth left the school. She entered a private school in the hopes of starting a new life, but soon the same patterns emerged of being ostracized and tormented. She began exhibiting self-injurious behaviors, isolating herself, and expressing suicide ideation. Elizabeth confided her behaviors and feelings to a new friend she had come to trust, only to discover that the friend had divulged her secrets and was part of the group teasing her. This accumulation of years of bullying exploded in rage at herself and this friend. Taking the family gun to school, she intended to shoot herself but instead shot her friend to "show her what she had done."

Elizabeth was arrested and is now incarcerated until age twenty-one. She feels her punishment is just and daily regrets what she did. Her reason for speaking about this school shooting is "to help other kids like her" who have been repeatedly abused by their peers.

Young people like Elizabeth who have been tormented by bullying may well have hidden rage that can surface suddenly and dramatically when they reach their breaking point. Children who have been victims of abuse, have a violent parent, hold a history of previous violent behavior, or are exposed to guns may be at risk. Boys and girls who join gangs or express interest in joining gangs, or those who isolate themselves, may be at risk.

WARNING SIGNS OF VIOLENCE IN CHILDREN

In a recent American Psychological Association (APA) poll, 40% of children polled said they were concerned about a potentially violent classmate and wanted to know the warning signs of violence. These APA warning signs indicate that "violence is a serious possibility" in children who exhibit them.

- Loss of temper on a daily basis
- Frequent physical fighting
- Significant vandalism or property damage
- Increase in use of drugs or alcohol
- Increase in risk-taking behavior
- Detailed plans to commit acts of violence

- Announcing threats or plans for hurting others
- Enjoying hurting animals
- Carrying a weapon
  (Child Violence: The Warning Signs http://www.msnbc.com/news/261462.asp)

PROJECTIVE TECHNIQUES FOR ANGER MANAGEMENT

Teaching children to work with anger in healthy ways that don't harm themselves or others is essential. Giving them positive alternatives to smoldering rage by incorporating projective techniques is important. These techniques allow children to safely place their feelings outside of themselves.

Children and teens can:

- Hit a punching bag in their room or their pillow.
- Scream into a tape recorder.
- Draw or write feelings or messages to someone who has been hurtful. This can feel satisfying and freeing. They can also keep a journal or write in a diary.
- Do something physical like running around the block, jumping rope, or playing sports.
- Learn self-defense techniques like martial arts or wrestling.

Young children can:

- Manipulate puppets to act out angry scenarios.
- Play with dollhouses and toys to show what happened. They can begin to release underlying feelings of terror and rage.
- Use a sand table to reenact a bullying episode on the playground. This allows children to play out the scene in a different way and safely strategize helpful alternatives.
- Make a bully out of clay and symbolically smash the figure. Children can safely vent hostility against the abuser.
- Read resources about anger with children, such as "Angry Arthur" and "The Hurt," which allow a pathway for children to openly and safely dialogue about their angry feelings.

An informative resource for adults in working with children and anger is the book *A Volcano in My Tummy* (1996). It provides concrete ideas and practical activities to help kids with anger management and positive alternatives to expressing strong feelings that can be hurtful.

CHILDREN, TEENS, AND GUNS

"Every day in the U.S. guns kill ten children" (*Prime Time Thursday, March 8, 2001*). "A gun in the home is 43 times more likely to be used to kill a family member or friend or to commit suicide than to defend oneself" (www.gangsandkids. comlstats.html. 02/16 /02). "Even though 66% of parents of 8- to 11-year olds said they had talked to their kids about guns in school, only half of their children remembered having such a conversation" (Dickinson, 2001, p. 82).

Our western concept of a gun toting anti-hero only magnifies and glamorizes an angry youth's attraction to guns. We must ask ourselves how much we can expect from our young people, who are developmentally impulsive and immature in their reactions to stress. Gun control is one timely argument to help stop the violence in our homes, schools, and communities.

Clearly, we must recognize this impulsivity of children and teens, and the allure and mystification surrounding guns in today's culture. Studies (*Prime Time Thursday*) show that our brightest girls and boys, when left alone with a gun, act impulsively and will play dangerously with it. *Prime Time* presented research that teenagers' blood levels and hormones actually increase in the presence of a gun. They seem to forget all of the adult warnings for that instant gratification of feeling all-powerful. If they have no access to guns, they cannot follow through by using them. *Prime Time Live, 2001* reported on March 8 that, "43% of American homes have guns," and explained that if your kids do not have them in their home, statistically, the kids in the house next door probably do. (Breaking the Silence, 2004, p. 94)

Children Witnessing School Violence

When children and teens witness a violent episode in a school setting, it becomes imprinted on their psyches. "These memories are not static photographic type images. They are fluid. Even infants and toddlers have the capacity to carry a 'movie' inside their heads, with repetitive 'showings' re-triggered by internal or external cues" (Gaensbaurer, 1996). Often the younger the child is the more he or she will internalize the experience and incorporate similar nonviolent experiences as the original violent trauma.

Children and teens witnessing a traumatic event may exhibit symptoms of trauma by reexperiencing, avoiding, or becoming numb to reminders of the incident. Crying a lot, withdrawing, isolating themselves, or being preoccupied with reasoning "why" may evolve as a trauma sign. Regression, and even disruption of natural developments such as toilet training or anger control may occur. Children may identify with the person that died and the way they died and become preoccupied with pervasive thoughts and even longings to be with that person.

The effects of witnessing violence can create self-destructive behaviors, anxiety, and increased aggression. Family members who have independently witnessed the trauma may demonstrate similar signs of hypervigilance and sleep disorders, reinforcing the conditions the child may already be displaying. Media portrayal of violence or other violent acts in the home or school may bring up memories and feelings related to the previous trauma that the child might interpret as the original event.

Trauma may not be only a psychological disorder, but a natural consequence to what is happening—a condition of life based on a real event. Trauma reactions can be innate and arguably healthy reactions to a survival or instinctual fear based on threatening circumstances.

THE EFFECT OF WITNESSING TRAUMA ON DEVELOPMENT

Shawn was a five-year-old who witnessed the violent stabbing of his older brother, Joey, at school. Mom had picked him up from his classroom for a doctor's appointment. As they were leaving the school building they heard screams and ran to the playground. A twelve-year-old boy was stabbing his brother. Shawn screamed and screamed "stop, stop, stop!!!" over and over again, and he and his mom rushed to get help. Joey was taken to the hospital and soon died.

The boys were fighting over a basketball and the interchange escalated into violence. Soon after the incident Shawn began to show signs of trauma. He became edgy, passing by students and hitting them as he went. When asked why, he said, "They don't like me. They would have hit me first." He cried a lot, began bedwetting, stayed up most of the night, and when he slept he frequently had nightmares. In many therapy sessions he would reenacted the scene continually acting out the stabbing. He even stabbed himself as part of the reenactment.

Shawn's Traumatic Signs

- Obsessive and intrusive thoughts: "Only for a ball . . . Only for a ball . . ."

- Re-enactment: "I'm stabbing the guy that killed Joey."

- Self-destructive behaviors: "I stabbed myself with a fork."

- Aggressive acts: "I hit him first because I thought he was going to hit me."

- Separation anxiety: "I want my mom. I know she is driving back to the playground and can get hurt."

- Sleep disturbance and hypervigilance: "I'm sleeping by the door to guard the house so no one can hurt us."

- Shared family trauma patterns: "My mom and sister stay up all night with me to guard the door against danger."
- Suicidal ideation: "I want to die and be with Joey. I know how I will do it. I'll stab myself."

Remind children that their intruding feelings and thoughts are not happening now.
Remind children that these intruding feelings and thoughts are connected to their past experience of trauma.
Remind children that they have survived the original trauma.

Random Acts of Violence: A School Shooting

In the fall of 2002, Montgomery County, Maryland, was terrorized along with neighboring Washington, D.C., and Virginia by a multilevel rampage of mass sniper attacks that kept a community hostage for more than three weeks. Residents were frightened to leave their homes, go to stores, eat at restaurants, or purchase gas. Killers assaulted victims in the most familiar of places: shopping malls, gas stations, public lawns, and schools. Tarps were placed over gas pumps to create the semblance of safety. Media shared daily reports about law enforcement progress in apprehending the snipers and shared evidence and clues as they emerged. Everyone was scared. Parents, educators, and children lived in fear that they would be the next victims, as these random acts of violence appeared in their neighborhoods, homes, and schools without warning.

Children became prime targets for fear during this incomprehensible siege. They felt the terror of the adult community as parents and teachers verbally and non-verbally shared major concerns for their welfare. When the gunman shot a middle school boy, the immensity of this violent episode became all too real for the children. Students realized if he could be shot, so could they. Parents escorted their kids to and from school. No one except faculty and students was allowed in or out of school buildings during the day. Sports teams couldn't play outside and games were cancelled. Police monitored the buildings. Outdoor recess was replaced by indoor play. Police patrolled the school grounds. School systems were on Code Blue, a system within a school where children remained inside for their own protection.

An educator reported the loss for the children of their day-to-day routine during the sniper attacks, as they searched to find meaning in a new world that didn't feel safe and restricted their familiar routine. She explained that it was like working in a dungeon because all of the windows and doors were shut tight due to Code Blue. The blinds had to be down at all times and any door with windows had to be covered with bulletin board paper.

TEACHABLE MOMENTS

Teachable moments are golden opportunities for immediate learning, timely processing, and important reassurance. They catch the flow of a natural point in time that spontaneously emerges during the daily routine. Educators can draw upon this learning opportunity in reacting to the situation as it occurs with interest and time. During times of crisis, teachable moments become a tool not only for the prospect of instantaneous understandings but also for needed assurances of safety and protection.

The following is an account of a school experience during the rampage of random sniper shootings and the thoughtful approach of one educator to a student's spontaneous response to the uncertainty around her. The teacher's wisdom in creating a teachable moment to reduce fear and educate students proved highly effective during the crisis situation.

Kerry, age 6, was so frustrated. She wanted to be able to go outside and play. Her school was on Code Blue alert and she was walking in line down the hall and talking to her friend, Charlene. "I used to have a favorite color but now I don't." When Charlene asked her what her favorite color used to be, she said, "It used to be blue, but now I hate blue because it means we are in trouble." When several of her classmates concurred with her statement, Mrs. Jones, her first-grade teacher, decided to have an impromptu discussion in the hallway about "feeling safe." The children readily shared concerns they were holding in about the sniper, Code Blue, and safety issues. They made a list of all of the ways their school was working to keep them safe and they left with Kerry telling Charlene she felt a lot better after she had a chance to talk about it.

A second-grade teacher, Miss Atkins, helped one of her students, Allison, with a teachable moment when Allison outburst of unexpected tears emerged during a classroom spelling lesson. Allison had heard on the news that day that the sniper had left a message that none of the children would be safe at home or at school. She had been worrying about it all day in school. As she began sobbing uncontrollably in  the middle of the lesson, Miss Atkins told the class to wait and took Allison into another room and asked her what was wrong. Allison couldn't talk but began drawing the picture shown here.

After she finished drawing, she began to explain. "I'm so scared I'll get hurt too." Miss Atkins gave her a hug and began explaining all of the ways the adults around her were keeping her safe. She decided to have a classroom discussion on safety and have kids brainstorm what they felt adults could do to help them feel safe.

CLASS MEETING: GRADE 2

Classroom discussions after a traumatic event provide the opportunity to give children accurate information. They create a forum to identify perceptions of the event, release shared feelings and normalize them, and reinforce concepts of safety and of the adult world working hard to prevent a reoccurrence.

The Sniper: "Your children aren't safe, anywhere, at any time."

Jaime Brinkman's second-grade class at an elementary school in Montgomery County, Maryland, had growing concerns about the sniper episode terrorizing their everyday lives, and especially the shooting of a child at a nearby school. Her six- and seven-year-old students were experiencing too many stomachaches, headaches, nightmares, and waking worries. She decided to implement a system for class meetings that would allow an open forum for discussion and processing.

The children were particularly anxious, active, and distracted on the day of the meeting. The media had shared the latest message from the invisible sniper: "Your children are not safe, anywhere, at any time." Most of the children had heard about it before they came to school, and those who hadn't soon heard from friends. Troubled by this threat so close to home, they wondered where they were safe and what they should do. Mrs. Brinkman formulated the following model that could be modified for any grade level to initiate and conduct a class meeting.

MODEL FOR CLASS MEETING SURROUNDING TRAUMA

A Second-Grade Class Discussion: The Sniper

1. *Question children about what they know.* This helps to understand their interpretations of the trauma and clarify any misconceptions. Teachers need to be prepared that some children might be upset by the conversation. Others may want to talk at length and those conversations can be deferred to a private time later. Ask the students, "Why have we been having Code Blue or lock down the past few weeks? What do you think has been going on?"

2. *Clarify what has taken place.* Explain to the children that a person has been making poor choices on purpose to hurt other people. This has made people sad, scared, worried, and even angry. The children may have heard people call this person a sniper.

3. ***Reassure children the adult world is working to create safety.*** Restore confidence for children that community agencies such as police, FBI, detectives, and government personnel are working very hard to keep everyone safe. These agencies are working around the clock (even when children are sleeping) to keep everyone protected.

4. ***Review existing school procedures for traumatic time.*** Code Blue is a plan for safety. We check to be sure that everyone is where they are supposed to be and also check to be sure the doors are locked to keep things extra safe. Also, remind children that Code Blue can be used for many things, including snow or a tornado or earthquake.

5. ***Allow children to brainstorm ways to stay safe.*** Walking home from school with friends or family members. Staying inside. Being sure someone knows where you are. Locking the doors of your home. Remembering in school that our building is made of strong things to keep us safe inside, just like at home or in other buildings.

6. ***Remind students:*** They are survivors of a difficult experience. How proud we all have been with them for working hard and learning when things are difficult. It is okay to talk about their feelings. It is okay to be afraid (or any other feeling) or maybe not to feel anything at all. Many people can feel many different ways. It is all ok and normal.

7. ***Encourage*** children to develop methods to feel better. Find a family member, teacher, or friend to talk with. Play with a favorite toy. Hug a stuffed animal or someone you care about. Listen to music. Exercise or dance or play basketball. Stop watching TV if it makes you worried.

8. ***Ask children if they have any questions.*** They might ask: Are they going to catch the sniper? Can he come to our school? Why is it taking so long? What are the police doing?

9. ***Support children in finding the positive in people.*** "Look for the helpers, you will always find people that are helping" (Rogers & Bluestone Sharapan, 2001). This is the advice given to Mr. Rogers by his mom to help him handle his discomfort when he experienced a public tragedy. Ralph spoke with admiration about Police Chief Moose and his diligence

and relentlessness in finding the sniper. "Not only did he work all the time until the murderers were caught, but he seemed so nice," Ralph explained. "I saw him cry on TV when he spoke of the boy that got shot."

10. ***Invite children to draw*** or write about how they are feeling right now.

The following are examples of children's drawings and writings as a result of the second-grade meeting at their elementary school. Some felt happy in school, some felt sad, and some felt like school was a safe place to be. Others worried what would happen when they left school to go home or went shopping at a mall and were afraid the sniper could hurt them or their loved ones.

Casey shares feelings of happiness and safety at school during the sniper siege.

Shantel feels happy and grumpy, too.

Bobbi and Toren feel sad.

Keale and Deion are scared and sad. All feelings are OK.

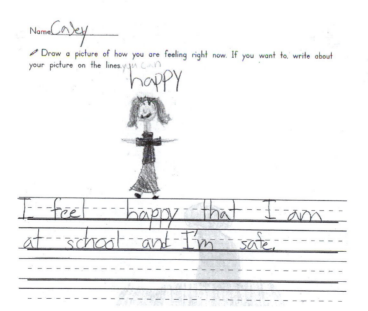

Name Casey

🖉 Draw a picture of how you are feeling right now. If you want to, write about your picture on the lines. you can

happy

I feel happy that I am at school and I'm safe.

By Shantel

grupey

Name Shantel

Draw a picture of how you are feeling right now. If you want to, write about your picture on the lines.

Rith now I am
feeling happy When
I am in school. I
feel saf when I am here

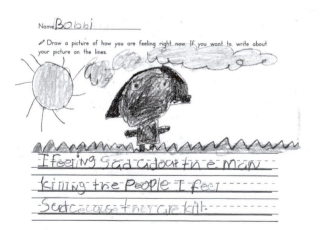

Name Bobbi

Draw a picture of how you are feeling right now. If you want to, write about your picture on the lines.

I feeling sad about the man
kiiing the People I feel
Sadcauusthey are kiil

Name Toren

✏ Draw a picture of how you are feeling right now. If you want to, write about your picture on the lines.

1 fell said ctry now.

Name Keale

✏ Draw a picture of how you are feeling right now. If you want to, write about your picture on the lines.

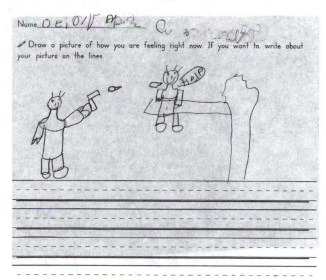

Name Deiolt PAP a

✏ Draw a picture of how you are feeling right now. If you want to, write about your picture on the lines.

AN EIGHTH-GRADE BOYS' GUIDANCE GROUP: REACTION TO VIOLENCE

During the sniper siege a sensitive middle-school counselor, Mr. Blake, noticed more edginess and hyperactivity in his eighth-grade boys and wondered if a guidance group would be of benefit. At the onset most of the boys were quiet, and there was little discussion. Then Thomas, a six-foot basketball player, admitted that "No one has asked me what I think about the sniper before." Mr. Blake then asked the boys the following questions, and the discussion became more lively and intense.

1. *What exactly do you know?*
2. *What do you imagine is happening?*
3. *How are you feeling?*
4. *What do you think about how the adults are handling things?*
5. *What have you lost out on during this event?*
6. *Is there anything you can do for yourself and others?*

Feelings emerged and more understandings unfolded. Douglas said he was angry he couldn't play football or practice outside and all of his games had been cancelled. Rick was upset that the class trip had been cancelled. Carlos confessed he was scared, and most of the others agreed. George said it made him nervous that a boy his age who looked like him got shot by the sniper at a school very much like his own. Mathew worried about his mom, who worked across the street from the gas station where the first victim was murdered. When time ran out and the boys were leaving, Mathew said he felt better and a little more hopeful. He left the group sharing his new perspective: "I think he will be caught."

Gangs and School Violence: A Special Issue

"Real power is having power over yourself, not over other people."

Stanley Tookie Williams (cofounder of the Crips, now on death row in San Quentin State Prison)

So often adults have the preconceived notion that gangs are born solely out of necessity for the poor, and that joining together creates a surrogate family needed to replace the support and protection missing in their lives. In effect, for many adolescents of all socioeconomic strata, gangs create a fertile ground for drugs, alcohol, violence, and a source of income through drug dealing and crime that they would not otherwise be able to attain. More and more, younger people from "supportive" families are finding themselves in ganglike activities and organizing into groups to protect themselves from each other.

The Arizona Attorney General Website for Teens reports in Arizona 13,497 children age 18 and under are gang members. Among ninth- and tenth-graders statewide, 7% are involved with gangs. The site presents the factors associated with youth joining gangs, described as *pulls* (status and prestige among peers) or *pushes* (social, cultural, and economic forces that lure kids into gang involvement). These factors include perceptions of a kind of love and structure, belonging, recognition, companionship, feelings of self-worth, acceptance, and a kind of pseudo-family involvement.

A gang is a group of people who want to be seen as different from others and want others to perceive them as a distinct group. They identify with gang names, colors, language or hand signs, and wear a certain type of clothing. They share the same kind of thinking, habits and lifestyle. Gang members are normally between the ages of 10 and 21 and come from every neighborhood, race, religion, culture, and economic level. These groups come together for the purpose of engaging in criminal activity. (Arizona Attorney General Website for Teens, http://www.ag.state.az.us/ChildrensPage/gangs/.html, p. 2)

Gangs operate through intimidation. As one ten-year-old told her teacher, "If they want something, you give it to them." Another teacher explained the allure for teens and preteens to look like gang members as a sign of status. Wearing their special signs and tattoos can be life threatening. One second-grader, Tommy, started doing the dance ritual that a local gang used after someone was killed. "You better stop doing that," his friend Sam warned. "You can get killed too if you do it."

WHAT MAKES A GANG ATTRACTIVE?

Today's youth face a lack of leadership and role models that forces them into situations in which they create their own. Gangs provide rules, boundaries, leadership, and the appearance of protection, giving members the false security that, as a group, they can do whatever they want and get away with it. Often gangs participate in some kind of illegal activity such as violent crime or drug dealing or both.

DIMINISHING GANG POWER

Adults can reduce the power of gang recruitment by becoming familiar with the signs of gang membership. School systems, parents, and police can work together to share information, create support groups for networking, act on information leading to identifying gang leaders, and create a nonviolent environment for gang members who are starting over. Because gangs symbolize "family" to their members, the bond is difficult to break. School and community systems need to create programs that provide the self-esteem and protection our youth need that provide an outlet for aggression, model nonviolent ways of life, and keep them safe from physical harm.

SIGNS OF GANG MEMBERSHIP

- Graffiti or "tags" on books and clothes to mark territory
- Bandanas, scarves, and emblems worn constantly
- Code words
- Handshakes and hand signals
- Staying out late and not coming home
- Extra money with no believable explanation
- School truancy and poor performance
- Sudden changes in friends

WHY JOIN A GANG?

Sixteen-year-old Sara had run away from home several times and was eventually placed in a residential treatment center for teens with emotional issues. She attended a support group for runaway adolescents with mutual problems and concerns. Group discussion began to center around gang membership and values. One twelve-year-old girl gave valuable input about her experience in a gang. Sara, although not a gang member, shared her opinions about why young people join gangs in the following way:

What Are the Five Best Things About Joining a Gang?

1. Protection

2. People are scared of you

3. Fun

4. Family

5. Get what you want

Why Join?

1. Lack of family: gang gives a sense of belonging

2. Media portrays gangs as being "cool"

3. Peer pressure

4. Have no other place to go: gang "family" functions as the provider

What Stopped You from Becoming a Gang Member?

1. I didn't join a gang because I have already lived that whole "street life"

2. I have things to live for. It's not worth having to look over your shoulder every minute.

Sara, age 12

TOOKIE'S STORY

Stanley Tookie Williams is the cofounder of the Crips street gang in Los Angeles, California, who is now serving his twenty-fourth year on death row. He tries to keep young people from the deadly path he chose by writing anti-gang books for children and promoting an anti-gang website, the Internet Project for Street Peace. This is Tookies self portrait at three. He drew it in solitary confinement where he was only allowed a 2 1/2 inch pencil without an eraser.

Tookie explains in one of his children's books, *Gangs and Violence,* his philosophy and warning about violence and youth. "We started the Crips to protect ourselves and our families from other gangs. We used violence against their violence. But starting the Crips only made things worse. The only thing that I was doing was destroying my own kind. I'd like to make amends for the madness, you know," Williams told CNN in an interview from his cell. (Lefeure 2004) The following is Tookie's advice to incarcerated youth, No. 1 (2001) which appears on his website. (CNN.com.usnews.lefeure, http://archives.cnn2000us/1202death.row)

Across this nation, countless young men and woman, like you, are vegetating in juvenile halls and in youth authorities. More and more prisons are being constructed to accommodate your generation when you grow to adulthood. The question is can you become motivated enough to defy the expectations that many people have of you? . . . It's time to flip the script. You or I can complain 24x7 about the problems of poverty, drugs, violence, racism and other injustices, but unless we choose to initiate personal change, we will remain puppets of unjust conditions. Unless we change, we will be incapable of changing the circumstances around us. (www.tookie.com/abouttc.html)

PREVENTING SCHOOL SHOOTINGS: A SUMMARY OF THE U.S. SECRET SERVICE SAFE SCHOOLS INITIATIVE REPORT, 2002

Several high-profile shootings in schools over the past decade have resulted in increased fear among students, parents, and educators. The U.S. Secret Service prepared a report summarizing findings associated with school violence. The findings indicated that knowledge about the attack had usually been given out, the violent act was often planned, no ethnic stereotype was evident, and easy access to guns and bullying were key factors.

FINDINGS OF THE REPORT

1. Prior to most incidences, the attacker told someone about his idea or plan. In more than 75% of the cases, the attacker told a friend, sibling, or schoolmate before taking action. In one case the attacker told 24 people about wanting to kill students, build bombs, or carry out an attack at school.

2. Incidents of targeted violence are rarely impulsive. In almost all cases studied, the attacker developed the idea to harm the target victim before the attack.

3. There is no accurate or useful profile of "the school shooter." Attackers varied in racial and ethnic background for ages eleven through twenty-one.

4. Most attackers had easy access to guns. In nearly two-thirds of the incidents attackers got guns from their own homes or relatives' homes.

5. Most school shooting incidents were not resolved by law enforcement intervention. More than half of the attacks ended before law enforcement responded to the scene.

6. In many cases, other students were involved in some capacity. Although the attacker acted alone in two-thirds of the cases, over half of these cases involved friends or fellow students who influenced or encouraged the attacker to act.

7. Bullying can be a key factor in the decision to attack. A number of attackers had experienced bullying and harassment that were longstanding and severe, which motivated their attack at school. Attackers described bullying as tormenting and as behaviors that would have met the legal definition of harassment in the workplace.

8. Most attackers engaged in some behavior prior to the incident that caused concern or indicated a need for help. More than 75% of the attackers had threatened to kill themselves during the attack, made suicidal gestures, or tried to kill themselves before their attack.

RECOMMENDATIONS IN THE REPORT

A U.S. Secret Service School Initiative report suggested recommendations to school systems based on their findings. They emphasized that an important effort in prevention may be to ensure that young people have opportunities to talk and connect with caring adults.

1. It is important that threat assessment inquiries involve efforts to gather information from anyone who may have contact with the identified high-risk student. It also is important to decrease barriers that may prevent students who have information from coming forward. In addition, both schools and investigators need thoughtful, effective system for handling and analyzing any information that is provided.

2. Plans to prevent school violence should involve adults attending to concerns when someone poses a threat (engaging in behaviors that indicate intent, planning, or preparation for an attack) rather than waiting for someone to make a direct threat (telling people they intend to harm someone).

3. Quick efforts to inquire about and intervene when knowledge is gained of intent and planning is extremely important. Inquiry should include investigation of, and attention to, grievances and bad feelings towards school.

4. An inquiry based on the student's behaviors rather than traits will be more productive. The aim is to determine if the student appears to be planning or preparing for an attack. If so, how far along are the plans, and when or where would intervention be possible?

5. A threat assessment should include investigation of weapon access and give attention to any communication about a weapon.

6. Schools can make the best use of their resources by working with law enforcement on prevention efforts as well as critical incident response plans.

7. Bullying played a major role in a number of school shootings, and a major focus of ongoing efforts should be to combat bullying in our schools.

8. This study indicates the importance of giving attention to students who are having difficulty coping with major losses or perceived failures, particularly when feelings of desperation and hopelessness are involved.

Conclusion

Although recent school shootings have raised safety concerns and fears of reccurrence, it is important to emphasize to children and teens that shootings are rare incidents. Because shootings such as the one at Columbine have drawn considerable national attention in the media, there appears to be strong public opinion to prevent them. "The actual incidence of targeted violence in the U.S. occurred in 37 communities across the country between December 1974 and May 2000" (Fein et al. 2002, 12). This indicates that school-based attacks are rare compared to other types of violent crime to which children are exposed.

Seventy percent of survey respondents believed a school shooting could happen in their community (Washington Wire, April 21, 1998). John Stossel (1999) critiqued television coverage of these infrequent school shootings and reported that the three major networks aired 296 stories on the Columbine shooting alone. He pointed out that lightning and bathtub accidents cause far more deaths for children but receive comparatively little media coverage. This validates the huge impact of the media's repeated images in inducing fear. This also confirms that our vigilance is important to remind our young people that the vast majority of students in our country will complete their schooling without ever being touched by peer violence.

In the wake of these infrequent but highly publicized school shootings, more pressure and public demand has evolved to prevent violent rampages in our communities. There is hope that the Secret Service findings will shed light on school shootings and the idea that they are more than random acts of violence; they usually are well planned and well executed, and involve a bully issue and guns. Many of the school shooters had difficulty coping with loss and failure, planned their acts of violence carefully, and told or included others. There is a strong recommendation to take any threat seriously and maintain a threat assessment program and communication with legal authorities. These are the very kids the report suggests need adult attention, caring, and connection. Emphasis must be placed on the internal and external environment that leads to school shootings rather than on the shooting itself.

Resources

FOR EDUCATORS ON SCHOOL VIOLENCE

Children Surviving in a World of Violence by McDaniel (2000) is a curriculum that includes 35 lessons for students in grades 5 to 9 for coping with a violent world.

Healing Images for Children by Klein (2001) presents activities to help children cope with stress and create positive outcomes.

Helping Teens Stop Violence by Allan Creighton (1992) is a practical guide for counselors and educators.

Picking Up the Pieces by Gabriel Constans (1997) is a book about violent death with interventions useful in working with middle-school students.

The Peaceful Classroom by Smith (1993) provides activities to teach preschoolers compassion and cooperation.

FOR CHILDREN AND TEENS ON SCHOOL VIOLENCE

Guns (1997) by R. Schulson is a story for young children that presents the facts they need to know about guns.

Just One Flick of the Finger (1996) by Lorbiecki is the story of a young boy who accidentally brings a gun to school and shoots a friend.

Just One Tear (1992) by K. Mahon is an honest account written by a fourteen-year-old of the overwhelming emotions after a boy witnesses his father being shot and fatally wounded. It includes accounts of the trial and its outcome.

The Boy Who Sat by the Window (1997) by Chris Loftis is an excellent book for young children. It tells about a boy who gets murdered and the cycle of violence that surrounds him.

When Someone You Know Has Been Killed (1998) by J. Schleifer is a book for middle-school children that discusses the emotions felt when someone experiences a murder and offers strategies to cope.

After a Murder: A Workbook for Grieving Children (2001) by the Dougy Center is an interactive workbook for children who have experienced a murder and the many issues that surround it.

ON GANG VIOLENCE

Bad Boy (1994) by W. Myers is about a boy who lives in foster care and becomes involved with gangs and drugs. He finally graduates from school, joins the army, and then begins to write books for children.

Life in Prison (1998) by S. Williams is a book of true stories about prison life. It is written by the author for middle-school children to encourage them to make better choices.

(Please refer to Chapter 12 for additional resources on gang violence.)

PART II

Working with Kids and Trauma: Home, School, Community

CHAPTER 5
Trauma Resolution Techniques: Helping Our Kids Succeed

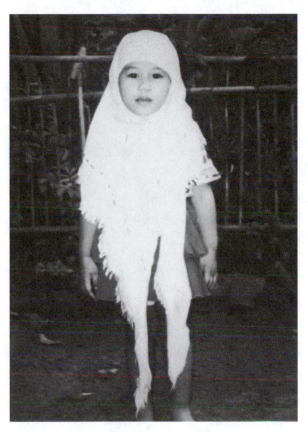

TELLING THE STORY • PROJECTIVE PLAY •
EMERGENCY PLANS • SAFE BOXES •
PUNCHING BAGS • PEACEFUL PLACES • PROPS •
WORRY BOXES • POEMS • LETTER WRITING •
MEMORY WORK

If opportunity doesn't knock, build a door.

Unknown

Children Feeling Safe in Today's World

The eternal question of how we can prepare our children to live in a world that we can't understand ourselves has been magnified for the generations of kids born into a personal and media-induced intimate experience of war, terrorism, random violence, and nuclear threat that the adults around them had never known. We ask ourselves what we can do for the children, and the response might well be to allow them to grieve their losses, help them reduce their fears, and instill in them again a sense of safety and protection in their homes, their schools, their communities, and their world.

Encourage children to remember that they are a part of a nation and a world that has survived challenging experiences. Remind them that human beings can work together and survive during difficult times. Throughout history many bad things have happened to good people and they and their countries have stayed strong and the world survived.

Activities That Help Kids Tell and Retell Their Story

One of the common signs of children under stress is that they may need to tell their story over and over again. We can help them do this by listening, sharing, and providing opportunities to help them retell and reframe their experience. Giving young people an open-ended avenue for relaying their experience of a challenging time is a key intervention. By allowing them to express their difficulties, share remaining worries, and present a new self-view, adults are giving them permission to recreate a worrisome experience. When we ask children to tell us about a day they will never forget, often they choose September 11, 2001.

CHILDREN TELL STORIES THROUGH DRAWING

Seven-year-old Victoria went to school in New York, and was close to the Twin Towers. She needed to share her story about what happened on the day of the terrorist attack, and she chose to draw the difficult images in her picture.

TEENS TELL THEIR STORIES

The following account by Max, a sophomore in high school, is an example of allowing kids to express their feelings and work with images that still stick with them.

A Time in My Life I'll Never Forget
By _Max_

My story first began when . . . .
the WTC buildings were attacked on Sept 11,

This is what happened . . . .
Our principal announced to us the disaster, I remember the tension of the community, the hysteria of the populace as events slowly unfolded,

The very hardest part was . . . .
Watching people jump from the World Trade Cent buildings. It instilled me with a shocking sensen of empath people being forced to take such turrible way out, normal people like me.

The best part was . . . . .
When people came together as a nation in support of those lost. It gave me a revival of the human spirit It amazed me that a group of over 250 million people could put aside political, racial or personal conflicts stand behind who truly needed it.

What still sticks inside of me are . . .
Images of the attacks happening and people running from the falling building. The pure magnitude of the attacks,

Now I see myself as . . .
a more cynical person. An experience like this forces you to approach it with some degree of cynicism so as to avoid certain emotional pitfalls that move as a side effect of the disaster.

PROJECTIVE PLAY

Projective play allows preschool through elementary children to release difficult times through role playing, acting out, or creating scenarios within a safe environment. Using projective props to recreate life experiences enables the child to work through challenging spaces without the need to directly verbalize them. Young children learn through play and grieve through play.

Helping figures, puppets, costumes, and building blocks allow children to construct their experience of what happened to them and work with what happened. Children feel empowered when they can imagine alternatives and possible solutions, release feelings, and create dialogue through projective play.

Many five-year-olds spontaneously built towers of blocks as the Twin Towers, and then knocked them down with an airplane to replay the attack. Alex explained to his nursery school teacher as the tower fell, "Airplanes make buildings go BOOM!"

Play techniques are especially helpful for processing grief and trauma. Preschool children may have a limited verbal ability for describing their feelings. Many girls and boys have a limited emotional capacity to tolerate the pain of loss. They can communicate their feelings, wishes, fears, and attempted resolutions to their problems through play (Webb, 2002).

Young children can recreate a disaster by using projective play. They are able to construct imaginary settings by using appropriate toy figures such as doctors, nurses, firemen, and policemen that enable them to construct the real-life scene they experienced.

Sally pretended to be a nurse helping those hurt at the Pentagon crash, and Jimmy put on a fire hat and gloves and said, "Don't worry, I'll save you." They felt empowered through play to take action and control over the difficult experience they had witnessed.

Jesse told her mom that she and her friends regularly play the "Let's Get the Terrorists Game" at lunch. She explained, "We make bombs. Some are filled with toys and food for the women and children at war, and if we think they are terrorists we put bricks in our bomb."

This child's game mirrors the very deep human conflict of war: defending oneself, compassion for those affected, and need for retaliation so basic to children and adults. Sometimes, what may appear to be a frivolous play activity can be an extremely meaningful outlet for children to recreate an event and safely express conflicting ideas.

POSTTRAUMATIC PLAY

Projective play creates situations in which children can safely express experiences and emotions using props, puppets, clay, and toy figures. This play allows and provides an outlet for thoughts and feelings and helps children adapt to their life situation. posttraumatic play can differ from projective play because it involves "compulsively repeating some aspect of the trauma" (Hamblen, 2002) without necessarily reducing anxiety or hypervigilance.

Tyler and Alan were twin six-year-olds who had survived the death of their dad. Dad was a fireman who was killed saving others. During a play therapy session, they repeatedly acted out the fatal fire, running back and forth into the building to save people. Alan explained that he needed to become "a fireman like his dad" and "save as many people as possible."

Kevin, age four, watched with the rest of his family in their car as their dad was murdered in a parking lot. His play presented constant replaying of the murder, and "good guy–bad guy" scenarios. He constantly took a toy knife and repeatedly stabbed it, saying, "you're bad, you're dead," over and over again. After the acting out, he would sometimes appear to be more anxious and want to leave the room.

PUPPETS, MUSIC, AND DREAM WORK

Puppets and stuffed animals are a safe way for children to speak of their trauma and release difficult memories. "I wonder what Bart [the dog puppet] would say about the trauma. Let's allow Bart to tell us his story." A statement like this is a technique of engaging children and freeing them from speaking in the first person. Puppets and stuffed animals can also be a source of nurturing and safety. Mary cried over missing her friend Ann who had died in a recent automobile accident. She shared their many times together and the things they would do. Then she put her arms around Bart, hugged him tight, and said, "I love you." Saying that to Bart made her feel better.

Jason loved music. His counselor, Mr. Price, asked his class to bring in music to help them describe their thoughts and feelings after 9/11 . One student brought in "God Bless America" and said she felt patriotic. Another brought in Bette Midler singing "From a Distance" and said he envisioned world peace. Still another brought in "My Hero" and said she felt sad about all of the firefighters who died to save others. Then Mr. Price took out some musical instruments (a drum, sticks, a tambourine, and a toy guitar).

"Can I hear what your feelings sound like?" Mr. Price asked. Jason began to bang on the drums as hard as he could, than he switched to a soft sad sound on the harmonica. His friend Sam shook the tambourine very loudly and explained, "This is how it sounds when the jet fighters fly over our houses. It's scary."

Dream work is another tool in allowing children to process difficult feelings. We can engage children in discussion about dreams by asking them if they have had any dreams they remember. Simply saying, "Have you had any dreams? Would you like to tell me about them?" allows an opening for the child to share and be listened to without judgment. Asking children how they felt in the dream or if they would like to create a different ending or change any parts of their dream can further dialogue. It may be difficult for some children to verbalize their dreams, and suggesting that they draw them may be a more comfortable form of expression.

Children and adults often feel survivor guilt after a sudden trauma. *Survivor guilt* can be sadness and depressing thoughts and feelings that surface after a tragic death. These thoughts and feelings can be accompanied by guilt that someone has survived while another person has died, and that the survivor did not or could not help the victim.

Tommy, age five, watched the news showing the plane crash into the building, killing his dad. Even though he knew his dad was dead, every time he watched the film he felt bad that he hadn't warned his father. The following dream by a traumatized child shows a common theme. Ten-year-old Justin explained that he continually revisited a nightmare after his uncle's sudden death at the World Trade Center. In the drawing shown here, he shares his dream and shows Uncle Tom calling out for help and his inability to reach him.

MEMORY WORK

Memory work can be a helpful tool to safely process the events of a trauma. Children can be asked the following questions as a foundation for discussion.

- Where were you when the trauma happened?
- What was your first thought?
- What are the facts about the trauma?
- What sticks with you now?
- Do you feel like you did anything wrong?
- What is it you still want to know?
- What scares you the most?
- What makes you feel peaceful?
- What can you do to feel better?

MEMORY BOXES

Memory boxes contain pictures and special objects that remind children of the person who died. They can be decorated with pictures and words that remind the child of their loved one or special containers meaningful to the person who died.

Chad's grandfather died when he was seven years old. His grandfather had been very sick for a long time in a nursing home. Chad spent lots of time with him and missed him very much. He wished that he could be with his grandfather again. One day we read together a book called *The Memory Box* and it was about a grandfather who died. His grandson made a memory box out of Grandpa's old fishing box. The fishing box was special to the little boy in the book because he and Grandpa had fished a lot together.

Chad decided to use Grandpa's special pipe box to hold treasured items. He put pictures of Grandpa inside, special letters Grandpa had written to Chad, and Grandpa's favorite ring. He kept the pipes displayed because he said Grandpa loved them so much and Chad liked to look at them.

The following memory book pages use September 11 for examples of children's attempts to make sense of their world when a disaster strikes. These pages help release feelings, tell stories, and express worries and concerns.

Draw Life Before the Trauma. Draw Life Now.

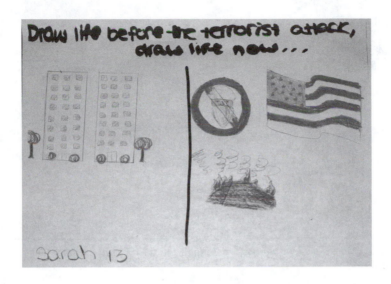

Tell Me What You Think Happened.

Tashika describes what she understood about the terrorist attack from watching TV and listening to other people. She thought it was a big fire in twin towers with people jumping out like dolls. *"When these people heard their was a fire, they jumped out of the twin towers. And it looked like it was dolls jumping out of a doll house."* (Tashika, Age 5)

TELLING THE STORY

Young children need to tell and retell their story or their interpretation of their story through words and drawing. Allison, age four, was very aware of the terrorist attack. Her dad was monitoring TV after the disaster and invited her to tell a story instead of watching the television. A short time later, Allison asked Dad if he would like to hear a story. She shared the four following pictures. Allison's story explained her feelings about 9/11, what she thought the terrorists did, and what she felt the solution could be. (Used with permission, Hogan, 2001, p. 5.)

This is a little girl crying when she is telling the story.

This is the plane, you can't see the bad guy inside.

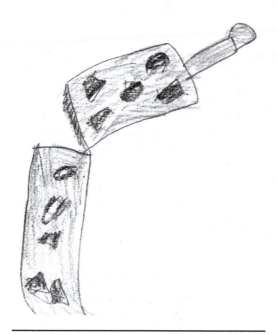

This is what they did.

Love and care. This is what America should do.

DRAWING PICTURES

If the Picture Could Talk, What Would It Say?

It is helpful for children to draw pictures of what happened to them. Sometimes the visualizations are difficult for them and drawing their perceptions of an incident is the first step in separating them from their traumatic happening. Shainna, age eight, was at her New York City school when the plane crashed into the World Trade Centers. Being so close to the trauma made her feel more vulnerable. She carefully drew the towers, the planes crashing, and people talking. Shainna said if her picture could talk it would say "trouble."

Where Were You When You Heard About the Trauma? What Did You Do?

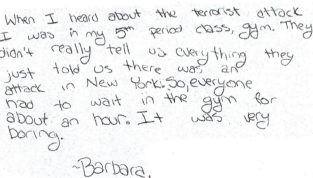

Where Were You When You Heard About the Terrorist Attack?

"It's still like a nightmare from last night. I remember I was in China. Becuse of the time difference, I was informed twelve hours later when I woke up in the morning. I heard my parents talking about the terrorist attack in a very confused manner and I thought it was a bad joke. Not until I listened to the newscast did I realize that it was true. I started collecting newspapers of that week and spent hours on the internet watching the NBC live. It scared me and everyone around me. Also, I began to contact my friends in Washington and New York to make sure they were alright."

What Did You Hear?

"It was Mom who woke me up that morning. She told me that two landmark towers in New York (she did not know they were the twin towers of the World Trade Center) were fatally attacked by two suicide airplanes the night before and toppled down in no time. She promised she wasn't kidding. I skeptically turned on the radio just to find out it was true. The newscast said it was during the working hours when two airplanescrashed into the twin towers, and a lot of people who were not able to escape were buried inside the ruins when the towers collapsed. I also heard that a third plane attacked the Pentagon in Washington, D.C., and destroyed one side of it. At the same time, there was a terrible plane crash at Pittsburgh, and had it not been for that land crash, another catastrophe would have happened somewhere else in the U.S. I was totally scared and I began to watch the online news coverage to keep being informed of the situation."

What Was Your First Thought?

"I suddenly realized it was September 11 (911!). My first thought was how the terrorists could launch such an attack that killed so many civilians, and how people and the government could be so defenseless that the terrorists had managed to create a disaster. But I was also 100% sure that the traumatized people would eventually stand up and fight back. Although it didn't happen in my country, it was an alarm to all around the world that the evil powers were always ready to encroach upon us."

Over and Over Thinking

Do you ever have thoughts that you go over and over and over in your head? Do you feel like you just can't make them stop? Do you see them in your mind like watching the news on TV?

What are your "over and over" thoughts?

How I would have felt if I had lost my mom. She works at the world Bank and I still remember how afraid I was at the thought that something would happen to her building/ organization (due to recent hatred towards the Bank) after the Pentagon was hit.

How do they make you feel?

They make me feel anxious and almost as though I have no control over it.

Jittery Feelings

Sometimes after something scary happens we might feel jittery, like we can't sit still and our minds won't stop working. It can be a nervous feeling inside or a fright from a sudden outside noise.

What makes you feel jittery?

I am a little jittery when I hear planes overhead. I am also a little scared about Flying overhead, especially after the plane crash a few weeks ago.

Dave, 12

What do you do?

I try not to think about it and that these types of things are very unlikely.

Dave, 12

What Do You Want to Know?

Andrea

What Do I Want to Know?

Sometimes kids may have questions about what happening in the world. Sometimes we can find out the answers and sometimes we can't.

What are your questions?

~~Wha~~ What measures can be taken
to prevent terroists to feel the
way they do about the US?

_____

What still bothers you? Write down your thoughts or draw them.

Although we have spotted the problem,
the US gov't still hasn't taken measures
to ~~refit~~ its foreign policy and treatment
towards less powerful countries. Also, the
fact that many terroists are living secretly
not just amongst us, but also abroad.
                                    -Andrea

What Is Your Biggest Fear?

One page in fourth-grader Alex's memory book asked this question. He responded in the following way. "My biggest fear is that someone might get some nuclear weapons."

What is your biggest fear about the future?

That someone might bomb us.

Adapted from *Breaking the Silence: A Guide to Help Children With Complicated Grief* by Linda Goldman, 2002, Taylor and Francis Pub. 1 800 821 8312.

by Alex   11/29/01

What Does Fear Look Like?

Can You Give It A Name?
ARACHNA

What Would It Say?
"I WANT TO HURT YOU!"

—TOMMY, AGE 11

What Do You Wish For?

Using a magic wand to ask children what their wishes are gives them freedom to express hopes in their memory book.

If you had one wish,
what would it be?

If I had one wish it
would be to change everything
that happend on Tuesday.

What do you wish the adults
around you would do?

I wish the adults around
me would stop talking
about the terrorist
attack because it sort of
scary.

~Barbara 11

WRITING LETTERS

Writing letters in memory books gives kids regained control to formulate and voice ideas and opinions and have them be heard.

9-21-a

Dear President Bush,
  How do you feel about what happened? I don't know why they did it. Do you know why they did it? I feel very sad for the people that died. If you feel mad or sad you should talk to your parents.
            Sincerely,
            Megan

Dear Mr. President,
  I think that you should talk things out with the terrorist. So we don't have another war because it kills alot of people.

            Sincerely,
            Barbara

POETRY AND CREATIVE WRITING

Use poetry and creative writing as an avenue of release for emotions and opinions. Andrew had watched people he knew grieve after a fatal car accident that killed a fellow classmate. He expressed his grief again through poetry in the following way.

Tears flow
As time passes
The relatives grieve
In love for the deceased

Andrew, Age 15 (personal communication,
December 11, 2001)

Activities That Help Kids Feel Safe

The eternal question of how to prepare our children to live in the world they were born into is magnified for our new generation of young people. Their complex world contains many challenges such as violence, war, and terrorism that seem to be becoming more commonplace. Equally challenging but far more satisfying is our task to develop resiliency in them.

Normalizing kid's feelings is important. We can do this by explaining that what they are feeling is very common, and reminding them that everyone has different ways of showing feelings and that is ok. Reassure children that caring adults are working at handling problems, and emphasize that they *are* getting through a hard experience. This helps to restore confidence after any kind of trauma.

Create discussion about the very low risk of being hurt by a traumatic incident. Children need to be reminded that the odds of being hurt in something like an act of terrorism are very, very small. Indeed, they are more likely to be hit by lightning, and that is very rare. When these incidents are replayed repeatedly in the media and constantly discussed, it seems that they are everyday occurrences instead of rare events.

Children can make a family collage with photographs of family members and their picture in the center. They can write or draw memories on the collage and keep it in their bedroom to visualize the love and safety surrounding them.

Creating a safe or peaceful box that children can go to with objects or pictures can help them feel protected. This box contains comforting objects that create peaceful feelings and thoughts. They can choose items that bring positive feelings of quiet and protection. When fearful or angry thoughts and feelings emerge, this box can bring calm and comfort to the children. Covering a shoebox with pictures from a magazine or newspaper or with stickers of things that make them feel calm, safe, and peaceful can create a sacred place to store special items.

Boys and girls can also make a safe or scary picture or object to carry with them in their pocket or purse. Following are pictures by Tony, age six, and Jon, age fourteen, of their safe and peaceful place.

Children can draw or visualize a scary place and then contrast it with a safe place that helps calm anxious and fearful feelings. Nine-year-old Shannon attended a New York school a few blocks from the Twin Towers. The following picture is her scary vision of that traumatic event.

First Lady Laura Bush suggested using family pets as a comforting, normalizing source of security for children. Hugging a dog, petting a cat, riding a horse, or feeding a fish are ways kids give and receive love that feels safe and protected.

Establish emergency plans with children by listing contact numbers, ways to communicate, and strategies for emergencies. Some people have suggested making a family emergency kit, including water, canned food, and medicines.

Preparation for Trauma

Emergency numbers

My family name _____

My phone number _____

My address _____

My community _____

My country _____

Ambulance _____ Mother _____

Fire _____ Father _____

Police _____ Friend _____

Suggestions for Kids to Help Themselves

Empowering children by creating expressions of feelings and thoughts about what can be done is essential. In this way they become valuable members of a larger community that honors their contributions and helps them to set ideas into motion.

1. Children can talk about their feelings. Allow children ways to tell their story as much as they need to. Draw pictures, create poems, write letters, and offer suggestions about ways to help. Writing letters in memory books gives kids regained control to formulate and voice ideas and opinions and have them be heard. Six-year-old Kyle decided he wanted to help the firefighters in New York. Here are his suggestions.

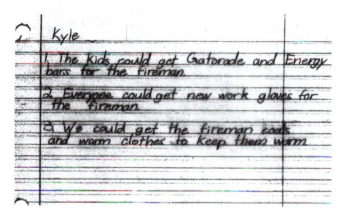

Kyle
1. The kids could get Gatorade and Energy bars for the fireman.
2. Everyone could get new work gloves for the fireman.
3. We could get the fireman coats and warm clothes to keep them warm

Kyle was given an opportunity to make suggestions, have choices, and feel empowered to be a part of a national grief team.

2. Create a worry list. Make a list of worries from 1 to 5. Number 1 is the biggest worry. Suggest children talk about this list with someone they trust, like their mom or dad, their sister or brother, their teacher, or a good friend.

3. Construct a peaceful or safe box. Ask kids to find toys, stuffed animals, and pictures that make them feel safe and peaceful.

4. Make a fear box. Cut out pictures from newspapers and magazines about what frightens them and paste them around box. Write down fears and put them inside the box. Tamara's fear box is shown below (see below). Her fears are written down inside.

Safe Box

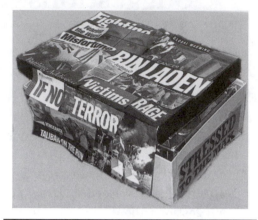

Fear Box

5. Read newspaper articles and discuss likes and dislikes.

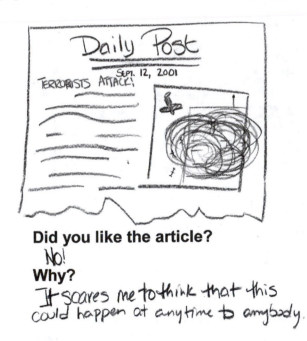

Did you like the article?
No!
Why?
It scares me to think that this could happen at anytime to anybody.

6. Help others. Help boys and girls give food or clothing to people that need it. Suggest that families might want to donate money to a good cause. Remind the children of President Bush's suggestion that every child give a dollar to help needy children.

7. Generate a fundraiser. Make flag pins or decorations and sell to get money for victims or community helpers.

8. Display an American flag or create an original global flag. Children can place these flags together outside their houses to remind everyone of their support for their country and their hope for world peace.

9. Make a memorial for the traumatic event.

10. As a family say a nightly prayer for world peace, and light a candle as a symbol of that.

11. Write a tribute. Angela, a high school student, lived in New York and attended school near the World Trade Center. The loss of the towers and the resulting ground zero became an integral part of her world. She decided to write a tribute to the Twin Towers and include her philosophy on that traumatic time.

Fallen Towers—Risen Powers by Angela

They stand adjacent to each other,
complimenting one another with style.
No one knew that soon they would be sentenced to exile.
They represented prestige and power,
but that came to a halt in the morning hour.

On September 11th, two planes descended
from the early heavens,
Hitting the World Trade Center.
The Twin that once graced New York
came crashing down,
making an unforgettable sound.

This day brought tears of pain and sorrow
For many there was no tomorrow.
Singed metal and burning debris
permeated the streets of New York for weeks.
The smell of death was everywhere.

This day tested many faiths and minds.
Some were weakened and some still blind.
Despite the tragedy, New York along with the world was united.
Something was ignited.
Through this loss, many things were gained.

Many faiths remained.
Churches have increased in size
And many nations rise.
God's hand is moving in the world.

Help Children Deal with Trauma

- **Talk** with them and listen to them.
- **Make sure** their understandings are accurate.
- **Stress** to them that they are survivors of an incredibly hard experience.
- **Find out** what still "sticks" with them after the trauma.
- **Help them** separate the past trauma from the present internal and external cues.
- **Support** them in creating the mental ability and emotional stamina to work with what life has given them.
- **Ask them:** "How are you now more wise, more strong, and more prepared if another trauma occurs?"
- **Ask them:** "How would you take care of yourself if another emergency situation occurred?"
- **Ask them:** "How could you now help family, friends, and strangers?"

Conclusion

Toddlers, preschoolers, and elementary, middle, and high school students need reassurance after a trauma that the event is finite and will not continually reoccur. Six-year-old Molly heard a balloon pop at a birthday party, which triggered her memory of the sound of the bullet that killed her brother. Too often, especially with small children, outer or internal cues may retrigger past traumas. It is essential that young people of all ages are aided in differentiating a present life experience from an earlier ordeal. All too often these events can be misperceived as a reenactment of the original trauma.

Children need to hear that they are safe, loved, and protected. Their visceral panic reaction can be used as a teachable moment to replace *terror* from another time with *support* in the present moment. Mary was panicked that Mom would be killed in a car crash similar to Dad's accident. She asked her mother to wear a seat belt and always use a vehicle with airbags. These safety measures brought Mary comfort, which eased her fears of her mother dying as her father had. Imprinting this new paradigm, through visualization of this positive experience, began to diminish the negativity of the past.

Children can feel empowered by being reminded that, even when alone, they are able to seek inner guidance. Tapping into a child's natural ability to access intuition and imagination by developing the concept that everyone has a wise place inside to guide them can foster self-reliance and strength. It is helpful for children to imagine asking an idealized parent, a teacher, God, or even a TV hero figure: "What would you do if you were scared?" They then can be encouraged to calm their mind while listening for the answer within.

When children manifest overwhelming feelings of fear and panic, they need guidance in separating the original occurrence as belonging to a distant event and not the current incident. In this way, we can begin to melt the "frozen hearts" of so many traumatized youths, as we create a path of replacing their fear with freedom.

Resources for Children on Trauma

About Traumatic Experiences J. Berry (1990) by provides answers to children's questions about trauma and traumatic experiences.

A Terrible Thing Happened by M. Holmes (2000) is a story about anxiety and anger after experiencing something terrible and learning how to talk about it.

Brave Bart by C. Sheppard (1998) is a story for traumatized and grieving children that can be used as a tool to safely project difficult feelings.

Reactions by A. Salloum (1998) is a workbook that helps young people who are experiencing trauma and grief express thoughts and feelings.

The Weather Kids by M.K. Jordon (1993) is a book for children who have experienced devastation caused by weather and earthquakes that helps them work through their traumatic responses.

CHAPTER 6

School Systems Respond to Crisis

CLASS DISCUSSIONS • LEARNING FROM THE PAST
PEER GROUPS • VIDEO CONFERENCING • PEER
MENTORS • WORDS TO USE • DEPLOYMENT
PREJUDICE AND RACISM • CHILDREN AND WAR
STUDENT INVOLVEMENT

Problems cannot be solved with the same level of awareness that created them.

Albert Einstein

could launch such an attack that killed so many civilians, and how people and the government could be so defenseless that the terrorists had managed to create a disaster. But I was also 100% sure that the traumatized people would eventually stand up and fight back. Although it didn't happen in my country, it was an alarm to all around the world that the evil powers were always ready to encroach upon us.

Draw a picture about it?

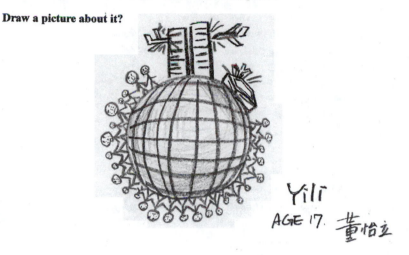

Yili
AGE 17. 董怡立

REPETITIVE THOUGHTS, JITTERY FEELINGS, FEARS, AND SCARY PLACES

Children share common responses to trauma. They may feel comforted to know that feeling panicky and jittery feelings, difficulty concentrating, desires to find answers, and reliving their event with "over and over again" images and thoughts are commonplace. As boys and girls process these new and sometimes disturbing feelings and thoughts, they may reexperience the past trauma and elicit honest responses concerning their future.

Children and War

Our children have faced war and threats of war throughout their lives. Many have had friends and family members deployed for active duty; some have returned, some have not. Stark images of bloody battles and demolished cities inundate our news, instantaneously bringing the war into our living rooms, sometimes with information that our servicemen have not received on the battlefield. Casuality listings of the missing, injured, or dead are broadcast daily. Our children watch and listen. What can we do?

The School Responds

One fifth-grade class was very concerned about the war in Iraq, and many students knew people who had gone there. The class talked about words such as *deployment*, *sand storms, temporary camps,* and *battle fatigue*. The children in the class made a list of what the children thought.

CHILDREN'S VOICES ABOUT WAR

- "I just thought it was a little bluff, or if it happened, it would be a little thing that would be over right away. The bombs exploding in fiery orange clouds on the first day of the war were the scariest part."
- "I was surprised to learn about some of the ways people were being killed in the war: helicopter accidents, U.S. soldiers and their allies accidentally shooting each other, soldiers accidentally killing Iraqi people who weren't soldiers."

- "I didn't realize it was going to be like this, like complete chaos. It's like gangs from different countries fighting each other."
- "I thought it would be where they go to a big humongous battle field and they say 'charge." (Shen, F. Kids Post, April 10, 2003, p. c15.)

Second-grade teacher Jaime Brinkman had a cousin in the marines who was stationed in Iraq. Her class spent time in their social studies unit reading the magazine *Time for Kids* and the feature article "Life for the Troops." The article was written at a second-grade level.

The children enjoyed seeing one picture of soldiers resting wherever they could, even taking a nap on the road after a nighttime battle. Another picture showed a soldier's gear that weighed 120 pounds. They even showed chow time and the U.S. military instant dinners of meat loaf and jerk chicken. Troops got to read letters from their sons and daughters and email them too. One soldier carries photos of his wife and ten-year-old son strapped to his arm. These pictures were helpful in reducing fears for the soldiers the children knew or saw on TV getting hurt in some way. By talking about the war and learning some of the facts about the life of a soldier, the boys and girls gained a deeper understanding of how soldiers feel and live during wartime. This helped to reduce the worry about them getting hurt.

The children decided to say thank you to the women and men in the military who were sacrificing so much to keep our country safe. Some of the students felt they would be helping their country if they wrote to the soldiers. Mrs. Brinkman's class wrote to her cousin. William and Italo sent the following letters.

Dear Will,
I hope you are not hurt. How large is a atomic bomb? thank you for keeping are country safe. IS it scary? Have you ever been on a helicopter? Have you ever used a gun? Have you ever been hurt? I hope not. have you ever seen an aircraft carrier? You are very fearles

From
William

May 5, 2003

Dear Will,

    Hi! my name is Italo.
Do you miss your parents? Thank
you for protecting our country. I know
that you are having a hard time
Mrs. Brinkman talks about you.
I know you have to be strong.
Good luck Will.

Sincerely
Italo

CLASSROOM DISCUSSIONS

Mr. Arnold's eighth-grade class held a meeting about the war. Emily's dad had been recently deployed and was to be in Iraq for a year. She cried a lot in school and talked about her dad all the time. She emailed or wrote him every day. It was hard for her to concentrate, and she said her Christmas was so sad without her dad.

The class met to discuss their feelings about the war and also see how they could help their friend. Arlene shared how it felt to have parents be divorced and not see her dad very much because he lived in another state. Steve talked about his mom's death when he was only three. Charlene said she had been adopted and wondered who her biological parents are. These preteens were surprised to see how many of their friends had had losses in their life. Emily explained it made her feel more normal to know other kids went through similar things.

Feelings About the War

The class began to share thoughts and feelings. Some teens said they wished they could fight, and others said they would be afraid. Carol decided to be the class secretary and write down some of the feelings and thoughts about war. Here are a few similar feelings expressed by young people in Teens and War (Seith 2003,).

- "We have to live in fear. We never know if a terrorist will come."
- "It certainly has been a distraction to schoolwork."
- "To tell you the truth, I'm scared of it, and I don't like it at all."
- "It doesn't bother me."
- "I can't take my eyes off the news coverage of the war."

Roger was a quiet kid and usually didn't share his feelings openly. He listened to people talk about the troops, weapons, prisoners, and destruction, and finally got up and asked Mr. Adam if he could write something on the board. He printed the following in bold black letters: "I feel sad about how many people were killed. I never wanted to be involved in a war but it seems now I am. I Hate War!!!!!"

Joey brought in a drawing from an Iraqi child attending a Baghdad elementary school that he discovered in the *Washington Post* Kids Page (Oct. 27, 2003). He wanted to share the Iraqis' child's view of war and help others understand war's impact. The following is a picture drawn by Wissam, age ten, sharing his images of Iraq's invasion.

(Permission granted by Puffin Foundation Ltd., Carl Rosenstein, and Patrick Dillon)

Deployment and Loss

Educators in the high school nearest Fort Hood, one of the largest military bases in the country, struggled with the huge population of their students affected by military deployment. Nearly 1,000 students, half of the student population, had a loved one deployed to Iraq, as did many teachers and staff. The school came up with an idea to help everyone feel that their loved ones were not forgotten: students walked through the halls with hundreds of stars hanging overhead. The stars were blue and gold, the school colors. On each one was written the name of a student and that student's parent or other relative deployed by the military.

Loneliness and anxiety gripped many of the students as they waited daily to hear of the safety and well-being of parents, siblings, and friends. Some of the older students were living alone because their single parent was deployed; others were living with relatives or guardians. The entire school mourned the death of a father who was killed in the war, and anticipated when the next tragedy would happen. One student said every time there was news of another soldier killed, "there is a gasp of breath here" (Hockstader, 2004).

One teen wore a dog tag with her dad's picture. "I was real, real mad when he left for Iraq, and now I am sad and angry mixed together." Her time was measured by what experiences her dad missed in her life, her first boyfriend, homecoming, and the holidays. She said her dad is her hero and she dreamed of spending a weekend with him. Another boy had a dad take part in the capture of Saddam Hussein. He called his son before dawn to tell him the news, and the boy said he was "in awe" of his dad (Hockstader, 2004, p. 1).

A SCHOOL SYSTEM ACCOMMODATES DEPLOYMENT

The school needed to modify schedules, curriculum, guidance services, and other resources to create an environment in which their students could live with and cope with their many losses due to deployment.

Student Reactions

- One student quit writing her father in Iraq because she was afraid it would jinx him.
- Many teens reported that television news accounts of the war had become an obsession.
- One fifteen-year-old got home every day by 4:15 to watch CNN news (Hockstader, 2004, p. 8).

School Changes

- Deployment had created a noticeable absence of fathers watching the school's games.
- At home, parents on their own lacked the support of their deployed partner in disciplining children and running a home. One mother pleaded with her husband deployed overseas to discipline her son who was acting out in school. He refused, saying he didn't want a possible last letter to his son to be a negative one.
- A deployed mom begged the guidance counselor to help her daughter with college applications since she couldn't be there to do it herself.

Displaying Patriotism

- American flag decals were stuck to window with the words "United We Stand."
- Stars hung from the ceilings dedicated to friends and relatives of students deployed by the military.
- The school is named for a retired four-star army general.
- Each morning The Pledge of Allegiance is said by the students
- Each morning there is a minute of silence remembering loved ones deployed.
- Each morning the name of one randomly selected parent or relative overseas is read over the public address system.

Identifying At-Risk Students

- Counselors intervened with two students whose dads were deployed, feeling the students were at risk for suicide. One student was hospitalized.
- Teachers reported an increase in discipline and academic problems.
- Staff described more truancy, vulgar language, wandering attention, and poor grades.

The school system continuously worked to help support its students facing losses of or harm to their loved ones or orders to be deployed overseas. Educators lived with the frustration that boys and girls would have more difficulty learning, more anger and frustration, and more sadness and loss as the war went on. "We can't bring their parents back or stop them from going over there," said a high school principal. But educators can create a sense of normalcy for all of the challenging issues their students face. They can help them believe they are part of a school community that supports the multiple losses and complex feelings associated with deployed military friends and relatives and make accommodations for their learning and mental health.

Prejudice, Racism, and Power

Five-year-old Tari, a Muslim child came to kindergarten the week after the terrorist attack and asked her teacher, "Are you still going to let me go to school here?" The children began talking about what they had heard on TV, from adults, and from friends.

CLASS DISCUSSIONS: A LESSON ON WISDOM

Tony's seventh-grade classmates began fighting after the war began in Iraq. Several of the students were from the Middle East. Angry conflicts arose with children of other nationalities. Some classmates blamed others for the war and terrorism. Name calling, punching, and racial slurs were a big part of the outdoor exchanges. Miss Brandt, Tony's English teacher, decided to create a special lesson. She presented quotes from famous people and asked students to share their reactions and begin to create more peaceful resolutions to differences.

Famous Quotes

"The future depends on what we do in the present."
Mahatma Gandhi

"Kind words can be short and easy to speak, but their echoes are truly endless."
Mother Theresa

"The harder the conflict, the more glorious the triumph."
Thomas Paine

"The greatest motivational act one person can do for another is to listen."
Roy Moody

"The best way to destroy an enemy is to make a friend."
Abraham Lincoln

Students vented their problems and their preconceived notions about each other. Some problem-solved about ways to change the world situation. Mary Ann blurted out "Isn't this what countries do, and then they go to war." Everyone stopped and sat in silence. These teens realized they were warring as much as the nations they saw on the news. It heightened their willingness to resolve their conflicts peaceably. Unresolved conflicts evolve into violence, hatred, prejudice, and war. Their homework assignment that evening was to write an essay on that topic.

HELPING EACH OTHER DURING TRAUMA

Billy didn't come to school the day after the Oklahoma bombing in Oklahoma City. Billy's grandfather had been killed in the disaster, working at the post office. Today was the day of the funeral. His second-grade teacher, Miss Thomas, began a class discussion on loss. She asked, "How many of you have had losses in your life? What are they? How did you feel?" Then she shared the facts about what happened to Billy's grandfather and asked the children, "What do you think Billy might be feeling?" The children began to respond. They talked about what they could say to Billy and ways they could help him when he returned

Children Can Help Grieving or Traumatized Classmates By:

- Knowing and understanding the facts about what happened to their friend
- Calling on the telephone, emailing, faxing, sending a note in the mail, or visiting a friend before they return to school
- Doing something for the friend, like making cookies or bringing dinner for the family
- Going to the funeral or memorial service
- Being prepared to help and support their friend with words to use when they return to school

  "We really miss you."

  "I'm so sorry your grandfather died."

  "I can't imagine how you must feel."

  "Do you feel like talking?"

  "I'm here if you need me."

  "Would you like to be alone?"

  "Would you like company?"

- Remembering that grieving or traumatized friends need friends. Some children feel isolated and alone. They may feel different and have a hard time talking about their experiences. Classmates can reach out to help them feel safe in school.

Include them in games.

Ask them to eat lunch with you.

Invite them over after school.

Offer to help them during school.

Be a good listener.

Don't be afraid to talk about the person that died.

Share a memory about the person that died.

Be a buddy to help with class assignments and homework.

Peer Mentors

Peer mentoring brings to children and teens on both sides of the interaction the capacity to grow in responsibility, empathy, and compassion. One young person commented after beginning her role as a mentor, "I was able to build a positive relationship with other kids because I've been through what they are going through . . . and I hope to help them know they aren't alone." Students can help others students in many ways. One way to help is individual sharing, another is group sharing, and still another is community sharing.

Mentoring programs can provide young people with confidence to overcome crisis, appreciation for sharing life experience, and gratitude for helping others. Sixteen-year-old Tommy became part of a school plan to have students serve as role models. Teenagers were asked to participate as mentors with younger children, sharing activities and personal experiences to create respect and friendship.

Tommy mentored eight-year-old Paul throughout the school year. He tutored Paul with schoolwork, emailed him messages, and played basketball with him during recess. They formed a strong bond because they shared so many similar life events: Tommy's dad had been killed in military service and now Paul's uncle was deployed for war. Tommy explained his relationship with Paul. "My role is to be someone for the younger kids to look up to and trust."

Younger children respond well to mentoring programs and often ask how old they need to be to become a mentor. Strong relationships are built between mentors and younger students, fostering an important sense of belonging. Mentorship is often empowering; as students fulfill the requirements of their responsibilities successfully and complete assigned jobs, they also can see they have made a difference in someone's life. Being a role model allows girls and boys to acquire a strong sense of dignity and worth for themselves as they earn the respect of those with whom they work. Teens and young children became transformed to sustain and survive future challenges.

Peer Groups

Peer support groups allow children to feel empowered and understood by their peers. This feedback for children is essential. By sharing their life issues with other kids their age, boys and girls get to see that they are not alone. They get needed support from kindred spirits who have experienced similar challenges in life. They gain an insight into common thoughts and feelings of grief and trauma that may otherwise seem foreign but are normalized by acknowledgment from others.

After the terrorist attack of September 11, many teens who had survived the death of a family member requested a group with others who had gone through the same experience. Schools with a large number of students having friends and relatives deployed for war created their own school support groups for deployment issues. Tom, age seven, said he felt comfortable in his school group talking about his dad being so far away, because the "other kids had been through the same thing and they just understood."

Studying Past Cultures and Trauma

Gaining a sense of history can help students understand that war and other public tragedies have occurred throughout time. They learn that civilizations and people survive. From underscoring these points during American and world history classes, to using resources that identify conflicts and trauma through time, a deeper understanding of mankind unfolds. Young people become more aware of universal triumphs and defeats from past to present, and mankind's ability to endure.

After the terrorist attack and the beginning of the war in Iraq, thirteen-year-old Gloria came to a new realization. When studying World War II in class, the events of Pearl Harbor took on a new meaning. "Now I understand what Grandpa Charles went through when he was young," she explained. "He must have been so scared when that happened. Then he had to leave his family and go far away to serve his country, just like Uncle Dan is doing now in Iraq."

Margaret thought about war and terrorism in her social living class. They spoke of man's nature that creates war and conflict and how it had always been a part of evolution. Her teacher, Mr. Owen, brought in a resource, *Bury the Dead* (Sloan, 2002), which described, through archeology, customs discovered through tombs, corpses, and rituals that developed understandings of cultures through time. Their classroom discussion emphasized that learning from antiquity can help normalize present challenging times.

Video Conferencing

High school students from Oklahoma City and New York City created a unique form of peer mentorship by using video conferencing to share experiences and provide hope with students who had lived through, survived, and grown from a public tragedy. Many of the students recently exposed to public and personal violence relating to the destruction of the twin towers verbalized feelings and questions to their peer group in Oklahoma regarding concerns, challenges, and expectations for the future.

The students in Oklahoma responded with firsthand experiences of their trauma, assurances of similar thoughts and feelings, and offerings of workable solutions of living with and coming through such an enormous national tragedy. One Oklahoma teen offered these words of advice: "Take your time, let yourself feel what you are going through. It just takes time."

The students from Oklahoma extended themselves to their New York peers as friends and mentors. They demonstrated not just their survivorship, but also their personal growth in strength, courage, empathy, and compassion. They modeled their ability to face fear and uncertainty after a trauma and emerge with optimism and confidence in their future, providing needed comfort and reassurance for the struggling New York teenagers.(In the Mix, Castlework, 2001)

Resources

FOR EDUCATORS

Managing Sudden Violent Loss in the Schools by Maureen Underwood and Karen Dunne-Maxim (1993) is a good resource on sudden violent death in school.

Breaking the Silence: A guide to help children with complicated grief, 2nd Ed. (2002) is a practical resource for working with completed staff issues.

Growing Through Grief (1989) by Donna O'Toole is an for excellent K-12 curriculum for helping children process loss nd grief.

FOR CHILDREN ON WAR, PREJUDICE, AND HISTORY

Bury the Dead (2002) by Christopher Sloan is a beautifully illustrated and executed book by National Geographic that gives insights for children from archaeology about customs and rituals throughout the ages.

Drawing Together to Accept & Respect Differences (2003) by Marge Heeguard is a workbook that helps children to communicate and learn to respect one another.

Feelings about War (1991) by Corder and Haizlip is a coloring book for young children that address questions and concerns they may have about war.

My Daddy Is a Soldier (2002) by S. and K. Hilbrecht is a story for young children that speaks to the many losses children face when their parent is a part of the military. Ages 4 to 7.

Sadako and the Thousand Paper Cranes (1993) by E. Coerr is a true story about a Japanese girl who is dying from her exposure to radiation from the bomb at Hiroshima. Her hope for peace and life is symbolized in her paper cranes.

The Skin I'm In (2003) by P. Thomas is a first look at racial discrimination for very young children.

PART III

Coming Together
to Create Change

C H A P T E R   7

Parenting Through a Crisis, Preparing for the Future

MATURE MODELING • NURTURANCE • LISTENING •
SUPPORT • MONITORING MEDIA • HUMOR • FAMILY
ACTIVITIES AND ROUTINES • DAILY RISKS • TEACHABLE
MOMENTS • EMERGENCY PLANS • CHILD
INVOLVEMENT • VALUES • SURVIVORSHIP • SAFETY

We parents are the holders of a priceless gift, a gift we received from countless generations we never knew, a gift that only we now possess and only we can give to our children. That unique gift, of course, is the gift of ourselves.

Fred Rogers

Providing a Strong Foundation

"There's no place like home."
Dorothy, in *The Wizard of Oz*

Parents may feel ill-equipped to know how to bring safety back to their children when they feel threatened themselves by the complex life situations that affect their daily life. We can allow children to express their feelings and emotions and model for them how we are bringing protection back into their lives as we bring it back to our own. We cannot promise them perfect solutions, but we can sit with them in the process of creating solutions. Sharing honestly our own human feelings and striving to hold the tension of events we cannot control allows our kids to do the same.

There is no place like home to create safety, nurturance, optimism and an environment of respect for young people as thinking and feeling human beings, capable and enriched by supportive parenting that allows for expression of feelings, a space to "just be," opportunities to offer creative solutions, and awareness of when and when not to press for responses. Empowering our children to become an essential part of the family team is the pearl of parenthood. Reinforcing to our children that we can live through challenging times, and exploring those times together, is medicine to their souls.

Children Are Survivors of Traumatic Events

ESTABLISH A SENSE OF ORDER

In an ever-changing and chaotic world it is important to maintain a sense of order in life. We want our children to realize not only that they are survivors of a difficult event, but also that their life still has continuity and meaning. Parents and educators can keep to the daily routine as much as possible. This allows children to feel a renewed sense of security.

ESTABLISH FAMILY ACTIVITIES

Family activities have a reassuring effect on children. Making meals together, eating dinner as a family, reading stories aloud, or playing family games brings continuity and a sense of normalcy back into their lives. Placing an American flag outside the house or donating food and toys for survivors or community helpers gives purpose and meaning through shared experiences.

Sometimes giving children special time for sharing thoughts and feelings about their difficult times is comforting to them. Reestablishing a schedule for normal routines and involving children in the process of maintaining the daily routine helps them feel more secure. Even giving girls and boys familiar chores like clearing the table or taking out the trash helps them feel they are a part of restoring normal family life.

Parents can create special time with children in the car, while making dinner, or at bedtime. Nyasa is an eight-year-old who attended school in New York. The sounds and sights of the city after the September 11 disaster left a deep imprint on her. Planes crashing, people jumping out of buildings, and her desire for it to stop is represented in her drawing of that occurrence. She decided to make her drawing just before bed and share it with her mom. It helped her to feel less scared to talk about it.

The trauma of the visual imprint was hard, and sharing thoughts and feelings with family helped to ease the fear and sadness she carried. Just being together at dinner, as a family, felt like a special event. She expressed in her poetry her perceptions of more parents spending more time together, especially quality time, with their children.

After the Disaster at the World Trade Center
Now families are spending more time together.
"It's really a long time since last I saw you."
I hear some people say some people
are getting off drugs every day.
More fathers and sons together spending quality time,
Now I don't have to worry.
Now I have a good night's rest.

INITIATE SAFE PLACES TO EXPRESS FEELINGS

Parents can initiate safe places for expression by simply finding a quiet time at home, in the car, or on a peaceful walk. Being with children without outside distractions can produce a comfortable climate to begin to dialogue. Matt confided to his dad on their walk in the country that a bully at school had been stealing his lunch money and he was afraid to tell. He had been carrying this secret a long time and it felt good to tell someone.

Bedtime needs to be reassuring, too. Parents can consider an increase in transition time, story-telling, and book reading to create a peaceful, uninterrupted nighttime environment. So often this is the time children choose to talk about their worries.

REINFORCE VALUES

Recognize and emphasize the importance of values such as compassion, empathy, and peaceful solutions. The battles of branding, bullying, and victimization, terrorism against citizens, and friend versus enemy can be discussed in our homes with renewed appreciation of your family's values. Through interventions and understandings that create a deeper understanding for one another, parents can nurture the human spirit and extinguish the very seeds of prejudice and intolerance that breed the endless cycle of turmoil in today's world.

Children can feel a deeper sense of gratitude that they survived a traumatic ordeal and appreciate another day to be with loved ones. Stacey-Ann, a seventeen-year-old, was a high school student in New York, very close to the World Trade Center. Six months after the terrorist attack, she expressed her renewed love for family in the following words.

The day when the Twin Towers were hit by terrorists

It felt like a dream I could not believe.

That night I was not able to sleep no matter

how long I laid in my bed.

Each time I closed my eyes I would see the image in my head.

Since that day, every day my family and I live

seems to be a great day.

We try to show love to each other in many special ways.

For if we do not show how we feel while we are alive,

We have no other way to prove our love no matter how much

we strive.

Stacey-Ann, a high school student

Stacey-Ann shared her appreciation for life and for being with her family. Her family's love for each other is evident, and the value they place on expressing this love to each other was deepened after the tragic experience.

MAINTAIN A SENSE OF HUMOR

Knowing how to laugh and seeing the humor even in the hardest of times is a helpful thing to model to our children. We let them know we don't always have to take ourselves so seriously, and that life can have lighthearted moments even in the toughest of times.

Marlys is an American mom living in Beijing, China, with her husband and daughters. The children go to Chinese schools and had experienced the SARS epidemic for quite some time. After so many cases of SARS became apparent, the schools were closed to stop the spread of contagion.

Marlys relayed the following scenario about an interaction with her daughters, Jessica and Jenny, which she found quite humorous. She explained that her daughters were having a conversation with a six-year-old Chinese friend who was playing at their house. She overheard the little girl saying, "I have a cold, but don' tell anyone. My parents said not to tell anyone." Right off the bat Jessica said, "Yeah, that's a good idea because if the first person heard you had a cold he would tell someone that you had a fever. That other person would tell someone else you had SARS. Then that someone would tell the next person you died!" The little girl's eyes grew very big when she heard that line, but they all had a good laugh out of it.

Sharing humor helped to reduce the anxiety of a scary event and create a sense of togetherness and understanding.

GIVE COMFORT: HUGS AND FOOD

Sometimes children and teens respond to a simple hug, an "I love you," or a home-made apple pie. These gestures of affection and nurturance provide symbolic reassurance during challenging times.

Scott was a fourteen-year-old involved in many activities after school and at night. He joined his parents after watching a broadcast on TV with a new request. "I just heard on the news if you want your kids not to join gangs, eat dinner with them. Can we eat together more?" he requested. The family began to do that.

PRACTICE MATURE MODELING

Parents are role models and primary examples from which children learn. Often they follow what we do as well as what we say. It is a primary role of parenting to be aware that what we do today, our children may do tomorrow. Sharing our feelings and thoughts honestly at challenging times, and working at staying present and productive while feeling sad or anxious, helps our children to know how to do the same.

After the assault on our nation, adults had many different reactions. One mom slept in her clothes with a packed suitcase next to her bed; another stayed in her pajamas and wouldn't leave the house for days; still another mom kept her child home from school all week. Parents are critical to their child's ability to recover from trauma. Steele (2002) presents the perception that parents are the single most important support for school-age children following a disaster. Steele (2002) explains a 1996 study by Byers on World War II, which showed that the primary factor in children's emotional well-being after the war was not the war itself, but the level of upset displayed by the adults around them.

We can use mature modeling of responsible roles for our children during traumatic times even while expressing that we may be scared, too. Children look to their parents' reactions and actions as a barometer of their own vulnerability or safety. Displaying calmness and an ability to serve allows young people to do the same. We can be honest about feeling afraid and still model behaviors in a calming way. (Mundy, Washginton Post, 2003).

Nadia and her family watched the terrible devastation of the earthquake in Iran in 2003. So many families lost homes, possessions, and loved ones. Dad and mom decided to help, and Nadia wanted to join them. The decision was agreed on to have a family rummage sale and to send all proceeds from the sale to the earthquake relief fund. Everyone worked hard to find belongings, label them, and get them ready for the sale that weekend. They raised $200, and Nadia proudly sent it along with a note of friendship from herself and her parents.

MONITOR TELEVISION

The young children sat, absorbing the mayhem. If their caregiver was unable, just now, to give care, Hollywood was happy to help.
Liza Mundy, *Washington Post Magazine*

Two-thirds of U.S. children live in homes where the television is left on at least half the time. Children aged six and younger spend about the same amount of time every day using screen media (1 hour, 58 minutes) as they do playing outside or reading. forty-three percent of children younger than two years old watch TV every day, and one in four has a TV set in his or her room *(Washington Post, 2003).*

Children absorb their surroundings and carry the experience. Elcy, age seven, drew a picture about how she was feeling after hearing about a murder close to her home. Her response was at the bottom of the picture, and she shared her perception of her parents' reaction to this violence in her picture.

Elcy's picture also shows a TV playing in the background with a scary movie. Unsupervised television watching creates a forum for a deluge of imagery and words that may be inappropriate, provocative, or terrifying to our children. The graphic display of "here and now" experiences, from war accounts as they are happening to violent news clips to real-time programs based on a fear factor, engulf children. They subliminally soak in impressions and many find them disturbing.

Carole watched a cow "go mad" as the news presented a story on mad cow disease. She ran to her mom crying, and sobbed, "I have a bad stomachache. I just ate a hamburger. Can I die?"

Studies indicate that the amount of time children and adolescents spent viewing television coverage of the Oklahoma City bombing of the federal building was positively associated with their degree of reported stress (Pfefferbaum et al., 2001). This research is a strong indicator to parents to limit exposure to TV coverage of traumatic events.

All too often, what young people see on television is so real to them that they feel they will immediately be impacted. They may think continuous replays are actually multiple occurrences of the event being pictured. Monitoring, limiting, and being available for discussion and teachable moments during TV viewing creates an environment of less fear and more safety for our children.

DISCUSS DAILY RISKS

Creating dialogue with children and teens about daily risks that are a part of life can help reduce fear during times of trauma. Remind them that although an event on TV might have happened once, it also may be replayed many times. These kinds of events happen less often then we think from our perceptions of constant viewing on TV. Daily activities such as driving in a car, crossing the street, and even riding a bike involve risk. We can remind children that we take precautions like using a seatbelt to keep ourselves safe, and then we can enjoy these activities that are part of our lives.

After watching the news with her eleven-year-old son, Nelson, his mother decided to intervene. "I can't believe there are so many murders and bad accidents. It makes me scared to go outside," Nelson explained. Mom reminded him of an incident when he was six and his dad was teaching him to ride his bike. "I'm too scared, I'm afraid I'll fall," was all Nelson could say as he pleaded with Dad not to let go of the bike. Nelson remembered his fear and also remembered his triumph on the day he first rode his bike alone. This seemingly simple task appeared life threatening to him as a child. After being reminded of his bike-riding experience, Nelson understood a little better that the day is filled with risks we overcome through using common-sense safety strategies and support from those we love.

CREATE TEACHABLE MOMENTS

Presenting words and images of famous people can inspire children to be true to themselves, succeed for themselves, and serve others. Make this a teachable moment at dinner, while watching TV, when driving in the car, or at bedtime.

Max, a twelve-year-old, talked with his dad on the way to school about an article he had read. It involved a high school football captain, David, who "came out of the closet" about being gay and shared fears of rejection and ridicule. His teammates surprised him by doing just the opposite. They surrounded him in a circle of protection and supported him on the football field in a show of affirmation the day after David's disclosure. Max shared with his father newfound insights into the plight of young homosexuals. His dad remembered a quote about courage—*"Courage is the power of the mind to overcome fear"*—and shared it with his son. Those words by Martin Luther King Jr. inspired a wave of feelings. Max wrote:

Courage seems very hard to come by these days. The world is becoming a much more conformist one. Now more than ever we strive to have more friends and to be more fashionable. . . . Then there are the people who don't feel accepted—because they express beliefs not accepted by society. But even though their lives are hard, they can't match the hardships that homosexuals can go through. First it is the mental torment that they feel different and then it is the fear of coming out. All these reasons force some homosexuals to have to live in secret; a terrible thing our society has imposed on them.

The real courage is in each and every one who is different, but especially those who are gay or lesbian. Because it is probably the hardest thing in the world to come out.
Max, Age 12

The following are other quotes to inspire young people in their life and through hard times. They can be woven into a teachable moment or used as part of a family discussion on bravery, perseverance, or social action.

Inspiring Words: Famous Role Models

"You must do the thing you cannot do." Eleanor Roosevelt

"Failure is the opportunity to begin again more intelligently."
Henry Ford

"Enthusiasm: a little thing that makes a big difference." Unknown

"Great things are done by a series of small things brought together."
Vincent Van Gogh

"Continuous effort is the key to unlocking our potential." Black Elk

"Courage is the power of the mind to overcome fear."
Martin Luther King Jr.

PREPARE A FAMILY DISASTER PLAN

Preparing for a natural disaster or national tragedy as a family helps everyone recognize that these things happen and provides an opportunity for children to be involved with their parents in locating resources they may need after the occurrence.

Parents can:

- Talk to children about consequences of disasters that could happen.
- Create a list of phone numbers of people to call or places to meet if family members are separated during an occurrence.
- Teach children how to call for help using 9-1-1. Write 9-1-1 boldly on the phone where the children can see it.
- Dialogue together and create supplies of food, water, radios, batteries, flashlights, candles, matches, and other emergency items that can be stored in a safe place.
- Allow children to be part of the decision-making process.
- Find personal items of value to each family member and secure them in an easy place that could be taken with them in case of emergency.
- Review procedures with children on responding to smoke detectors, fire alarms, or local community warning systems.

STRESS TO CHILDREN THAT THEY ARE SURVIVORS

Children used coping skills to help them work through all of the hard feelings of loss and fear after the attacks of September 11. They are living through war and threats of biological harm and still having productive days. Sometimes it is helpful for our children to look at the gains as well as the losses to assess their experience. A life and loss timeline is an activity to help children understand that their life keeps going despite their losses. After living through a traumatic event, children may feel scared about the future, and afraid to look forward. By creating a lifeline of past, present and future life events, traumatized children gain a sense of the continuity of life.

Twelve-year-old Benjamin made a "loss and gain collage" after the sniper siege in Washington. Although he expressed sadness and fear about the random acts of violence, he was surprised to see that he felt "stronger after living through this trauma," safer as more safety and protection measures were initiated during the crisis, and protected by various police and government agencies that worked together to catch the criminals.

Patriotism in a Global Community

Being part of a global community and having a sense of commitment to country bring comfort to many children. Stimulating an awareness of measures taken to reduce fear and increase safety is valuable in diminishing children's anxiety. Discussing increased security at airports, stronger cockpit doors for pilots, wartime procedures to find terrorists, and health measures to identify and deal with anthrax bring assurance to our youth that the adults around them are working toward their well-being. They are survivors of a very difficult ordeal.

Creating teachable moments to expand patriotism is also valuable to children. Jamal was visiting New York with his parents and took the boat ride to see the Statue of Liberty. The sight of this beautiful figure inspired Jamal to ask questions about how it was made and what it meant to the people of America. His dad explained that it was a sign of hope for many foreigners who came to this land seeking solace from traumas and tragedies in other countries and the vision of a better life.

When Jamal arrived home he was pleased to find a *Kid's Discover* magazine that had devoted an entire issue to the Statue of Liberty (February 2004). One article explained the history of its creation, another discussed how it was being restored, and a third contained stories of inspiration from those who had been oppressed. Discussing the material in this  publication at dinner, in the car, and even before bed became a lively interaction for Jamal and his parents and shaped a new paradigm about patriotism with deeper understanding about the Statue of Liberty.

Parents as Mentors

Shri was a mother of three, forced to leave her country and her children to come to America in search of an income for her impoverished family. She learned the language, gained citizenship, and worked diligently for more than fifteen years, sending money back home so everyone could live and grow. She called, wrote, and visited as often as she could, and watched her children grow into responsible young adults.

Her oldest daughter, Luzviminda, graduated with a doctorate degree and her mom was able to be there to see it. Luzviminda gave her mom a hug that day and said, "Your hard work gave me the gift of this accomplishment. I love you."

Shri's power as a mentor is apparent through her unconditional love for her children from a distance. She taught them by example, modeling hard work and self-sacrifice to benefit others.

Parenting Immigrant Children

There are many losses associated with immigration for children. It is an issue affecting growing numbers of children. These young people experience multiple losses in an unfamiliar world, losses including family, home, language, culture, and country. These boys and girls often feel different in looks, dress, and familiarity with conventional ways of being. As one immigrant child explained, "When I first came to America, the only word I knew was 'Hi'" (Fassler & Danforth, 1993, p. 114).

Parents foreign to the school system may have difficulty helping their children navigate their educational world and the work it requires. Often immigrant children benefit from support groups with children from their native country, educational programs for their parents, ESL (English as a second language) programs within the school that works with foreign students, and resources such as *Coming to America* (Fassler & Danforth, 1993) that deal with the issues they face as immigrants.

Involve Children in Solutions

Liuxinsiao was a twelve-year-old concerned about the possibility of getting SARS. He lived in Beijing and worried that he or someone close to him would get sick or die from the disease. Fear of contagion had gripped the nation. Liuxinsiao felt more panicked when all of the schools closed and he needed to work with school lessons by watching them on national TV.

Wanting to do something to help others and also help himself, he began to observe what his mom and dad were doing to help stop the spread of the virus. His parents invited him to join them in the fight against SARS and he felt a sense of pride and

accomplishment in the effort. He explains in the following pictures what his parents modeled to create optimum health situations in their home and environment. He then became actively involved in a solution for SARS by being sure he created sanitary conditions when he was outside by wearing a mask and keeping the streets clean. When he stayed home, his mom had explained how important it was to keep the windows open and let fresh air in. He did this every morning.

Dad talked to Liuxinxiao about keeping his hands very clean by washing them to stop the spread of germs. He began washing his hands several times a day when he realized that it was an essential tool in the prevention of SARS.

By modeling his parents' behaviors Liuxinxiao became an advocate to stop the SARS disease. And by applying his parents mentoring and their provision of an appropriate way to become involved, he began to see himself as an active force in eliminating the virus.

Emphasize the Enormous Outreach

Emphasize the enormous outreach of help human beings give to each other during times of crisis, signaling ways their community, their nation, and their world came together during a frightening time. This serves as a model of how adults can react maturely and responsibly under great distress. Firemen and policemen bravely rescued victims, sometimes at the loss of their lives. Movie stars, sports figures, and moms and dads joined to raise money and give time to rebuild what had been destroyed; the police and fire safety people and hospitals all had their plans to help people. Many countries gave money and military aid to help the United States stop terrorism. They joined in their own national commemoration to pray for and send support to America during uneasy times.

Conclusion

Parents can offer their children hope for the future and empowerment to reach their goals. Nurturing children's capacity for hopefulness encompasses the ability to support their creation of goals and further their competency to realistically achieve these goals. This is fundamental for their human learning, especially during stressful times. Strategies that help develop this nurturance for hope include learning self-talk about succeeding and reframing difficulties through a perspective of incorrect strategies rather than incompetence (Snyder, 1995).

Parents can help children achieve hope by providing mentorship and promoting their ability to create their own solutions. By giving them choices and encouraging their active involvement, we empower our young people to bring some sense of control back into their lives. Reenforcing their sense of survivorship is crucial during difficult experiences.

Resources

FOR CHILDREN

Statue of Liberty (February 2004) is a full issue of *Kids Discover* magazine devoted to the history, renovation, and inspirational aspects of the Statue of Liberty.

Necessary Noise (2003) by M. Cart (ed.) is a compilation of stories for middle-students school and older that deals with real-life situations in today's families, including a sibling's overdose, life with two mothers, and a dad visiting his son on death row.

The Little Engine That Could by Watty Piper (1954) is a story for young children that identifies the value of perseverance and positive dialogue as the little engine repeats "I think I can" until he accomplishes his goal.

FOR ADULTS

Your Guide to a Happier Family (1990) by A. Faber and E. Mazlish presents practical interventions with personal accounts of ways to create a peaceful family environment.

The Best Things Parents Do (2004) by Susan Issacs Kahl creates 40 essays that help parents remember what is important in working with children and provides practical techniques to create a loving environment.

(Please refer to Chapter 12 for additional resources on adults.)

Educators at Work: Meeting the Challenge of Traumatic Events

SCHOOL MEETINGS • CLASS DISCUSSIONS • GUIDANCE
GROUPS • STUDENTS GRIEVE • FUNDRAISING AND SPECIAL
EVENTS • MEMORY WORK • SCHOOL PROJECTS • STUDENT
INVOLVEMENT • HELPFUL SUGGESTIONS FOR ADULTS •
IDENTIFYING AT-RISK YOUTH

Do not confine your children to your own learning, for they were born in another time.

Ancient Proverb

School Involvement with Trauma

In today's world, school systems suffer trauma as well as the students they serve. School shootings, snipers, suicide attempts, terrorist threats, and random acts of aggression on students and faculties create an environment in which educational populations are thrust into danger at unsuspecting moments of the day. As prepared as many systems have become, the unexpected drama that instantly unfolds in today's schools leaves kids, teachers, and parents shocked and vulnerable. Absorbing the mayhem, integrating it, and focusing on responding to students when teachers and principals are themselves traumatized is indeed a challenging task of our present age.

Responding to 9/11: a Student Grieves

Julia's elementary school was devastated by 9/11. Her best friend Zoe and her parents were killed on the doomed flight that crashed into the Pentagon. Not only did boys and girls and their teachers watch and process the events of the terrorist attack, but being a school near Washington, D.C., they felt its impact in a very personal way. Many of Julia's classmates had family and friends who worked in the Pentagon or near the Pentagon in downtown Washington, and they feared for their safety and their own.

The terrorist assault presented new and uncharted challenges to students, teachers, and counselors. Michelle Brown was Julia's guidance counselor, and she learned of Julia's loss the next day when Julia got off her bus. Mrs. Brown greeted her and asked her how she was doing. Julia began to sob and relay the story about her friend.

THE IMPACT OF IMAGES

Julia's usually cheerful ten-year-old nature was replaced with overflowing feelings of shock and deep sadness. She was haunted by the visual images that haunted so many children in our country as they witnessed the media output again and again. For Julia, watching the plane crash into the Pentagon was not only a frightening drama, but a continuous reenactment of her friend being killed again and again and again while she helplessly watched. It was paralyzing. The horror of the event was magnified a hundredfold as she personalized the deaths of Zoe and her family in her mind.

DAILY COUNSELING SESSIONS

Julia worked with Mrs. Brown, her guidance counselor, on a regular basis at school. Within each session she would share feelings about Zoe and her death and its huge impact on Julia's life, her school, and her country. It was difficult for her to handle feelings about the death of her best friend when she learned that Zoe's picture was displayed in a national magazine as "among the dead." She wondered how something so private could become so public. Grieving the sudden and traumatic death of a best friend is difficult for any child, but having that death become part of a national tragedy involving extreme fear, distress, and constant publicity complicated the natural grieving process.

SHARING FEELINGS

Many counseling sessions were spent on Julia's feelings of fear, anger, and sadness. Working with clay, artwork, poetry, and writing offered a nonthreatening avenue for the release of complex feelings. Julia drew her body and used different colors to indicate where she was feeling things inside. Sometimes she would play the "Top 10" game of telling her top ten funny memories of Zoe. Sometimes after sharing memories she would decide to rest and hug a favorite stuffed animal, Sammie the Seal. "I like thinking about memories . . . it gives me a break from being sad."

Poetry was a creative outlet for many of Julia's difficult feelings and thoughts. She created the following poem about Zoe, revealing her love, how much she missed Zoe, her difficulties and pains, and her future hopes of healing and change.

Julia
Active, funny, kind
Good Friend of Zoe
Loss, anger, grief
Who misses her funny, caring and silly ways
Who worries about war and our President
Stomachaches, headaches, muscles get tense
Who heals by reading, laying down, talking
Remembers by memories and hearing her name
Who wishes for peace and unity
Strong
(Living with Grief: Coping with Public Tragedy. Hospice Foundation of America. Licht, & Doka, Eds., p. 146)

Julia had complained of increased stomachaches and headaches as the threat of terrorism and increased military involvement with the potential for war loomed heavily in the daily news. She was becoming increasingly angry that "we are doing to them what they have done to us." She decided to write President Bush about it and this letter evolved into a four-page book with illustrations. She said she felt better after writing it.

FINDING OUT THE FACTS

Julia pondered and verbalized thoughts that emerged in her mind, similar to the questionnaire in the following figure, and shared a question that is foremost in the minds of survivors of a traumatic death: "Did my person suffer? Julia was thirsty for any and all factual details about Zoe's death, and the adults around her helped gather that information. She made a list of questions: "If Zoe knew what was happening? Was she sitting with her parents? Did she feel any pain?"

What Do I Want to Know?

Sometimes kids may have questions about what happening in the world. Sometimes we can find out the answers and sometimes we can't.

What are your questions?

Did she Know what was happening?
Was she sitting with her family?
Did she suffer?

What still bothers you? Write down your thoughts or draw them.

This is what I see in my head all the time:

Adapted from *Breaking the Silence: A Guide to Help Children With Complicated Grief* by Linda Goldman, 2002, Taylor and Francis Pub. 1 800 821 8312.

WHAT WERE THEY THINKING?
BEFORE THE CRASH

PARENT INVOLVEMENT

Julia's parents were actively involved in her grief process and the counselor communicated with them on ways to help. They decided to make a "no TV policy" in the house for a little while after the plane crash to avoid the visual input and retriggering of the traumatic event. Communication was ongoing about Julia's needs being met within the school setting.

The school developed a poster contest entitled "What the World Needs Now." Julia's loss of Zoe was a motivation to create this project, and she was eager to participate. She became the judge of the contest, and this role not only allowed her to use her intelligence and sense of humanity in choosing a special poster, but created an active involvement as judge that allowed a degree of control to be placed back in her life as she made choices and became involved in a cause that could help provide ideas to bring order and hope out of a chaotic experience.

MEMORY WORK

Julia loved to talk about Zoe and share memories. Mrs. Brown gave her a homework assignment to begin to gather meaningful items to create a memory box of precious items reflecting her friendship.

After learning about Julia's plan to make a memory box for Zoe, her parents contacted Zoe's grandmother, who graciously sent a package to Julia. It contained precious pictures and mementos of their time together at church summer camp and a beautiful note to Julia from Grandma about how much Zoe loved her and was proud to have her as a friend. She put the kind letter into her memory box, with the pictures of Zoe and Julia, her top ten list of what she loved about Zoe, her letter to President Bush about her, and other special items. She considered her memory box a comforting and safe place to return to.

Each time a new development on bioterrorism emerged, a new notification of code orange or yellow issued, or new updates of death and destruction from the war were released, Julia was greatly affected. Memories would resurface and events of September 11 were re-triggered, especially the death of Zoe. Her grief was private, public, ongoing, and exacerbated by world happenings, making it almost impossible to put a sad event somewhat in the past because of the ever-present reminders wherever she turned.

As Mrs. Brown states so eloquently about her new paradigm as a school counselor after the national tragedy: "Having a school full of mourners has proven to be both challenging and rewarding. This national tragedy has birthed a nation of grievers and I am just beginning to learn how to ride the 'wave of grief.'"

School Systems Cope with Trauma

Schools systems throughout the country struggled to cope with students and faculty so impacted by public tragedy. How could they allow children to process the enormity of such an event and still focus on schoolwork and learning? One school's response to this challenging question was to involve students in learning activities that allowed them to process thoughts and feelings and also become involved as concerned citizens on the planet. Writing poetry, drawing posters, creating fundraisers, and promoting dialogues on topics of war, terrorism, prejudice, and peace were useful and inspiring.

A WALL OF THOUGHTS

Children in the school were encouraged to participate in a Wall of Thoughts that held students' thoughts and feelings about the terrorist attack. Joanna Shea, the writing lab teacher, involved students in writing assignments in the school. The subject matter was modified to allow the students to explore creatively their processing of this huge and sudden experience. Their compositions were posted and shared with other students. The Wall of Thoughts became a part of the school's writing lab and was decorated with work posted for all to read.

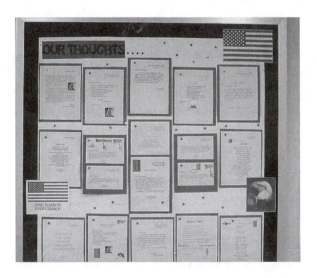

The following are meaningful examples of children's thoughts during that time. Roxana describes the chaos around her, and Kate speaks lovingly of those who helped.

All on This Beautiful Day
People gasping, people crying,
People scared, people in fright.
Twin towers falling,
People screaming.
All on this beautiful day!

The Pentagon on fire,
People jumping.
People emailing.
People calling.
All on this beautiful day!
Why Did This Happen?
Roxana, Grade 5

The Fire of Love Is Burning
The fire of love is burning
Although you didn't have to
You risked your life to save others.
Inside you, you left the fire of love burning.
The fire of love is burning: that fire can never go out.
If you want to know why, it's because that fire is YOU.
Kate, Grade 5

CLASS DISCUSSIONS ON BRAVERY, HONOR, PREJUDICE, AND WAR

New classroom discussions emerged as students attempted to make sense of the unthinkable. Debates emerged over retaliation or nonretaliation, revenge and forgiveness, prejudice and equality, patriotism and human rights, and war and peace. Douglas, age twelve, felt a new awareness surface as he realized he had a new interpretation of what a hero is. He realized events only read in history were now making history and he was a part of it. He expressed his understanding in a letter to rescue workers.

Dear Rescue Workers,

I'm proud that you guys are risking your lives to rescue people. First, I thought that only sports stars could be American heroes, but when I saw you guys in the news . . . I know who the true American heroes are. I hope that you guys find a lot of people. You are very brave. If I could do something to help, I would. I hope this never happens again. When I heard the news, I was shocked. I didn't really think it was that bad, but when I watched the news, I was horrified. Nothing this bad has ever happened in my life.

I remember reading about the attack on Pearl Harbor, the British attacks in the 13 colonies, but nothing this bad happened to the United States. When I hear the word military, I remember what happened last week and Pearl Harbor. I will never forget this day. When I saw the American heroes on the news, I knew that they were brave. I know that they wanted to risk their lives for innocent people, but as long as the American flag is still standing, the United States is not beaten and will never be beaten.

Sincerely,

Douglas, age 12

POSTER CONTEST

The school challenged its students to participate in a poster contest with the theme "How Kids Can Make a Difference." Julia became the judge and admired many concepts of children having bake sells to help victims and helpers, cleaning up their environment, standing united or manifesting cooperation, respect, and kindness. The following are examples of these posters.

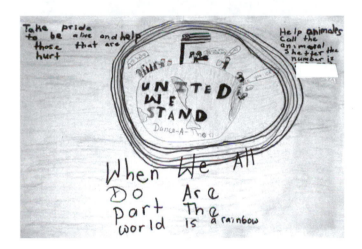

FUNDRAISING

Students decided to become involved in a fundraising service project to raise money for victims of the tragedy. The entire student population voted on the title of the dance, and their choices were "Dancing to Make a Difference," "Red, White and Blue," and the winning name "United We Stand." After morning announcement, teachers were asked to take a quick "hands-raised-eyes-closed" tally vote and have results counted and announced.

Students decorated the gym, sent out flyers, and joined together in fun and celebration to raise money for a good cause. The fliers explained the United We Stand Dance-A-Thon and invited families to attend in order to benefit the September 11th Victims Relief Fund. Fliers were made encouraging students to participate in the "Kids Making a Difference" poster contest to be presented the night of the dance, and giving instructions, the due date, and information about the winning award presentation that night.

Save-the-Date
Wednesday, December 19th, 2001

Get your dancing shoes ready!

Your family is invited to

United We Stand Dance-A-Thon
Wednesday, December 19th, 2001
7:00 pm - 8:30 pm

To benefit the September 11th Victims Relief Fund

Students earn a family "ticket" by raising a minimum of $4.00

Free babysitting for children over 3 years
Free beverages for dancers
Delicious baked goods on sale
Macarena, Electric Slide, Chicken Dance & more!

Please see attached pledge sheet for details

"KIDS MAKING A DIFFERENCE"
POSTER CONTEST

All posters entered in the contest will be on display at the
United We Stand Dance-A-Thon
Wednesday, December 19th

Winners will receive a special award and have an opportunity to dance on stage!

Important Instructions:
1. Your poster needs to include the title "Kids Making A Difference."
2. Draw a picture illustrating what kids can do to make the world a better place. (Hint: If you need help, think about our All-Star themes of Cooperation, Respect, Kindness and Perseverance.)
3. You may use crayons, colored pencils, markers, or paints.
4. Please check your spelling.
5. You will be judged on creativity and effort.

All finished posters are due to Mrs. Brown by
THURSDAY

The dance-a-thon was a huge success that created a forum of joy and giving in the midst of upheaval and confusion. The school auditorium was filled with kids and their families, faculty, and friends, and all felt a great sense of pride and accomplishment in raising money to help others.

The winners of the poster contest were announced that evening. Julia proudly informed her classmates that the winning poster was made by Shantal and Da'Imah.

"What can we do to make the world a better place?" was the question these young people asked. They answered it themselves by volunteering with time and money to help those who were in need. They became the answer to their own question. By developing new ideas, putting these ideas into action, and bonding in friendship and service they became a caring community of young people. They spontaneously found themselves in roles they had previously only imagined as heroic.

School Activities for Helping and Healing

HOMEWORK ASSIGNMENTS: EMERGENCY PLANNING

Children can be given a homework assignment to help them be prepared for any kind of trauma. Having them find out important telephone numbers and places in case of any emergency and record them in a safe place becomes a valuable tool to bring assurances and options back into their lives. They can also create ideas for an emergency kit. As a homework assignment, students can choose needed supplies such as water, canned goods, and medicinal needs and bring them to class. Then they can choose a designated place to keep these supplies in case they are needed.

PERSONAL TRIBUTES

Anthony's uncle died in military service in Iraq. Anthohy created his own tribute in honor of Uncle Frank by lighting a candle and playing TAPS on a trumpet. Anthony shared this tribute during his fourth-grade meeting time.

STUDENT INVOLVEMENT

The SARS epidemic created panic and stress for school children around the world. Students in China cleaned their classroom as part of their normal assignments for the day. To avoid contagion during the SARS epidemic, Chinese boys and girls did an extra special job of sanitizing their classroom and became active participants in its prevention.

Jessica, age nine, is an American child living in China and attending a Chinese school. She explains through the following picture how she and her classmates helped to prevent SARS in their classroom.

SCHOOL BOOK VENTURES

One educational system created a literary project as an outlet for thoughts and feelings, a sharing of ideas, and a coming together of the school community that allowed students to feel connected to a larger purpose. Their creativity and flexibility allowed for a teachable moment to modify the present curriculum to include a writing lab focused on the tragic events of 9/11. The book was written and illustrated by students and contained thoughts and feelings through poetry and artwork. It became an important resource that spoke of the terrorist attack through the eyes and ears of the children. The following is an example of the children's

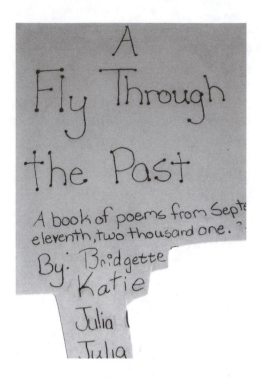

poetry and drawing in the book titled *A Fly Through the Past,* written, designed, and illustrated by Bridgette, Katie, Julia, and Julia.

MEMORIAL PROJECTS

Butterflies

I once saw a butterfly flitter
Out of its wings came color and
glitter
I think they are the souls of people
That are passing by on their way to
heaven where they watch us day by
day.
In death they live on in a beautiful
way.

School systems throughout the country adjusted classroom lessons and curricula to allow students to process thoughts and feelings related to the public tragedy. Children became involved in the formation of creative projects as the work to produce them became part of classroom lessons. One twelfth grader, Yili, was given the assignment in civics class to develop a memorial for 9/11 to share with the class.

A ninth-grader, Jon, decided to memorialize the Twin Towers by painting a picture of them as part of the New York skyline. It became the cover of his school's student magazine of poetry and drawings, becoming a memorial of 9/11 for the entire student body.

(Painting by Jon Goldman)

Many school systems had multiple members who were injured or killed in the attack. Four members of one school community died in the terrorist attack. Students and faculty decided to create a memorial project that would become a part of their school. All of the children participated in constructing a memorial path of footprints displayed through the grounds of the campus, and then chose appropriate flowers to plant. It was a constant reminder of their loved ones and a source of pride in a project well done by the entire school population.

Schools Provide Child Trauma Information to Community

Montgomery County school systems felt an enormous impact after the September 11 disaster due to the close proximity of the Pentagon and Washington, D.C. Through the beginning days of shock and grief they struggled with ways to respond to the community with ways to help the children. The following is a guide for parents, educators, and other caring professionals given out by the school system to increase understanding about traumatized children.

SUGGESTIONS TO HELP TRAUMATIZED STUDENTS

Share the facts in a calm and caring manner.

Remind children that teasing and taunting people from diverse cultures is not tolerated.

Provide a vehicle for expressing fears and anxiety, such as journal writing or drawing.

Ensure that the information you give is appropriate to the developmental level of the child and is stated in a vocabulary that can be understood.

Clarify misconceptions and restate information as necessary.

Allow for opportunities to talk about the situation. Listen closely to fears and concerns.

Control panic among children by remaining calm yourself.

Be flexible and allow time in your routine to address concerns as they arise.

Reassure children that their emotional responses are normal responses to an abnormal situation: to some extent, everyone is afraid. It's all right to be afraid and to talk about it.

Acknowledge that there is some uncertainty about what will happen next, but that many adults are working together to ensure everyone's safety.

Ask children what things they have done in the past to help them through difficult times. List these activities and encourage the use of similar strategies.

Encourage children to make healthy choices in what they eat and drink and to allow more time for sleep and relaxation.

Tell children that it is okay to turn off the TV or to change the channel so that they don't become overloaded with disaster information.

Don't overlook the positive events. Point out that although many people were hurt in this tragedy many were not injured and many of the injured will recover. Look for stories of heroism and bravery in the face of the disaster and talk about how this crisis brought out the best in people from all over the world who want to help.

Assure children that they will be all right and life will continue.

Be alert for children whose reaction seems especially intense or unusual.

Consult with the school counselor if you have concerns or questions. (This material was developed by the Montgomery County Public School, Department of Student Services, 2001)

SCHOOL SYSTEMS AND EMERGENCY PLANNING

Many schools had been preparing themselves for crisis interventions before the terrorist attack, but crisis planning took on a new dimension after 9/11. Few systems, including schools, were prepared to deal with a population of children and teens traumatized by a national event they were directly related to by knowing someone impacted by the trauma, being close in proximity to the trauma, experiencing this trauma vicariously through the media, or by being citizens of the United States.

Many schools located near the sites of the terrorist attacks and surrounding states were greatly impacted. One nearby school had many students with parents working near to or inside the disaster area. Many families had relatives or friends affected by this traumatic event. Emergency procedures on the day of the event involved counseling, communication with parents, and safety measures.

This school decided to invite its present and past community for a meeting to commemorate 9/11 . The weekend after the attack, the school held such a meeting for students, families, alumni, and friends to come together to mourn the shocking events of the past week. More than a hundred people gathered together, candles in hand, and members of the group shared spontaneously their feelings and thoughts and experiences about September 11. It was a solemn and sacred sharing, whereby strong bonding strengthened the deep feeling of community as people came together to honor each other, the victims, the helpers, and their country in mutual respect and caring. The power of this sharing emanated throughout the evening and the gift of this coming together was a renewed strength that enabled them to begin to move forward after such an overwhelming challenge.

Throughout the year this school maintained a program allowing children to voice feelings at weekly meetings and provided education for parents on how to help the students during this difficult time. Threats about anthrax in neighboring post offices and code orange terrorist alerts kept the image of 9/11 ever present for many. The school began to take steps to secure the safety of students and employees on both campuses.

A committee was created to formulate a comprehensive crisis management plan that outlined protective measures against a variety of specific threats, including biological, chemical, and radiological attacks. The finished product also discussed defense against fire, earthquakes, tornadoes, bomb threats, and armed intruders. In addition, the plan detailed administrative structures and procedures for centralized decision making and schoolwide communication during a crisis. Emergency managers were identified for every building on both campuses. Specific routes for evacuation and the seeking of shelter were identified. The school assembled well-stocked emergency kits to be stored in strategic locations.

The writing of this crisis management plan was accomplished in part through the assistance of the Office of National Preparedness in the Federal Emergency Management Agency (FEMA). The plan was reviewed and commented on by FEMA officials and shared with more than twenty-five schools across the nation.

The head of the school sent a letter to parents, faculty, staff, and alumni and includes the preceding information. Additional information included some emergency situations that might require that students remain on campus inside buildings until the emergency is over. In these cases, the school would try to inform parents whether and when they could pick up students. To the extent possible, given the nature of the emergency, news would be disseminated through the school's website, the emergency extension on the Parents Association information line, and local radio and television stations. The head master ended his letter with the following words, which seem to personify the wish of all educators caught in the challenges of any ever-changing world.

I know that contemplating such dangers as discussed in this letter is extremely difficult for us all. Nevertheless, the school must take steps to secure the safety of everyone. I earnestly hope that friends will never have to implement any of the measures outlined in the crisis plan, and I know you will join me in that ardent wish. It is essential, however, that we be as prepared as possible.

RESEARCH ON STUDENT AND TEACHER REACTIONS TO 9/11

Research presented by Noppe et al (2004) in "Adolescents' & Teachers' Responses to September 11: A Qualitative Study" offers survey data after the terrorist attack on 8th and 9th graders and their teachers in Wisconsin. Findings indicated fear and concern from students, worry about the future of the country, greater amount of television viewing by the students than prior to the attack, and increased thoughts of terrorism and war. Students questioned used coping strategies such as talking to family and friends, and participating patriotic activities. Findings indicated that girls experienced more concern and anxiety than boys. Also, high school teachers allowed more TV watching during school than those teachers of younger grades.

The most common initial response of adolescents to the tragedy was shock, anger, and confusion. Some students indicated they were tired of hearing about September

11th; others seemed very angry. Students indicate parents and teachers were the most beneficial in helping students understand what happened. Activities to cope with the stress of 9/11 included acting "normal, sending aid, or shielding oneself from the unfolding drama." Noppe et al. presented key themes of adolescents as predicting things would return to normal or believing more terrorism, war, and death would occur. Students wanted to be given information and at the same time expressed a desire to be sheltered. A great number of adolescents spontaneously indicated anger, a need for revenge, a desire to make sense of the events of September 11th, and a desire to "do something," whether it is a military response, bringing people together, creative expression, or supporting patriotic activities.

Teacher responses ranged from telling students nothing to giving them as much information as possible and using the experience as a learning opportunity. Teachers emphasized they needed to maintain a routine and reassure their students. They observed increased angry responses in students and were often told by administration to minimize information given to students. Some were frustrated with some student's lack of outward concern. Teachers noted the historic significance of the events of 9/11, and despite awareness of a change in world events, many teachers voiced a need to move forward and emphasized American's resilience.

Research Conclusions

Even in the absence of physical proximity to New York, Washington DC, & Pennsylvania, it was clear that September 11th had a significant psychological impact on Midwestern adolescents. Although many of our adolescent participants could not identify with specific individuals, many viewed the attack as one on America in general. Both students and teachers were acutely aware of the change in the world order and this was reflected in many concerns about "What will happen next?". Much of the anger voiced by the Midwestern adolescents in the survey appeared to stem from the perception that the attacks were deliberate, intentional, and planned.

Adolescents commented about how shocked they were at the news of the attack. Both teachers and adolescents suggested that the continuing interest and media coverage of September 11th needed to end.

This research (Noppe et al: 2004) also indicates a tension between social isolation and the need for social connection in many adolescents after 9/11. Teens sought peers and family; yet they also isolated themselves in solitary activities. Young people wanted adult guidance; yet they also expressed the need to be left alone as adults were making it worse for them. Adolescents suggested they understood what happened and still felt confused. They wanted information and honesty, but were tired of media reports. Young people attempted to rework their sense of identify with their fear of losing themselves. They expressed the need to do something but also claimed people were overreacting. They stated they were coping and had confidence in their future, yet they also worried about the future. Students desired to go to war and show our nation's power; but they also wanted to be sheltered and kept safe.

The findings of this research conclude the adolescent experience of September 11th presents issues and concerns for them that are unique to their developmental period. Physical proximity does not preclude psychological proximity, as many Midwestern adolescents were profoundly affected by the terrorist attack. Schools and teachers provide both support and resilience during public tragedies. The public nature of this tragedy added another layer of understanding to adolescents' evolving understanding of death (Noppe et al; 2004).

At-Risk Children

Important factors indicating difficult outcomes for children after a traumatic experience are a history of prior traumatic experiences, their anxiety level prior to the trauma, and their continuation of stress reactions after the first three months following the traumatic event. Following public tragedy children may be at risk for developing posttraumatic stress symptoms as well as other behaviors and thoughts that create distress and negativity for them. The majority of children with posttraumatic stress reactions return to normal functioning within three months following the tragedy. LaGreca et al. (1998) concluded that continuing high levels of posttraumatic stress reactions three months after the tragedy was a high predictor of children who would persist in having these reactions. Girls generally have a greater degree of more intense and long-lasting reactions than boys and they are at greater risk for developing posttraumatic stress disorder (NASP, 2002).

Posttraumatic stress symptoms include reexperiencing, avoidance of reminders, numbing of general responsiveness, and increased arousal. Often depression, feelings of guilt, searching for reasons, and disruption of developmental issues such as toilet training and anger control become a common by-product of trauma. Children can show increased aggression and self-destructive behavior that affects interaction with others. The independent impact of a trauma on other family members and the extent to which a trauma may bring up memories and feelings related to previous trauma can increase stress signs of physical ailments, hypervigilance, startle reactions, and reenactment.

Imprints of traumatic memories deeply affect the child, as they continually reccur without warning, as if they were a continuous movie on a screen. Even infants and toddlers have the capacity to carry this movie inside their heads and continually replay it when similar instances occur in their life.

IDENTIFYING CHILDREN AT RISK

At-risk behaviors may surface after a traumatic event. The frequency, intensity, and duration of these signs are important factors to consider. Children may experience posttraumatic stress, revisiting the traumatic event through outside stimulus such as photos, music, and media videos, or reliving the sights and sounds of the tragedy in their minds and re-creating earlier stress symptoms. Prolonged anxiety from continuing apprehension about future attack, ongoing war, and threat of biological harm heighten and maintain these traumatic signs.

Angela walked out of class and said she didn't want to live. It was five days after the terrorist attacks and her social living class was talking about the tragedy. "I don't want to talk abut it, and I don't want to talk to anyone!" she shouted as she ran down the hall. Angela's dad had died in a plane crash two years earlier, and images of the 9/11 horror rekindled her past trauma. The principal called Angela's mom and described the incident. Her mother explained that Angela had begun to show the same signs of trauma she displayed after the death of her dad. She barely ate, barely slept, and didn't want to go to school or be with her friends. The school decided to schedule a meeting to discuss, identify, and suggest a plan to work with Angela and the at-risk behaviors she displayed.

Educators, parents, and other health care professionals can establish tools to identify children at risk. Celotta, Jacobs, and Keys (1987) explain findings from their research in the article "Searching for Suicidal Precursors in the Elementary School" and point out that two questions at-risk children respond to positively 100% of the time are: "Do you feel hopeless?" and "Do you feel sad?" These responses were part of a checklist given to elementary school children to identify depression.

Educators, parents, and health professionals can also develop a simple at-risk tool to help target children who are traumatized and may be at risk. We can help locate some of the areas of concern or distress in their lives by asking simple questions, such as the following, and asking children to draw or write their responses.

- What makes you feel panicked?
- What makes you feel jittery?
- What makes you cry?
- What makes you really angry?
- What do you think about over and over again?

Teachers and counselors can also ask the two questions that at-risk children constantly answer yes to:

- Do you feel sad all of the time?
- Do you feel hopeless all of the time? (Celotta, Jacobs, & Keys, 1987)

Educators have a responsibility to monitor how children are coping after a traumatic event. Teachers and counselors need to identity at-risk behaviors, involve parents with those children they identify, and schedule appropriate follow-ups for the findings. It is essential that teachers, counselors, and parents educate themselves on the warning signs of children experiencing difficulty in coping. Some may repeatedly relive the trauma through thoughts or repetitive play and demonstrate hyperviolent responses and appear highly reactive. Others may be unable to return to their level of functioning in school and home prior to the event. The following behaviors may also indicate that the child may need professional help.

- Sudden and pronounced change in behavior
- Threat of suicide or preoccupation with or creation of artwork or writing indicating the child doesn't want to live
- Harmful acts to other children or animals
- Extreme confusion or incoherence
- Substance abuse
- Sudden change of grades
- Avoidance or abandonment of friends
- Angry or tearful outbursts
- Self-destructive behavior
- Inability to eat or sleep
- Over-concern with own health or health of a loved one

- Creation of a will or giving away important possessions
- Sudden unexplained improvement
- Depression, isolation, or withdrawal (Goldman, 2001)

Conclusion: The Responsibility of Educators

Educators carry an enormous responsibility in working with children after a trauma. Their role is to function as nurturers and providers of safety, sources of accurate information, oases of release for stored and confusing thoughts and feelings, indicators of at-risk students, and providers of emergency planning offering appropriate procedures, resources, and follow-ups.

Boys and girls often feel helpless, hopeless, and powerless to change what happened or to stop their intrusive thoughts and feelings after a traumatic event. They manifest startle responses, sleep disorders, physical ailments, hypervigilance, aggressiveness, and repetitive reenactments in and out of the classroom.

"Responding to Terror: The Impact of September 11 on K-12 Schools and Schools' Responses" (Auger, Seymour, & Roberts, 2004) indicates that students clearly had heightened responses during the days immediately following 9/11. The average K–12 student in their study was exposed in school to 3 hours of live television coverage of these attacks. These researchers noted a disparity between the substantial level of student distress seen by the respondents and the very low numbers of students who sought school-based support. They urge after a national traumatic event for "school counselors to actively seek opportunity to assist students and staff" and suggest activities such as "proactively visiting classrooms, roaming halls looking for affected students, and organizing supportive activities (p. 229)."

Schools must remind students they are survivors and can get through challenging experiences. Educators must create learning to accommodate the complex issues facing our children today and their reactions to them. They must restore confidence that adults are working to keep students secure, and that there are many good people trying very hard to help others during these hard times. Only then can our young people move forward with increased assurance of safety, protection, and hope.

Resources

FOR CHILDREN On 9/11

Fireboat: The Heroic Adventures of the John. J. Harvey (2002) by M. Kalman is a story about a fireboat that becomes a hero in New York by helping after the terrorist attack.

September 11th, 2001 (2001) by N. Pottenger is a book made by children to share their experiences of 9/11.

It's Still a Dog's New York (2001) by S. Roth is a story of two dogs after 9/11, expressing their feelings and recognizing the heroics that took place and the hope of rebuilding and going on.

FOR EDUCATORS

A Student Dies, A School Mourns (2000) by Ralph Klicker helps prepare educators for a death in the school community. It offers ways to assist the school in creating and implementing a crisis response plan.

The Art of Healing Childhood Grief (1993) by Anne Black and Penelope Adams is a school based expressive arts program for the grieving child.

When Death Impacts Your School: A Guide for School Administrators (2000) by the Dougy Center is an excellent resource when death affects a school.

C H A P T E R 9

Community Action: From Fear to Freedom

COMMUNITY RESPONSE • TRAGEDY ASSISTANCE
PROGRAMS • BALLOON RELEASE • UMBRELLA
PROJECTS • MEMORY ACTIVITIES • CONFLICT
RESOLUTION • LETTERS • GRIEF CAMPS • PEER
MENTORS • ROLE MODELS • VIDEO CONFERENCING
SUPPORT GROUPS

Few things help an individual more than to place responsibility upon him, and to let him know you trust him.

Booker T. Washington

Responsibility of a Community-Based Outreach Program

After children experience personal or public trauma, they often feel alone and different. Frightened because their once comfortable world now seems unpredictable and unsafe, they may react in ways that we as adults can truly not judge, understand, or anticipate. All too often I hear children and teens say, "No one understands what I have been through. There is no one I can talk to. I feel weird and I just want to feel normal."

Knowing that these thoughts and feelings are common for those young people who have been exposed to traumatic grief, community outreach programs for grieving and traumatized children can use this knowledge as a framework to create safe havens for expressing, reflecting, and processing incredibly challenging events with others having similar issues and life styles in order to heal.

A primary goal of any community-based outreach program for children with traumatic grief is to provide an oasis of comfort where young people feel supported and understood by others they can identify with and relate to. Support groups and camp situations provide an "extended family" of reassurance, which includes other children and adults sharing similar events. This allows them to normalize scary and new feelings that surprisingly turn out to be common to so many others. After the terrorists' attacks in Washington, teenagers who were survivors of parental death consistently expressed strong feelings that they needed to be in a teen support group with others whose moms or dads had died in the Pentagon attack. They felt they were the only ones who could truly understand.

By incorporating peer mentors and big sister and brother systems, community outreach programs provide further identification that both adults and children can truly understand. Nick was seven years old when his dad, a policeman, was killed in the line of duty. He missed his father so much. The police force offered Nick a big brother named Willy. Willy was another policeman, giving his time to a boy who needed a male figure in his life. Nick loved Willy's visits and the shared understanding of Dad's work, his uniform, and simple familiar activities like playing ball and eating hot dogs. Nick felt Willy really understood.

Allowing children to openly grieve and share in activities designed and shaped by the special social and cultural patterns unique to their lifestyle and their loved ones is essential in creating a familiar environment that encourages freedom of expression. Many times a grief therapist searches for specific groups to meet specific needs of a young client. Ten-year-old Evan suffered over his dad's imprisonment and felt embarrassed to talk about where his dad was and why he was there. He withdrew from friends and isolated himself. Finding a peer support group for children whose parents were incarcerated provided a resource for Evan with other kids who also felt embarrassed and afraid to reveal their life issues for fear of judgment.

Establishing memorials and rituals that provide children and teens opportunities to be part of a community-based grief team is extremely powerful. Dan's dad died in the Vietnam War. On his dad's birthday, Dan and his mom and younger sister, Susan, went to the Vietnam Memorial and said a prayer for Dad. They came home and took out the flag they were given at his funeral and placed it outside the house. Dan felt proud of Dad and was glad he could remember him in this way.

Mary's mom died of cancer when Mary was sixteen. She participated in and raised money with thousands of others in a bike ride to find a cure for cancer. She felt comforted by being part of a larger community group striving together to find answers to an illness that had caused the death of so many loved ones.

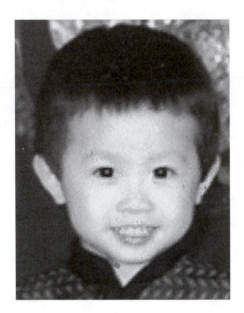

Tragedy Assistance Program for the Military

CHILDREN'S OUTREACH

An organized community program respects and includes children with traumatic loss and serves as a liaison to communicate to other members of the community through providing education and creating a forum to memorialize for their unique population.

An important part of the Tragedy Assistance Program for the Military (TAPS) is their outreach program for children who have had a loved one die in any branch of the military service. Surviving parents often indicate the most critical need for their children who have experienced a traumatic death is an organized program of assistance. These children of military families have specific concerns and issues that many outside of the military might be unaware of or unconcerned about.

GRIEF SUPPORT CAMP

Infants, toddlers, children, teens, and young adults need support to express grief with others, sharing similar experiences to help normalize difficult feelings. The surviving youth are taught coping skills, provided outlets for grief, and given methods of stress reduction through a camp for grieving military children. They learn how, as a nation, to honor all of those who have served in the U.S. armed forces and died.

The Good Grief Camp is held for one weekend each year during the TAPS National Military Survivor Seminar each Memorial Day weekend. Children feel pride for their loved ones as their courage and honor and ability of their military duty are stressed. By sharing their pain with other military children around the country they are able to feel less isolated and alone and are provided with a support group with other children who have had similar experiences throughout the country. Adult survivors have opportunities to share with other adults through adult peer support groups and workshops. They also learn about their grief and the grief of their boys and girls.

Groups for children provide an opportunity for children to create a special military connection as well as develop a sense that they aren't so different. The groups help children to normalize military grief. During one camp experience Jon and Adam realized their dads had died on the same plane and that they lived near each other. They became fast friends, bonding deeply on the similar special issues they had both encountered. The boys continued to support each other throughout the year.

HONOR GUARDS AS MENTORS

Using a respected and familiar adult who represents their unique community as a mentor provides children with adult companionship and protection they need during their grief process.

Military honor guards representing every branch of the U.S. armed forces volunteer each year to serve as mentors for the children, each becoming a big brother or a big sister to a young girl or boy. They come early to the camp and receive training in helping children cope with traumatic death. The honor guard's regular job is to pay tribute to any member of the service who has died in the line of duty in Kosovo, Afghanistan, Iraq, or any other of the many hot spots in today's world. They adhere to a strict code of conduct that honors a fallen soldier, and train extensively to respectfully handle the casket of the deceased. They present the American flag to the family, perform a 21-gun salute, and escort the parent or spouse of the service member who has died.

During the weekend of mentoring the children, they perform a formal silent drill team to honor those who have died. Wearing white gloves and dress uniforms, and carrying their rifles, they present a shiny and polished performance for the youngsters. They then spend time sitting and talking with the youth. Some kids get hugs; others sit on the laps of the honor guards.

A nineteen-year-old female honor guard was part of the search and recovery team after the Pentagon attack. She had nightmares and anxiety after her duty. She became very cognizant of the grief and loss issues and sensitive to the children's feelings. Working with the children provided a tremendous space for her to feel safe to work through some of her own trauma.

These honor guards are unique women and men. They understand the huge sacrifice that military personnel make while serving their country and the honor guards realize how important they can be to the surviving kids. They donate their time to the children in respect and admiration for their fellow soldiers, sailors, and airmen. One honor guard was sixteen years old when his own dad died in the military. Now he is twenty-four years old and able to give back and share his experience with the young survivors.

Another honor guard knew a little boy's dad who had died in the war. The boy's dad had been the honor guard's commander and he was able to share precious stories about the father with his son. He said he felt privileged to do so. Stanley asked his honor guard as he was getting ready to go home, "Will you be my dad?" Then he hugged him tight and begged him not to leave.

Most honor guards are touched by their powerful experiences in grief camp. It means so much to them that they can make a difference for grieving boys and girls in the military. One explained his feelings in the following way: "When I hear the kids, it gives me hope and makes me confident that the honor guards would be here for me and my kids—and they would offer them warmth and support if they needed it.

PEER MENTORS

Other children who have experienced similar events and can serve as models of survivorship and growth provide one of a child's most powerful supports. Another component of the weekend support group is the peer mentoring program. Many children who have attended camp come back as assistants and mentors. Others mentors may be adults whose parents were killed many years before the camp began, such as in the Vietnam War. Still others may be older children who want to give back after several years of being away. Sixteen-year-old Simon explained that he wanted to be a peer mentor because the children's group "felt like a place that feels like home—where people understand your loss and no one makes fun of you."

MEMORY ACTIVITIES

Grief activities for children need to be designed and shaped by the specific social and cultural patterns unique to them and their loved ones. These weekend groups include many activities for children and sometimes include adults as well. Pool parties, the Marine Corps parades, and the closing ceremonies are just a few examples. On Memorial  Day, the children, mentors, and other family members venture to the Tomb of the Unknown Soldier to commemorate their loved ones in a sacred way. Two of the children are chosen and trained in the correct procedure to place a homemade wreath on the Tomb of the Unknown Soldier. Two others are selected and trained to carry the TAPS flags and the American flags during the Memorial Day ceremony at which the President speaks. They are greatly honored and recognized as being an important part of the day.

Sometimes the children venture to the zoo, the park, the Smithsonian Institute, or visit the White House. They experience outings together that help to solidify friendships. Other times they just have fun running relay races, jumping on moon bounces, or eating at a barbecue.

There are also many activities specifically for the children. A simple drawing exercise can prove very meaningful. One-eight-year old, Sally, was drawing a picture about her dad. A helper asked her what she needed to finish her picture. "I need a silver crayon and there isn't one." She replied. "That doesn't matter," was the response. "Yes it does!" said Sally. "My dad was a Lieutenant Colonel and he had a silver oak leaf." Sally and the helper went to the kitchen to get aluminum foil to complete the drawing. The unique understanding of the military and military children is a special part of the TAPS children's program.

One activity for all ages was group puppet shows. Infants to teens were included. Babies and toddlers watched as preschoolers sang "God bless Daddy in heaven." Kids wore halos they had made out of pipe cleaners. Elementary-aged children shared with puppets the scenario: "Want to play ball with my dad. Dad isn't here. Want to go fishing with my dad. Dad isn't here."

Preteens performed a scenario about what it was like when they heard their parents died, and older teens gave a play about what it was like a week and a month after the death. They shared how it "still feels like a fog but it's a little easier. We can laugh a little and have a little fun."

Each participating child was given a blanket from Project Linus, a national organization that donates handmade blankets for those who have had someone important die. Children snuggled with the blankets for security during their time together, and then treasured the blanket as a linking object when they got home. The blanket comforts them as they remember their weekend experience. Every boy and girl is given a TAPS tee shirt to wear during the weekend. This serves as a reminder throughout the year of their meaningful time. Other activities include making buttons with pictures of their loved one that died. The children can wear and share memories safely throughout the weekend and feel understood and acceptance.

THE UMBRELLA PROJECT

Symbolism is a powerful tool for communication and expression of grief. Even when the child is too young to know the appropriate words, art and other forms of expression help children heal. The Umbrella Project was inspired by the huge degree of grief experienced by children and their families after the terrorist attack on America. During the TAPS Good Grief Camp 2002 National Military Survivor Seminar in Washington, D.C., international artist Matt Lamb created an original way for children to express their grief and trauma through art. Children who were survivors of service members who died through military service used umbrellas as a vehicle for expression. The umbrella is an international symbol of protection, and children decorated and painted them inside and outside to display their own inner and outer feelings. The underside stood for vulnerable, unexposed grief and trauma, and the outer side represented a shield of protection. This project gave them strength and hope, and allowed them to share their pride in their loved ones who had died.

Each child sat with a mentor and was given paint and an umbrella. They were asked to talk about what it feels like on the inside when we grieve and what it looks like on the outside. They decorated their umbrellas with inner and outer grief, let their paintings dry, and signed their names.

Then the forty children and their forty mentors paraded their painted "umbrellas of safety" throughout the hotel where the camp was taking place, singing "When the Saints Come Marching In" on their way to meet their families. They brought smiles and tears to those they passed, and inner satisfaction to themselves in being able to join with kindred spirits in an open display of love for those they had lost. The umbrellas where transformed into a unique sculpture displayed in the Sam Rayburn Office in Washington, D.C. and other places throughout the country and the world. This project earned a grant from Newman's Own Awards for Military Community Excellence in 2002 for its role in improving the quality of life for children and families of the military who sacrifice so much.

BALLOON RELEASE

Providing a group ritual of symbolically remembering a loved one allows children to feel comforted and reassured that life and death can be a mystery shared by others. One of the culminating activities for the children was a balloon release with the entire group including the honor guard mentors. Children received what they called a "healing balloon" and wrote a note inside. Very young children to older teens were involved, as one by one they let their balloons go, symbolically carrying a message to their special person.

CHILDREN'S VOICES: LETTERS TO TAPS

Letter writing provides a concrete forum for shared reflection within a group, helping children to normalize uncomfortable thoughts and feelings while respecting their own uniqueness and individuality. Children's voices were valued and shared in many ways. Some wrote letters expressing their deep love for a parent who died during active duty in the armed forces. Others spoke of concerns about their health, their surviving parent, income loss, and the loss of moving away from the military life they had known. They explained how they heard about their parent's sudden death and the impact it had on their lives. Physical ailments, embarrassment, and fear emerged. So did love, respect, and hopes of seeing their person in heaven. Each child appreciated their group of military peers who understood the special issues surrounding the death of a loved one in the armed forces.

As you read the following letters, the common signs of grieving children are evident, coupled with the unique circumstances of the death of someone special to children who are military dependents.

Dear TAPS,

My dad was a Major. I am very proud of him! He made me feel like I was the most important person in the world. I miss him a lot and will never forget him, ever. I wish I was here with him now . . .

Since my dad was in the military I only got to see him in the early morning, afternoon and on some weekends. He worked lots of long hours. Sometimes I used to hide his hats, so he couldn't go to work without telling me good-bye! I miss him a lot. Sometimes when I am sad about my dad's death, I remember that he and his hat are waiting for me in heaven! . . .

Carolyn, Age 9

 Dear TAPS,

My dad died when I was only 8 months old, and I never knew him.

I have lived 13 years of my life without a father. I wonder many times, why did it have to happen to me? And why can't I just be like my friends? But then I realize that if I would have had a dad I wouldn't be who I am.

I am always embarrassed if someone asks me what my dad's job is. I don't know what to say except the truth — that my dad was a doctor in the Navy but he died.

Will

Dear TAPS,

The day I remembered the most was the day that my Dad died. It happened in Camp Pendleton, California, a year ago.

I was sick in my bed. My brother came in and said, "Michael, Michael, Dad is missing!" I said "What?!" Then my Grandmother walked in and said, "Michael, your Dad is missing, "No!! Where's Mom?" I said. Grandma said she was in the living room. When I got there I said, "But Mom. Why?" She said, "Come here, Michael," and we talked through the night.

Later that night we heard that Dad had died. They said it was an accident and that a flash flood destroyed a bridge he was standing on. "But where?" I asked. It happened at a training site at Camp Pendleton. I felt sick that night. I had a dream about my Dad, but it felt real. It was that my Dad and I were talking about things together. It seems that when I saw Dad he wasn't dead. So I said, "Can we go tell Mom?" He said, "Yes!" Then my dream stopped and I woke up.

After that I said to myself, "Why, why, why did it happen?" I told myself it wasn't my fault and I couldn't do anything about the bridge.

Michael

Dear TAPS,

My father was killed in the first AWACS plane crash ever on September 22, 1995. It has been almost a year now.

I wasn't really sure if it was real or just a dream. My friends and I just hugged and cried. After a while the truth sank in, I was scared. What were we going to do for income or where would we live now that my father was dead?

Laura

Dear TAPS,

My name is Tyler and I am 9 years old. I am the oldest of 5 kids. When I was 6, my dad died in a plane crash in Germany. That day I had a tooth pulled and he was late for the appointment. Later we went to his office. My mom went in and all five of us waited in the car. Then, some guys came out with my mom's keys and we were scared that they did something with my mom, but they were nice. They took us into the hanger and we saw my mom crying. I asked her what was wrong,

but she didn't answer. So, we played around airplanes with some of my dad's army friends. Then about an hour later, we had a drink of pop.

My mom and some other people told us that my dad was killed in a plane crash. I was bawling and I didn't believe my mom and kept saying it was a lie. A couple of days later, I woke up and my legs hurt so bad that I couldn't walk. My mom took me to the doctor, but he said nothing was wrong. Even sometimes now when I think of my dad or hear about him, my legs start to hurt again. I have a hard time when my friends ask about my dad and also when we do Father's Day at school.

I came to TAPS last year and it was good, because I never knew anyone else who had their dad die in the military and it helped me express my feelings and talk about it. It was nice to talk to people who have gone through the same thing. It has been 2 $\frac{1}{2}$ years now and my mom is dating a real nice guy and he sometimes makes me think of my dad. I can't wait to see everyone this year.

Tyler, Age 9

FAMILY COMMUNITY OUTREACH

Community-based supports can provide all family members a shared place to participate and process their grief and trauma, and a mutual support network for the future. The Reed family attended the weekend grief conference and children's group for many years. Within that structure they were able to come together to have family time, participate as cherished members of the military community, and separate from each other to participate in individual and peer group activities. They each had unique experiences, yet the entire family became part of a larger grief community.

The children of Joseph Oliver Reed, III, missed their dad very much. He had died during his military service and all of his children were greatly affected by his sudden, traumatic death. He was killed in a helicopter crash when two helicopters collided during training in Texas on April 15, 1996.

Junior, now ten, had great difficulty after his dad's death when he was in first grade. He seemed sad a lot and had difficulty concentrating in school. At the end of first grade he attended his first grief camp with TAPS. His mom reported that he was much happier after that experience and did better in school the following year. Junior explained that "being with other kids who had dads die in the same way just felt better." He looked forward to going back to the grief camp each year and reconnecting with his friends from TAPS.

Jasmine was sixteen months old when her daddy died, but five years old when she first went to TAPS. She told Mom she was "going to be shy" when she went to grief camp. When her mother left her there for the first time she felt a little worried about her making new friends and sharing. Mom returned to pick her up only to find Jasmine conversing with a four-star general. She talked and talked to him about her dad and he commented later about how impressed he was with her enthusiasm. "You should be so proud," he said to Jasmine's mom. The entire family felt grateful that someone so important took the time to ask, listen, and care about the Reeds and their feelings. Next time Mom came to pick up Jasmine from a group activity, she almost pushed Mom out of the door and exclaimed. "I have friends and stuff to do. You go do your own thing."

Jessica was the youngest daughter, and Mom was pregnant with her when Dad died. When she first came to the grief camp a person on staff said, "She looks like she wants to grieve, but doesn't seem to feel like she is entitled to be a part of it." Having never known her dad, Jessica's hidden feelings of not deserving to grieve unfolded. She was paired with a mentor, an honor guard given to each child. Soon her pride for her dad emerged as she happily told him, "You are like my daddy, and you go to West Point too." She felt special enough to be able to talk about things she never spoke of before. Jessica now represents TAPS as their cover girl on the TAPS website and in pictures with Senator Bob Dole. Jessica had no pictures of her and her dad in the house, but now she had wonderful photos in TAPS literature showing her sharing her love for her father.

Mrs. Reed was proud of her husband too. She shared many special things about him, as did his West Point peers in a website they created in his honor. His last evaluation from the military was very meaningful. Captain Reed was "able to excel, calm and unflappable in stressful situations, and willing to stand up for what is right. He makes things happen right—a true leader and professional with unlimited potential." How healing these words are to the family. An Excellence in Engineering Award is presented in Captain Reed's name each year at West Point.

Activities to Help Children Participate in World Events

Children can create rituals that allow commemoration and avenues to voice feelings. Lighting candles, planting flowers, writing letters, raising money for victims, or saying prayers for survivors or world peace allow children to be recognized mourners. Thirteen-year-old Helen lived in a New Jersey community where many families, especially those of firefighters and police officers, had been deeply affected by the September 11 disaster. "Let's make brownies," she told her younger brother and sister, "and sell them to raise money for the firefighters. Everybody likes brownies."

Teachers can create a global flag project in their classrooms. Students creatively design a global flag and think about their own vision of world peace. One high school senior pondered a strategy for peace. "Suppose we had one million people walk across the Afghan border, bringing food and clothing and only wanting peace. I wonder what would happen."

School systems can create assemblies about their multicultural populations to better help students understand cultural diversity. Sharing ethnic food, inviting guest speakers from different countries, and creating panel discussions on multiculturalism can enrich acceptance and appreciation for values and concepts from different groups of people. Programs on bullying and victimization policies, prejudice and intolerance, mediation and conflict resolution, and school and community harmony can also be implemented.

One school created a "Peacemaker of the Century" contest. Each student pretended to be a famous peacemaker. They explained why their person deserved to win the prize and presented the philosophy, skills, and goals of their peacemaker. Benjamin became Nelson Mandela, using his native costume, customs, and practices. He won second prize.

Communities can involve children in fundraisers for the survivors in New York and Washington, or for special groups like the firefighters and police officers. Making patriotic pins and selling them to raise money to help victims and survivors, creating websites for world peace, or having a poster contest at school on "What We Can Do To Feel Safe" are ways to give children back a sense of control and participation in their lives.

Community rituals and shared memorializing can have a powerful impact on our youth. During times of public tragedy the spontaneous outpouring of feelings and remembering of loved ones reminds everyone of the huge communal loss. The following photos were taken after the terrorist attack in New York. This community response included letters and pictures placed at the train station in the heart of the city. They represent a "grief community" coming together after a national tragedy.

Shortly after 9/11, a group of students from New York University put out lengthy sheets of butcher paper in Union Square. People who passed by lit candles, taped on posters with pictures of people who were missing, and added drawings. They

wrote a wide variety of messages, including expressions of sorrow and condolence to those who had lost loved ones. Some messages included a personal response to the tragedy or a political viewpoint. Messages were posted from individuals of many backgrounds and in many languages. At times, people disagreed through "fights on paper." These murals became a forum for community debate as well as a mechanism for the community response.

Media can provide valuable information for children. Newspapers such as the *Washington Post* contain kids' sections that actively involve children in the news of the day. This is an excellent vehicle for children to feel included as part of the larger community and can be used as a forum for discussion and education.

Remind children that our nation has the support of many people throughout the world. People all over the world are sad and are praying for America and are helping the United States to find the people responsible for 9/11 and stop them. Point this out as you are reading the follow-up stories in the newspaper. Karen, a sophomore in high school, was amazed that all of England stopped the day after the terrorist attack to commemorate the loss in the United States. Schools, traffic, and government froze as all gave moments of silence for what had happened to their American friends. Reassure them that we have many friends throughout the world working together to help solve problems. Encourage children to remember that they are a part of a nation and a world that has survived difficult experiences and is stronger for it.

The drawing to the left is an example of how a child in Panama felt after watching the terrorist attacks on the United States. He told his mom how sad he felt for the people in America and drew this story to share with them.

Talk to children about strategies. Ask them if they have been thinking about the world situation and if they would like to help change things. Begin to brainstorm ideas.

"What kinds of things can you do to help yourself?"

"How would you go about doing this?"

"What kinds of things can you do to help others?"

"How would you go about doing this?"

Kids can feel more empowered to create change in themselves and their world if they are given a forum for discussion and action.

Archiving Children's Artifacts After 9/11

The New York State Museum has acquired a significant collection of letters, drawings, quilts, banners, and other artifacts that were created by adults and children in the aftermath of the terrorist attack. Carla Sofka, a volunteer at the museum working on this project, shared stories and pictures of the many forms of community outreach by children being documented and preserved as an unprecedented response to a tragedy in American history. Carla explains some of the altruistic gestures of children in the following accounts.

Shortly after September 11, 2001, Haley, a 7-year old girl from Brooklyn, began gathering inscriptions and signatures of support in a notebook that would be delivered to Engine 54, Battalion 9, known as "the pride of midtown Manhattan." She included drawings, photos of herself, and pictures of community events. Haley walked throughout her neighborhood and school, gathering signatures from people in various parts of her communities. Although these different groups of people never met in person, the pictures from her book joined together all of those individuals who signed it and the members of the firehouse who had the opportunity to view it.

(Permission to reprint from the New York State Museum.)

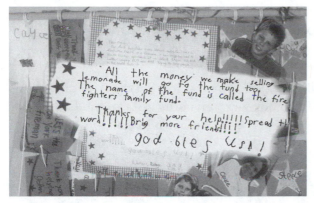

(Permission to reprint from the New York State Museum.)

In Nashville, Tennessee, several girls and boys decided to raise money in their neighborhood for the World Trade Center Relief Fund by selling lemonade. They took a wooden dowel and attached photos of themselves. The children provided small rectangles of red paper for people to write notes of support after donating money. A sense of community was created as people stopped to buy lemonade and then write their messages for a good cause.

A large banner was created by students who were members of a service club, the Interact Club, at Fort Myers High School in Florida. Students in this club felt the need to do something, and Heidi, its vice president, came up with the idea of making a flag banner out of white canvas and paint. Red handprints would form the stripes and blue and white paint would be used to create stars. Along with the handprints, members of the club and members of the Rotary would write inscriptions to be sent to the people of New York.

Once the banner was completed, it was sent to New York and was delivered to the recovery efforts. The banner hung in the Hilltop Café until the café was dismantled and then was taken to the New York State NYS Museum, where it hung in the permanent exhibit on 9-11-2001 until the summer of 2003. In August, I had the honor of taking the banner back to Fort Myers to reunite it with some of the students who created it.

The assembly at the high school was an amazing event. Heidi described the motivation behind creating the banner; she hoped that the banner would illustrate that her generation truly did care about what was happening in the world. As Keith told the story of delivering the flag, you could have heard a pin drop in the auditorium. Several hundred high school students were silent, hanging on his every word.

During the assembly, I announced that the NYS Museum had given me permission to leave the banner in Fort Myers until the anniversary of 9-11 had passed. Within five minutes of the end of the assembly, members of the Interact club and their advisor, representatives from Rotary, and members of the Red Cross had developed a plan to display the banner on 9-11-2003. As I watched them working together, the following question came to mind: Does a community create an artifact, or does an artifact create community?"

The following are quilts made by children in appreciation for the firefighters and other community helpers during 9/11. They were given as gifts to the fire station by Mrs. Owen's class and are now a part of the museum archives.

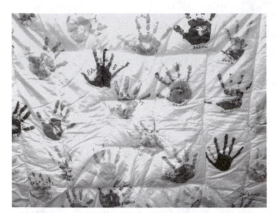 

(Permission to reprint from the New York State Museum.)

The significance of the museum's archive of children's work after 9/11 is enormous. Preserving the outpouring of caring and support made by girls and boys to help others and thank them during times of crisis gives a strong message to our children that what they do is significant and has great meaning. Acknowledging their efforts as helpful and important reinforces to all that young people are an integral part of a community team during difficult times.

Resources for Adults About Community Tragedy

Living with Grief: Coping With Public Tragedy (2003) by K. Doka and M. Licht takes a comprehensive look at the many ways children and adults lived through and coped with the terrorist attack.

Loss of the Assumptive World: A Theory of Traumatic Loss (2002) edited by J. Kauffman presents a diversity of perspectives and interpretations of the concept of the loss of the assumptive world facing many people.

Trauma of the Century (2000) is the story of the Taiwan earthquake told through pictures and words.

When a Community Weeps (1999) by E. Zinner and M. B. Williams presents case studies in group survivorship in trauma and loss.

CHAPTER 10
Enhancing Resiliency in Children

SOCIABILITY • OPTIMISM • SELF-CONFIDENCE •
COMPETENCE • FLEXIBILITY • PERSPECTIVE •
SELF-CONTROL • SURVIVORSHIP • PERSEVERANCE •
SUCCESS • HUMOR • SERVICE • INSIGHTFULNESS •
CHOICE • COURAGE • SPIRITUALITY

How wonderful it is that no one has to wait, but can start right now to gradually change the world! How wonderful it is that everyone, great and small, can immediately help by giving of themselves.

Anne Frank

What Is Resilience?

Resilience often is referred to as the resources one uses to cope with difficult times and the ability to bounce back from these hard situations. Triumphing over pain, overcoming challenges, accomplishing through adversity, and developing strength through suffering are familiar descriptions. The *American Heritage Dictionary* defines resilience as "the ability to recover quickly from illness, change or misfortune; buoyancy." As parents, educators, and other caring professionals, we may ask how we can identify, nurture, and instill the qualities of adaptability, tolerance, patience, and fortitude in our children within their ever-changing environment.

Resilience and Youth

Memories of traumatic events deeply affect the child, as they continually reccur without warning as if they were a continuous movie on a screen. Even infants and toddlers have the capacity to carry this movie inside their heads and continually replay it when similar instances occur in their life.

The concepts surrounding children and resilience have become popular topics in today's world. We not only identify what characteristics are incorporated into those children who are resilient to adversity, but also explore what qualities parents, educators, and professionals can instill and model for children under stress and adversity. Taking resilience a step further, we may strive to create models for all children, not just for those especially predisposed to be at risk.

Children in the twenty-first century face obstacles and pressures that create stress, tension, and grief in their daily life. Their ability to cope, strategize, and adapt to everyday challenges with a resilient quality breeds success in the present and for the future. We may ask ourselves what qualities give certain children and teens the inner strength to cope successfully with the daily demands of life in a fast pace, media stimulated, often violent environment where day-to-day bullying and threats of terrorism are as commonplace as divorce, pressures for good grades, and social status. We may wonder how we can stop the current trend for many of our kids to become products that only "look good," with the right SAT score and the wrong values or fiber to move them through life. A ten-year-old explained that he needed at least three extracurricular activities for his résumé for college.

Parents, educators, and other caring professionals can contribute in creating resilience for the children and teens around them by facilitating their positive adaptation to life adversities. Three important factors contributing to resilient children are their perception of and involvement in the world, the social support and resources available to them, and the coping strategies accessible to them.

Children are living with adversity, stress, and anxiety with outer world pressures and inner expectations placed on them by themselves and others. We may imagine a world where these very children are strong enough, capable enough, and fulfilled enough to process their inner and outer experiences in ways that strengthen their self-concept and serve the larger community.

Adults As Models

One practical way to build resilience is for caring adults to provide interactions and modeling that strengthen a child's ability to meet challenges with confidence, purpose, and compassion. Teaching coping skills, stress management, anddecision making, and providing ways that young people can share with others, enhance friendships, and become responsible citizens in the community and the world is another.

Masten (2001) shares the view of many researchers about the special quality resilient children possess. "Resilience appears to be a common phenomenon that results in most cases from the operation of basic human adaptation systems. If those systems are protected and in good working order, development is robust even in the face of severe adversity; if these major systems are impaired, antecedent, or consequent to adversity, then the risk for developmental problems is much greater, particularly if the environmental hazards are prolonged" (p. 227).

Adults play a powerful role in nurturing a child's or adolescent's choice making and processing of problems, and in providing the educational setting to allow this processing to unfold and develop with learning that can be used when the next problem arises. Being models that give children the confidence that adults in their lives can handle difficult times and can take care of them during these situations is a powerful message.

Keys to Resilient Children

Why is resilience important to talk about? How can one use it to help children once it is explained? A major aspect of resilience may be the feeling that "I'm not totally alone against the world—that somehow, somewhere, I'm part of something bigger than me." Regardless of which lens it is viewed through—spiritual, religious, social, community, or family—resilience provides and encourages altruistic urges to help others and to make life work.

CHOICE

 The last of human freedoms is to choose one's attitude in a given set of circumstances.

Victor Frankl

Victor Frankl exemplified the human spirit and its struggle to survive and eventually thrive in intolerable situations as a long-time prisoner in a Nazi concentration camp that stripped him to a bare existence. In his classic book *Man's Search for Meaning*, Frankl describes the struggle and power of choice, telling us that even the very tiniest choice can create freedom and power. Dr. Frankl was asked why he didn't just kill himself, and answered the question by explaining his process of "weaving slender threads of a broken life into firm patterns of meaning and responsibility" (Allport, preface). For him the ultimate choice was between life and death, and he chose to live. He demonstrated the triumph of human dignity in holding fast to images of love and hope, and the power of the mind to create that attitude of optimism.

Simon was a fifteen-year-old exhibiting adolescent behaviors and sometimes difficulties. Although he had many friends, a loving family, and a bright mind, he often felt alone inside, and remarked repeatedly that there was nothing good in his life. Although we did regular reality-checks with him to confirm that there were positive situations and people all around him, he persistently maintained that he could see none. The concept of choice in the thoughts one uses was introduced and repeated in our many times together, explaining that negative talk and self-defeating phrases were often unconscious but that their repetition could create the perception that they were true. Simon's patterns still seemed to continue.

After many discussions about the power of these unproductive messages and the ability to interject positive ones, a casual incident identified a change in understanding. Simon greeted me after school with a smile. Asking how his day went, he replied "good"—a response he did not often make. He then proceeded to explain that he had "decided to be happy" and how lucky he was that he "learned this at such a young age." The power of choosing our thoughts and the impact of positive messages had become a viable tool for resilience for Simon.

OPTIMISM

Resilient children have hope for the future or a willingness to let others hold that hope for them. They also understand that they can create a happy attitude by looking for the good and creating positive outcomes—saying a kind word or noticing a kind deed.

Mary's dad died. She was very sad. Her friend Tony's mom had died the year before. "You will feel better Mary. It takes time," he explained. She sighed for a moment and felt comforted by his words.

Twelve-year-old Alice's parents got divorced. She felt different from other kids who lived with both parents. She needed other preteens to talk to. She decided to put an ad in her school newspaper for other middle-school children to meet together and created a "Divorce Club" that met at lunch time to talk about their life situation.

COURAGE

Resilient children act even when they are afraid or unhappy. They often overcome their fears to work for a helpful cause.

Tanya's fifteen-year-old brother Henry got killed in a ride-by shooting. She was devastated. She wanted to do something to stop the violence in her neighborhood. Her community was having a town meeting on violence and her pastor asked her to talk about her brother's death. She was shy and felt scared at the thought of speaking in front of so many people. Having the courage to be afraid and still "step up to the plate" highlights Tanya's strength in the face of fear.

REALISTIC GOALS

Resilient children face goals realistically and choose options that coincide with self-knowing of strengths and weaknesses. Tommy was a high school senior preparing to enter an Ivy League College. He had become increasingly depressed, realizing that he didn't want to attend the school that had been a family tradition for his parents and grandparents. He decided to tell his parents he couldn't go because he didn't feel he could fit into the environment there that wasn't right for him. He loved art and graphic design and chose a school that met the needs of his special talents.

HUMOR

Resilient children can see the humor in themselves and sometimes in difficult situations surrounding them. Their ability to laugh during challenging times can help lighten them. Amy, age eight, shared her account of a bullying event in her life. Although she was very disturbed by a bully who continually annoyed her and her classmates in the classroom and on the playground, she was able to see the humor in the following bullying scenario.

You know how there are basically two types of bullies in your class, girl bullies and boy bullies? When I was in first grade there was a kid in my class named Merissa and she was such a bully. She hit, punched and kicked all the other kids. She pushed and used bad words. I stood up to her but she didn't listen to me so I told a teacher. By that time my teacher was fed up with her as well. She said, "Merissa, go to the principal's office!" Merissa refused. So the teacher tried to drag her by the arm down to the principal's office. Merissa grabbed onto the bookshelf! Slowly, with the teacher still pulling, the bookshelf went after her down the hall to the principal's office. It was quite a vivid memory. So you see sometimes what starts out as bullying can end up as comedy.

MY FIRST GRADE BULLY
BY AMY

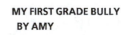

SELF-CONFIDENCE

Children who have a flexible nature and are willing to experiment allow new experiences into their life that breed self-confidence. Eleven-year-old Thomas discovered a program for his age group that created camps for world peace in foreign countries. One campsite was in the mountains of Japan, and Thomas initiated a campaign to convince his parents this would be an authentic adventure in his best interests. The group that went was composed of delegates from nine countries and appropriate chaperones for a one-month period. He industriously created a contract for his parents, promising to clean his room, brush his teeth, and walk the dog. Still his mom and dad declined. Finally Thomas began his verbal advocacy. "I know I can do it and I know it will be great!" His mom responded, "Why not go to camp like all of your friends in the state where we live?" "Mom," he explained, "when I grow up and my kids want to go to Mars, do I tell them they can only go to the moon?" Thomas went that summer and it was the adventure of a lifetime, opening new vistas of internal growth and greater cultural understanding.

APPRECIATION OF SELF

Resilient children feel they are special in certain areas and draw from this self-concept to create change in their lives. Sometimes they may even view problems and difficult times as a challenge rather than a barrier. By having the ability to learn from their mistakes, resilient children can use past errors to develop new coping strategies.

Mattie was a young boy living with a rare form of muscular dystrophy and the grief associated with the loss of his three siblings from the same life threatening disease. He became a courageous, award-winning poet, inspiring others by his deep well of understanding, immense insightfulness far beyond his years, and optimistic outlook through his heart's journey. He was the author of many books, including *Heartsongs* and *Journey Through Heartsongs,* in which he expressed his life struggles, hope, wisdom, and humor in a delightful and thought-provoking way. He was a perfect example of a child who took the difficult challenges presented to him and used them to bring new lessons and dialogues into the world to help others. Mattie donated a portion of his profits to various charities and spoke on television shows, seminars, and conferences, inspiring children and adults to find the place within where sources of conflict in life can be transformed to higher levels of understanding and appreciation.

The following is one of Mattie's poems. His words personify the resilience of a young boy living with a life threatening disease filled with gratitude for being alive and cherishing the ever-present moment (Mattie died at age 14).

The Daily Gift

You know what?
Tomorrow is a new day.
Today is a new day.
Actually,
Every day is a new day.
Thank you, God,
For all of these
Special and new days.

(From *Heartsongs* by Mattie J.T. Stepanek. Copyright © 2001 Mathew Joseph Thaddeus Stepanek. Reprinted with permission from VSP Books/Hyperion.)

ACCEPTANCE AND COMFORT

Resilient children know themselves in a realistic way. They recognize their strengths and talents as well as their vulnerabilities. They feel comfortable with themselves and peers, and ask adults for help.

Ariel was a sixth-grade girl who experienced the death of her dad when she was ten. She had been part of a grief support group and shared her feelings with peers, friends, and relatives for quite a long time. When she was ready to give back to school, she contacted the counselor in her school to ask if she could be a peer mentor, and was disappointed there were none at the time. Finding my website about children and grief on the Internet, she decided to contact me to ask if there was any way to help her create a mentoring program for grieving children. She explained on the phone that she felt she had "worked through a lot of grief feelings about her dad and now she was ready to help others."

Ariel was entering a new junior high school in the fall. We devised a plan for when she began the new year. I would call her new counselor as a liaison for her to see if a peer mentoring program in grief would be helpful in the school. This counselor was open and willing to provide time and space for the project. Ariel loved to write, and wrote an article for the school newspaper explaining her program and welcoming participants. Her ability to solicit adult help, coupled with her own creative talents and desire to help, inspired others to join a peer mentoring grief program that served a useful purpose in her school setting.

PROCESSING LIFE THROUGH PRODUCTIVE ACTION

Resilient children learn from processing past experiences and building on them. They are capable of taking productive action to realize their goals and are self-assured in creating ways to work through adversity.

Research after 9/11 indicated adolescents demonstrated important resiliency skills for coping with trauma. (Noppe et al., 2004). Findings frome Noppe's study demonstrate that students exhibited engagement in many activities ranging from patriotic to spiritual that were helpful to others. Many sought solace from family and friends. Others attempted to construct a meaningful narrative from what happened by explaining events and their personal ideas on future social and political change.

Sixteen-year-old Andrew was angry when he witnessed the terrorist attack on TV. Living in Washington, D.C., he knew many people affected by the assault on the Pentagon. He adamantly explained to friends and family that he wanted to go to the Mall in downtown Washington to show the terrorists that he wasn't afraid and he wasn't going to change his routine or lifestyle because of them. He stated boldly, "They can't win. They can't tell me what to do." He didn't want to talk about any other feelings. A year later, Andrew still felt strongly that he would not be intimidated by terrorism. He shared these feelings in his poetry.

When terrorists provoke fear they win
Their victims aren't the deceased
Their victims are those who change their lives due to
The fear stemming from the terrorist
To be scared is to lose
To lose is to die

Andrew, Age 17

His strong stance for individual freedom and a proactive life has led him at seventeen to pursue certification to become an emergency medical technician after admiring the heroism of so many emergency personnel.

Liuxinyn was a teenager living in Beijing during the SARS epidemic. Living in a panicked environment with schools and other public buildings closed for fear of contagion, he displayed the universality of adolescent action by claiming in the following picture, "I know I can win!" against SARS.

Mohamad, age ten, goes to school in Baghdad. He illustrates American soldiers giving food to the people of Iraq after the invasion. His drawing depicts a scene of cooperation between soldiers and Iraqis as they appear to be working together during adverse situations to rebuild the country. (Permission by Puffin Foundation Ltd. Carl Rosenstein and Patrick Dillon.)

CREATIVITY

"The only difference between you and Woody Allen is that you think you can go to a movie and he thinks he can make a movie. But you could make a movie too," a former teacher of creative writing once told me. Creativity is a self-esteem booster for children, encouraging them to explore parts of themselves in appealing ways. It is often a healing outlet for troubling areas and a means of self-expression that is as unique as each individual.

My own experience with creativity proved enlightening as I looked back at my life's journey and a high school English experience. At fifteen I enjoyed writing, and an English teacher gave a class assignment to choose from three subjects and incorporate original ideas into an essay. Choosing the topic of death, I proceeded to express my evolving outlook on the subject and how I could work with it. I was delighted with the results and glad to see a concrete formulation of my own thoughts on the subject. I was sure the teacher would appreciate it too.

When papers were returned and I looked at mine, I was astonished to see an F and the words, "I do not agree with your philosophy." (I later found out the teacher's grandfather had just died). Perhaps my teenage mind hadn't explained it as clearly as I thought I could, and I proceeded to counsel, teach, and write throughout my adult years in an effort to refine my thoughts and articulate my perspective on the subject of death and dying.

SPIRITUALITY

Children's individual and meaningful belief systems can create a strong framework to positively cope with life issues. Ellen's mom died in a car crash and Ellen was devastated. She missed her all the time. Her mom loved butterflies and so did Ellen. Every time a butterfly went by, Ellen thought it was her mom sending her a message. Dad respected this belief system and made her a butterfly necklace to wear to feel close to mom. She felt comforted by the symbolism of mom's presence.

Teenage Thomas was angry at God. He entered his grief therapy session one day and asked, "Why did God have to kill my mom in that plane crash?" I couldn't answer the question but we could begin to discuss Max's anger toward God, his strong feelings about his mom's sudden death, and his spiritual belief system.

Adults can respect children's spiritual belief systems. Some children may feel comforted by thinking about their feelings about God, and may choose to express these feelings. They can light a candle or say a prayer. Second-grader Shainna, age eight, created her very own prayer as reassurance during public tragedy. She was attending school in New York a few blocks from the Twin Towers when terrorists attacked: "Lord, Father thank you for giving us strength to go on after such a tragedy. Bless everyone. Amen."

Six-year-old Christina drew a picture about her spiritual perspective after 9/11. Although the towers are burning and people are sad, she seems comforted in feeling that angels are watching and God knows everything is OK.

once a reat a pon a time angels wr watching god knew That everuthing was fine

Shannon, age ten, drew a picture of the planes crashing into the Twin Towers, a disaster that occurred a few blocks from the school she was attending at the time. Shannon explained her comfort in believing that God would take care of the United States and drew a picture of the terrorist attack with the words "God Bless" and "Peace" —a reassurance to her that life would be ok again. Shannon's classmate, Tisa, added this prayer: "Why Lord why, did this happen to my world? But thank God, the terrorists cannot destroy our souls."

Six-year-old Julian explained how people could feel safe after 9/11 by going to a temple or church. "It feels good to be with God when you are scared. I feel safe when I'm inside my temple." He shares that in the drawings.

Tran, an Asian American teen, did not relate to religious thinking. When asked about God she would say, "I don't believe or disbelieve; I just don't think about it." But Tran had a deep respect for life: plants, animals, and people. She valued kindness and felt sadness for everybody hurt during the terrorist attack. She helped collect money for victims and families and helped her class make a giant "thank you" card for the police and firemen in New York. Her caring for others was her spiritual outlook during a tragic time.

SERVICE

Giving to others allows resilient children to feel a part of a larger family and community and give and receive love and support while helping to make a situation better. Madeline was a nine-year-old child who had lived with her grandmother's illness for quite some time. When asked what worried her the most, she said it was when someone is sick, and began drawing a picture of her grandmother in bed with a thermometer in her mouth.

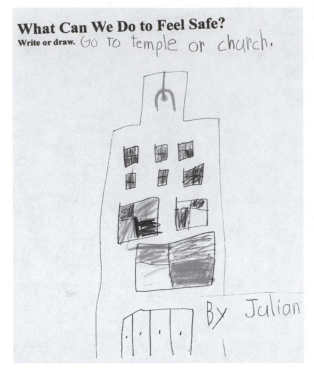

I asked her if there was any way she helped her grandmother with her illness. She began to smile, realizing she was playing an active role in her care that actually made her feel good and was meaningful to her grandmother. She seemed almost surprised to realize how much care she gave her grandmother. Watching TV with her, making her a card, and bringing her a drink are a few of the many loving activities Madeline drew.

She explained after a visit to Grandma, that she "made her happy that day and that made me happy." When Grandma thanked her for her kindness, some of her worry "seemed to disappear" and she felt appreciated and loved and important for giving to another person.

Making a Difference:
Mara's Story

Mara was thirteen when her older brother, Chris, died of suicide. He suffered from depression and anxiety attacks throughout his life. Mara is the youngest of eight children and was determined to raise awareness and money for suicide prevention. Her brother's tragic death influenced her future goals to speak out about suicide and depression in this country. Mara has spoken many times about Chris and written much on the subject of suicide. She volunteered as in assistant in a children's grief camp and has joined the speaker's bureau for SAVE, Suicide Awareness Voices of Education. Mara speaks in schools, churches, and civic groups and feels these activities help her stay connected to her feelings and her brother, even though she still has days with tears and questions of "why."

OPTIMISM

Through her speeches and writings Mara hopes others will become more knowledgeable about depression and suicide. She also enriches her own school health curriculum on these subjects. Her perseverance, optimism, and service to others have exemplified her inner goal that "one person can make a difference."

PERSEVERANCE

Mara's perseverance was apparent in her determination to participate in a walk to raise money for suicide awareness. "They weren't going to let me go on the walk because I'm under eighteen, so I wrote them a letter, and got the participation age changed to thirteen," explained Mara. This important achievement not only raised awareness for teens to become a part of this community action, but also allowed Mara to raise more than $2,000 dollars for the cause. She hopes to keep on working to create new ways to help others, and feels there is so much more she can do.

One idea is to create an organization in her school to help kids deals with depression and let them know that "there is always help, even if you don't see it."

PARENT MODELING

Mara's family was devastated when the shocking news came of Chris's suicide. They chose to share the facts about Chris's death instead of trying to hide it. Chris had openly discussed his depression with his family; although he was a happy person at times, he sometimes felt followed by a dark cloud that was so much a part of his disease.

Mara's family provided the honesty, love, and positive attitude to allow their daughter to go out into the world as an advocate for suicide prevention and a loving presence for their son Chris. Her mother's words of pride for her serve as a model for all of her children of what they can do with conviction and goals. "I'm proud of Mara. She is a great example of showing people you don't have to be ashamed and that this can happen to anyone."

Chris's mom and dad wrote a message to Chris in his memorial booklet that caringly stated their deep feelings of love and understanding for all to know on that day of remembrance.

Chrissie Boy,
We will celebrate your newfound peace,
We will try to understand your pain.
And we will always love and forgive you.
Mom and Dad

INSIGHTFULNESS

Mara wrote many poems, essays, and journals that reflected her deepest feelings during the long periods of grieving for her brother Chris. She shares her reflections willingly with others in the following poem to her brother, giving the gift of her insight and thoughtfulness during these times.

Thoughts and Memories
Sitting here in my room,
Thinking about the past.
Knowing your life ended so soon,
And knowing mine will last.

Trying to remember the sound of your voice,
Feeling the pain of knowing I can't
Thinking about your last choice.
And my wishes no one can grant.
Remembering the good times we had together.
And trying to forget all the bad.
Remembering feeling under the weather
And trying not to feel so sad.

Thinking about your beautiful smile,
And how you were always with a grin.
Knowing I won't see you for a while,
'Cause my life has yet to begin.
I never got the chance to say goodbye,
But I always told you that I cared.
Now I'm left with the question 'Why?'
And realizing life's not fair.
But I'll be all right,
I'll be okay.
I can be really strong,
But, just not today.

Please don't worry about me,
I told you I'd be fine.
My whole life is ahead of me,
It's all in a matter of time.

(Copyright ©2003 Mara Katherine Mattis)

This picture of Mara and Chris is the only one of them together and it is very precious to the family. Mara is only three months old in this photo and she is lovingly held by her big brother.

EMPATHY

"I hope the suicide rates go down or get people to get help. I don't want people to go through what I went through," Mara stated. At thirteen years of age she and her family participated in a 26-mile walk to raise money and awareness for suicide prevention, Out of the Darkness, she explains, is an event about "addressing the issue of suicide head on with determination, dignity and hope. It's a statement that it is not ok that someone dies of suicide every 17 minutes in this country. It's about using the rising sun as a powerful metaphor to shed light on an issue that had been dark for too long."

SOCIABILITY

Mara invited others to join her in raising money and awareness, with a pledge to "walk not only for the memory of Chris, but in memory of all whose inner pain has stolen them from us." She invited others to "share their names with me and I will carry their names on my t-shirt for you." This promised pledge to others evolved from her participation in the marathon and her willingness to walk not only for her brother Chris but for all those who suffered a similar death of a family member but couldn't actively participate.

COMMUNITY SUPPORT

Mara and her family joined 2300 others to walk in memory of Chris and speak of suicide. Joining together with so many others in the community gave them an inner sense of power and comradeship that soothed and stimulated them to share their stories and their passion for helping others create change.

Mara wrote a thank you to all who helped by participating or donating money toward her journey of healing. She told of the love in her heart as she walked and talked, laughed and cried with so many others until they reached their goal of the Washington monument as the sun was rising. "It was incredible . . . the exhilaration and the pain." She chose to share the following words spoken at the closing ceremonies of the walk in the shadow of the monument that so inspired her and the community of marchers for suicide awareness.

In a world blinded by the pursuit of pleasure, I am here to say that people are in pain. In a world rushing to get ahead, I am here to say that people are being left behind. In a world obsessed with the value of the market, I am here to speak for the value of life . . . and I am alive. This will be no quiet fight, for I am the voice of audacity in the face of apathy. I am the spirit of bravery in a world of caution. I am a commitment to action in the face of neutrality. I am alive. (Out of the Darkness Walk, closing ceremonies, 2002)

Methods of Promoting Resilience

- Increasing children's self-esteem
- Changing the harmful series of life events
- Providing alternate directions for success
- Remove the stressor
- Maintaining nurturing relationships
- Creating positive peer and adult interactions
- Sustaining a feeling of connectedness

Models Promoting Resilience

The key element in parental mentoring is to grasp the concept that being a mentor is not something you do to a child; it is something you do with a child. The goal is to encourage our sons and daughters to develop strengths and achieve self-confidence that is lifelong. By enjoying their uniqueness, honoring their timing for learning, respecting their thoughts and feelings, allowing opportunities for creativity and self-appreciation, and offering encouragement and support for who they are, their capacity to solve problems and live through life's challenges will amplify.

MODEL EMPATHY

Dr. Daniel Goleman defines empathy as one of the cornerstones of emotional intelligence. It is that ability to put ourselves in another's place and see their situation through their eyes. Developing empathy lays the foundation for productive interpersonal relationship skills so important in nurturing the resilient mindset. Listening closely, validating thoughts and feelings, and avoiding judgments are essential. Mary couldn't understand her biology homework. "Read it again," was her mom's response. Mom could have said, "Sometimes biology homework can be hard, and lots of kids have trouble at times. Let's figure out what we can do to help."

OFFER APPRECIATION AND ENCOURAGEMENT

Children need times at home and at school when they are given special recognition for a job well done, or motivational support for a new idea or creative endeavor. Providing them with time alone before bed or in the car creates a perfect time for listening and positive feedback. Dinnertime talks and hanging out on weekends provides "spontaneous precious moments" of recognition that reinforce self-worth. Eight-year-old Angie was in her room drawing when her dad stopped into to say hi after dinner. "What a beautiful picture," he exclaimed. "Your talent in art always amazes me." Angie smiled and went back to drawing, full of happiness from her father's recognition of her abilities.

BECOME AN ADVOCATE

Becoming advocates for our children is twofold: it allows us to be present in a situation where they may need adult help, and it creates a model for them to emulate and incorporate into their learning. Julie's son Fred had been complaining for two years of continually being bullied at his school, and he was increasingly feeling that the adults at his school were incapable of helping. Eleven-year-old Fred believed aggressive students at his school were targeting him and that it had snowballed. He believed the targeting was exacerbated because Fred needed to carry an electric writer in school to compensate for his learning disability. He also believed he was further targeted because he expressed a large and varied vocabulary, was an avid reader, and was in many accelerated classes.

During the past two years Fred had reported physical abuse. He said, "Every day somebody hits me." Fred explained to his mom that students came up behind him in the halls and hit him on the back and neck. He said the barrage of comments directed at him and meant to be insults included assertions that he was stupid, gay, or ugly. Although staff had from time to time intervened, Fred felt that the retaliation it caused afterward made his ability to feel comfortable and safe at school impossible.

A recent incident resulting in the suspension of the perpetrator (who had been suspended four times previously) resulted in further harassment by students sympathetic to the perpetrator: harassing phone calls, insults, surreptitious assaults in the hallway. Fred had been able to maintain an adequate level of school performance while enduring such bullying in the past, but he no longer felt that he could continue.

Julie felt sad and angry at her son's plight and decided to take steps to help him. She felt Fred had exhausted all possible solutions without adult intervention. He couldn't sleep, couldn't concentrate, and didn't want to go to school. She began a series of interventions.

1. Called the teacher, counselor, and principal
2. Requested a conference to discuss the problem
3. Wrote letters to proper channels to have Fred's school changed
4. Accomplished Fred's transfer of schools for Fred

Julie had received many calls and she participated in conferences over the past years. She too realized that the bullying problem was not changing in this school environment. She explained to Fred, "If someone was harassing an adult, stalking them, stealing from them, or physically or verbally abusing them, the adult would call the police for help. It is against the law." She felt it was impossible for Fred to remain in this environment and that it was time for action. She proceeded to write letters and initiate contacts to complete a transfer. Fred's new school was very freeing for him. He made new friends and was respected for his intelligence. He felt a sense of accomplishment and gratitude for his mother's advocacy, realizing how important her strong stance was in creating change. He also felt he was not alone in his predicament.

ENHANCE FLEXIBILITY AND LEARNING FROM PAST EXPERIENCE

Help children brainstorm alternatives to a problem and realize that there may be more than one possible solution. Create discussion on mistakes and share times that mistakes have led to embarrassment or significant learning for future use. This is another way to emphasize that resilience and the development of optimism, choice, and inner discipline is a continually evolving process.

PROMOTE SELF-DISCIPLINE

The model of creating children with good self-esteem and the ability to make realistic choices can be enhanced by creating skills that allow children to verbalize problems and various decision-making choices. Allowing kids to be part of the decision-making process at home, in school, and in the community enhances self-esteem and builds confidence that empowers them to achieve self-responsibility. Thirteen-year-old Mike wanted to stay after school. His mom wanted him to let her know his plans. "What do you think is a reasonable time to call?" Mike responded, "5 o'clock," and stuck to the decision and time he created. Had his mother told him the time, the dynamic might have changed into a power struggle. Instead, Mike felt confident in adhering to the time that felt right for him.

SUPPORT OPPORTUNITIES TO BECOME RESPONSIBLE

Children need to feel they are making a meaningful contribution to home, school, community, country, and planet. Young people respond well to being part of a mentoring system, support group, or volunteer community program where they can share life experience and help others. Self-esteem grows as they realize they can actively participate as members of a larger group for the good of themselves and others.

Together we can fight SARS. Everyone has to take responsibility.

Li ChenXue, age eight, asked her mom why there were so many cases of SARS. She lived in China and went to school with many friends who knew people who had SARS. Even a boy in the sixth grade, Le Shen, and a math teacher, Miss Chen, were sick with SARS. Mom explained, "Before people knew about the disease they might sneeze on each other or forget to wash their hands. Now that it has spread so much, we all have to try and keep very clean so that no more germs spread. If everyone does that it can help stop the spread of the virus."

Li ChenXue responded, "I know what to do to make this bad virus go away." And she began to draw the following picture and wrote her answer in Chinese, which is translated below her drawing.

OFFER INSPIRING RESOURCES

Because of the disturbing images they see of people in danger, screaming, and sad, children need parallel experiences that provide uplifting imagery. Hogan and Graham (2001) suggest that young children can benefit from reading classic stories like *The Little Engine That Could* or "The Tortoise and the Hare" that present enduring messages about overcoming difficulties through patience and perseverance.

For middle-school children there are wonderful books about hope through endurance, such as *The Diary of Anne Frank*, which shares Anne Frank's positive attitude while hiding during her teen years during the rule of Nazi Germany. Reading about her life under the most difficult of experiences creates a model to look up to during challenging times. Older teens can learn from reading the philosophy of mentors presented in books such as Victor Frankl's *Man's Search for*

Meaning, which tells of Frankl's plight in a concentration camp, as real-life teachers of heroism and bravery moving children to follow in those footsteps.

CREATE GENERATIONAL FAMILY ROLE MODELS

A Grandfather's Inspiration

Family members can become mentors to children, especially grandparents who have acquired wisdom through time. At ninety, fifteen-year-old Jonathan's grandfather often shared his personal philosophy of life, one his grandson admired and hoped to emulate. His grandfather, Poppy Jerry, had recently experienced the death of his wife and been diagnosed with kidney disease, but still volunteered his time at a hospital. Pop wrote his thoughts in a letter to Jonathan. His cherished words inspired optimism as Jonathan reflected on his positive outlook. "I only hope I can have as great an attitude as Pop when I grow up. He is amazing! "

The following are Jerry's words of encouragement to his grandson and a picture that reflects his inspiring mental outlook at age ninety:

Dear Jonathan,

I have adopted two words since my teenage years — "Never Better," with a smile. It means to always keep in good physical health, especially when you are a senior citizen.

And you will always feel "Never Better." We all have injuries and tragedies during our lifetime. Be grateful for the parts of your body that are in good health.

After a tragedy, be thankful for the good years you had with your departed loved one, and you will feel "Never Better."

A family is the most precious gift on earth. They give you love, devotion, and compassion — a life of happiness that is "Never Better."

Use the words "Never Better" with a smile and a helpful lending ear that is your invitation to the human race.

Try it, it works!

Love,
Pop

Activities to Promote Resiliency

- Define resilience: Talk to children about strength, leadership, courage, and stamina. Define resilience as the ability to keep going during very hard times. Then ask them to make their own definition and explain why.

- Create a dialogue: Young children can read a resource such as *The Little Engine That Could* or *Courage* and then draw or write what that story means to them. Use a quote such as "Courage is the power of the mind to overcome fear," from Martin Luther King, and ask middle and high school students to respond as to what that means to them.

- George didn't like high school. He worked hard at not doing anything. It took three schools and six years to graduate college. He not only survived but began to thrive, finding work that he loved and a new sense of responsibility within himself.

- Tell me about a time in your life you felt you were resilient.

- How did people respond? What did they say?

- How did that make you feel?

- How does it feel now?

- Is there anything you wish others had done?

- Can you use what you learned from this experience now?

A Resiliency Questionnaire

1. What is your position in the family? Oldest? Youngest? Middle? Oldest girl? Oldest boy?
2. Do your have any memories or recollections about what your mother or father said about you as a young baby? Or anyone else?
3. Did anyone ever tell you about how well you ate and slept as a baby?
4. Do members of your family and friends usually seem happy to see you and to spend time with you?
5. Do you feel like you are a helpful person to others? Does anyone in your family expect you to be helpful?
6. Do you consider yourself a happy and hopeful (optimistic) person even when life becomes difficult?
7. Tell me about some times when you overcame problems or stresses in your life. How do you feel about them now?
8. Do you think of yourself as awake and alert most of the time? Do others see you that way also?
9. Do you like to try new life experiences?
10. Tell me about some plans and goals you have for yourself over the next year. Three years. Five years.
11. When you are in a stressful, pressure-filled situation, do you feel confident that you'll work it out, or do you feel depressed and hopeless?
12. What was the age of your mother when you were born? Your father?
13. How many children are in your family? How many years are there between children in your family?
14. What do you remember, if anything, about how you were cared for when you were little by mom and others?
15. When you were growing up, were there rules and expectations in your home? What were some of them?
16. Did any of your brothers or sisters help raise you? What do you remember about this?
17. When you felt upset or in trouble, to whom in your family did you turn for help? Whom outside your family?
18. From whom did you learn about the values and beliefs of your family?
19. Do you feel it is your responsibility to help others? Help your community?
20. Do you feel that you understand yourself?
21. Do you like yourself? Today? Yesterday? Last year?
22. What skills do you rely on to cope when you are under stress?
23. Tell me about a time when you were helpful to others.
24. Do you see yourself as a confident person? Even when stressed?
25. What are your feelings about this interview with me?

Source: Reprinted from C. F. Rak & L. E. Patterson (1996). Promoting resilience in at-risk children. *Journal of Counseling and Development, 74*(4), 368-373. © ACA. Reprinted with permission. No further reproduction authorized without written permission of the American Counseling Association.

- Resiliency questionnaire: The following resiliency questionnaire (Rak & Patterson, 1996) works well with middle and high school students. It serves as a tool to identify and dialogue about their levels of resilience.

- Support resiliency in school. The school environment can be an important support system for helping children cope with tragedy. Research indicates that the school is a resource for promoting resiliency after 9/11 by allowing teachers to provide information abut the attacks, reassure students that they were safe, interpret the events as they were unfolding, and normalize the school routine as much as possible. (Noppe, et al. 2004).

- Survive/thrive chart: Ask girls and boys to think of a time that was hard for them in their life. Make a chart with "Survive" as one title and "Thrive" as the other. Have children list what things they did to survive or make it through and what things they did to grow and learn that brought new meaning to their life.

- Join in social action and volunteerism. This promotes support for children and teens to become "agents of change." Organizations such as "Kids Can Free the Children" encourage more than 100,000 members to become "peace builders" and activists on a postcard level by raising funds and shipping supplies to children around the globe (Burrell 2004, 23).

- Share a role model: Young children through teens can choose a family member or famous celebrity who represents a special quality of resilience to them. They can share a picture with others and explain what that quality is. We can then help them identify that quality in themselves by asking them, "Tell me about a time when you displayed that quality in your life."

- Resiliency inventory: Present a resiliency inventory for preschool and elementary children. Have them identify a difficult time in their life when they used strength and courage to make it through. Explain that as resilience. Help them identify these attributes and relate them to present and future uses.

- Community resources and guest speakers: Invite guest speakers to share ways that they used the qualities associated with resilience and overcame challenges throughout their lives. Help children to identify those qualities. Examples can range from the school principal to a TV anchor or home team sports celebrity.

- "My Hero" contest: Teachers can have a "my hero" contest in the school. Children become the person they emulate, dressing like them, using their mannerisms to present a dialogue representative of their hero to other students. The class votes on the winner. Barry pretended to be a favorite teacher, Mr. Pollard, generally respected for his fairness and good sense of humor. Barry told a funny story he had heard from Mr. Pollard. The class enjoyed a long and hard laugh, and Barry won the prize for his presentation.

- Resiliency awards: Children can list all of the attributes they understand as resilient. The students choose a classmate they feel exemplifies this quality. That classmate is given the award for that attribute. Every child receives an award for some positive attribute, even if it is for the attribute of "patience" for the last child.

Signs of a Resilient Child

- The ability to bounce back
- The capacity to have courage
- The motivation to move forward
- The power to stay centered
- The awareness of knowing themselves
- The gift of laughter
- The potential of showing promise
- The capacity to ask for help
- The tenacity to accomplish goals
- The willingness to share feelings
- The capability to connect with others
- The inspiration to give back

Children throughout the planet are learning universal lessons in resilience from their survival of public tragedy. From SARS to terrorism, war, and violence, children manage not only to survive but also to thrive. Mentors and role models in daily life can inspire them to get through difficult times and achieve goals. When the chaos and confusion around them is transformed into planned action, children can then become a part of a global community of citizens working toward the betterment of themselves and others, remembering that all of us need to take responsibility for the complex world we live in.

Conclusion

Never doubt that a small group of thoughtful, committed citizens can change the world. Indeed, it's the only thing that ever has.

Margaret Mead

The new frontier our children face is not one of rules and regulations their parents and grandparents lived with or understood. Living under the new fear of personal attacks and vulnerability in our country creates both fear and hope for what might be. Our role is to protect and prepare our children to be able to accept present circumstances, to adapt in an ever-changing world, to nurture our kids to thrive and grow to their greatest potential, and to help them create a future vision of global unity.

We ask ourselves what we can do for the children. The response might well be to allow them to grieve their losses, help them to reduce their fears, instill in them a sense of safety and protection, and empower them to imagine a future of peaceful coexistence for all human beings.

From the trauma of bullying to the threat of terrorism, random violence, and war, many of our children watch or experience apprehension daily. They fear assaults from foreign strangers, threats from unknown figures, and harassment from well-known classmates, siblings, and adult figures. If we can help our young people to see the relationship between terrorist attacks, violence, bullying behaviors, and issues of power and control at any cost to another human being, we can begin rooting out evil behaviors not only through military means, financial holdings, and global cooperation and unity, but through the very roots of behaviors that create oppression, prejudice, misguided rage, and destruction of people and property as a justification for a cause or self-serving purpose. We can help children understanding mediation and conflict resolution techniques that respect each other's differences and empower them without harm.

Responsible adults need to help girls and boys cope with these life issues. By providing information, understanding, and skills, we can aid them in becoming more compassionate, caring human beings and thereby increase their chances of living in a future world of inner and outer peace.

By building on experiences of successful survivorship through trauma, we can promote a sense of optimistic confidence. We can help establish the belief that the future difficulties will be flexibly and creatively overcome.

To do what is needed after the crisis interventions are over, we must develop increasingly comprehensive training in schools and universities to prepare to work with children in the context of a new paradigm of trauma and stress. Using skills of resilience, our goal is to transform our young people into mature, responsible citizens. Educators, parents, health professionals, and all caring adults must become advocates in generating understandings and procedures to work with our children who are facing a present and future so different from the past. Our task is to help our youth to stay connected to their hearts and consciousness during these complex times. By planting the seeds of empathy, compassion, and understanding, we facilitate the flourishing of our most prized possessions—our children.

We are now a community, a nation, and a world of children struggling and succeeding in living within a complex environment without definite answers or roadmaps for success. This knowledge helps us hold the ambiguity of many parallel ideas as we search for useful answers to the confusion and upheaval surrounding our children and ourselves. We can begin to transform our initial understandings into higher learning, greater humanity, and a wiser way of cohabitation on our planet.

We hope to raise our children to be centered in a solid core of safety and nurturance and still be able to float in a world of imagination and hope. Giving the children roots to stand firm and wings to fly high can be our greatest possible gifts.

We hope to create resilient children and teens who can meet the challenges of life in the twenty-first century. This resilience doesn't mean that young people will not experience anxiety and stress during difficult life situations. It does mean that although these events may be disturbing, ultimately they will feel they are surmountable. Building our children's capacities to positively endure, adapt, and overcome life adversities with optimism is our ultimate goal.

Resources

FOR CHILDREN ON RESILIENCY

Character Building by M. Heegaurd (2004) is a workbook for children that allows them to process character building tools through drawing and writing. Ages 5 to 10.

The Big Box by T. Morrison (1999) is a story about children put in a box by adults and their strong desire to gain personal freedom. Ages 5 to 10.

Oh, the Places You'll Go by Dr. Seuss (1990) uses his magical creativity to inspire young and old to succeed in life, despite the many ups and downs they face. Ages 5 to adult.

Heartsongs by M. Stepanek (2001) is a compilation of poems written by a young boy expressing hope and optimism for the future. Ages 6 and up.

PART IV

Resources and Information

Oases of Safety: National Resources That Help

ORGANIZATIONS • HOTLINES • INTERNET
RESOURCES • SUPPORT GROUPS • BOOK SERVICES

Organizations

FOR GRIEF AND TRAUMA

ASSOCIATION FOR DEATH EDUCATION AND COUNSELING (ADEC)

639 Prospect Ave.
Hartford, CT 06105
203-232-4285

BATON ROUGE CRISIS INTERVENTION CENTER

4837 Revere Avenue
Baton Rouge, LA 70808
504-924-1431

CHILDREN'S HOSPICE INTERNATIONAL

11011 King Street, Suite 131
Alexandria, VA 22314
800-2-4-CHILD

COMPASSIONATE FRIENDS, INC.

National Headquarters
PO Box 1347
Oak Brook, IL 60521
312-323-5010

GOOD GRIEF PROGRAM

Judge Baker Guidance Center
295 Longwood Avenue
Boston, MA 02115
617-232-8390

GRIEFWORK CENTER, INC.

PO Box 5014
Kendall Park, NJ 08824
732-422-0400

HOPE FOR THE GRIEVING HEART

PO Box 41064
Brecksville, Ohio 44141
330-476-3535

HOSPICE EDUCATION INSTITUTE

PO Box 713
Essex, CT 06426-0713
800-331-1620 Computerized "Hospice
    LInk"

HOSPICE FOUNDATION OF AMERICA

2001 S Street, NW #300
Washington, D.C. 20009
800-854-3402
www.hospicefoundation.org

INSTITUTE FOR THE ADVANCEMENT OF SERVICE

PO Box 19222
Alexandria, VA 22320
703-706-5333
Mental Health Information Center
800-969-NMHA
www.nmha.org

MINNESOTA COALITION FOR DEATH EDUCATION AND SUPPORT

PO Box 50651
Minneapolis, MN 55405
763-391-3051

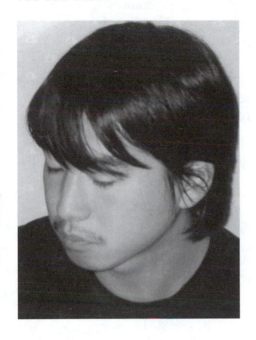

NATIONAL HOSPICE ORGANIZATION

1901 N Fort Myer Drive
Arlington, VA 22209
703-243-5900

NATIONAL MENTAL HEALTH ASSOCIATION

1021 Prince Street
Alexandria, VA. 22314-2791
703-684-7722

NEW ENGLAND CENTER FOR LOSS AND TRANSITION

PO Box 292
Guilford, CT 06437-0292
800-887-5677

TEEN AGE GRIEF, INC.

PO Box 220034
Newhall, CA 91322-0034
661-253-1932

WILLIAM WENDT CENTER

730 Eleventh Street, NW, 3rd Floor
Washington, D.C., 20001
202-624-0010

WORLD PASTORAL CARE CENTER

1504 N. Campbell St.
Valparaiso, IN 46385
219-531-2230
800-638-8078

FOR CHILDREN'S ISSUES

ADVOCATES FOR CHILDREN AND YOUTH, INC.

300 Cathedral Street, Suite 500
Baltimore, MD 21201
410-547-9200

AMERICAN ASSOCIATION FOR PROTECTING CHILDREN

c/o American Humane Society
63 Inverness Drive East
Englewood, CO 80112-5117
303-792-9900

ASSOCIATION FOR THE CARE OF CHILDREN'S HEALTH

7910 Woodmont Avenue
Bethesda, MD 20814
301-654-6549

CHILDREN'S DEFENSE FUND

25 E. Street NW
Washington, D.C. 20001-0500
202-628-8787

CHILD WELFARE LEAGUE OF AMERICA

440 First St. NW, Third Floor
Washington, D.C. 20001-2085
202-638-2952
www.cwla.org

DOCTORS WITHOUT BORDERS USA, INC.

6 East Street, 8th Floor
New York, NY 10016
doctor@newyork.msf.org

SAVE THE CHILDREN

2000 M. Street NW Suite 500
Washington, D.C. 200031
202-293-4170

UNICEF HOUSE

3 United Nations Plaza
New York, NY 10017
212-326-7000

FOR DISASTER

AMERICAN RED CROSS

1709 New York Avenue NW
Washington, D.C. 20006
(800) HELP-NOW
www.redcross.org

FEDERAL EMERGENCY MANAGEMENT AGENCY (FEMA)

P.O. Box 2012
Jessup, MD 20794-2012
www.fema.gov

FOR SCHOOLS

AMERICAN SCHOOL COUNSELOR ASSOCIATION

801 N. Fairfax St., Suite 310
Alexandria, VA 22314
800-306-4722
www.schoolcounselor.org

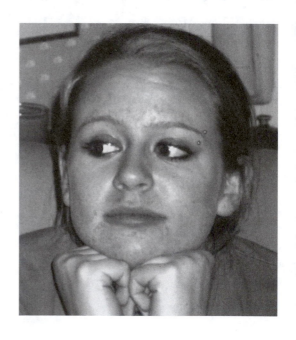

EDUCATORS FOR SOCIAL RESPONSIBILITY

23 Garden Street
Cambridge, MA 02138
617-492-1764
www.esrnational.org

INTERAGENCY ON CHILD ABUSE AND NEGLECT (ICAN)

4024 Durfee Ave.
El Monte, CA
www.ican–ncfr.org

NATIONAL ALLIANCE FOR SAFE SCHOOLS

PO Box 1068
College Park, MD
301-935-6063

NATIONAL EDUCATION ASSOCIATION

1201 16th St. NW
Washington, D.C. 20036
202-833-4000
www.nea.org

NATIONAL SCHOOL SAFETY CENTER

141 Duesenberg Drive, Suite 11
Westlake Village, CA 91362
805-373-9977
www.nssc1.org

SAFE ALTERNATIVES AND VIOLENCE EDUCATION (SAVE)

201 West Mission Street
San Jose, CA 95110
408-277-4133

ZERO TO THREE

2000 M Street NW, Suite 200
Washington, DC 20036
202-638-1144

FOR PARENTING

FEDERATION OF FAMILIES FOR CHILDREN'S MENTAL HEALTH

1021 Prince St.
Alexandria, VA 22314-2971
703-684-7710
www.ffcmh.org/enghime.htm

PARENT ENCOURAGEMENT CENTER (PEP)

10100 Connecticut Avenue
Kensington, MD 20895
301-929-8824

PARENTS ANONYMOUS

National Headquarters
22330 Hawthorne
Boulevard, Suite 208
Torrance, CA 90505
800-421-1325

FOR MENTORING

BIG BROTHERS BIG SISTERS OF AMERICA

230 N. 13th Street
Philadelphia, PA 19107-1538
215-567-7000
www.bbbsa.org

GANG RESISTANCE EDUCATION AND TRAINING (GREAT)

Bureau of Alcohol Tobacco and
   Firearms
P.O. Box 50418
Washington, D.C. 20091-0418
800-726-7070
www.atf.treas.gov/great/great/htm

MENTOR: THE NATIONAL MENTORING PARTNERSHIP

1400 I Street NW, Suite 850
Washington, D.C. 20005
202-729-4341
www.mentoring.org

FOR RESILIENCE

ADOLESCENT SOCIAL ACTION PROGRAM (ASAP)

Family Practice Building, Third Floor
2400 Tucker NE
Albuquerque, NM 87131-5241
888-738-2940

NATIONAL FAMILY RESILIENCY CENTER, INC. (NFRC)

2000 Century Plaza #121
Columbia, MD 21044
410-740-9553

RESILIENT YOUTH PROGRAM AND CURRICULUM

2122 South 850 East
Bountiful, UT 84010
888-667-7934

FOR THE MILITARY

TAPS TRAGEDY ASSISTANCE PROGRAM FOR SURVIVORS, INC

National Headquarters
2001 S. Street NW, Suite 300
Washington, D.C. 20009
800-959-TAPS (8277)

FOR TRAUMA AND VIOLENT DEATH

AMERICAN TRAUMA SOCIETY

1400 Mercantile Lane, Suite 188
Landover, MD 20785
800-556-7890

CHILDREN'S DEFENSE FUND

25 E. St. NW
Washington, D.C. 20001-0500
202-628-8787

CONCERNS OF POLICE SURVIVORS (COPS)

9423 A Marlborough Pike
Upper Marlborough, MD 20772
301-599-0445

CRIME VICTIMS LITIGATION PROJECT

c/o National Victim Center
4530 Ocean Front
Virginia Beach, VA 23451
804-422-2692

MOTHERS AGAINST DRUNK DRIVING

669 Airport Freeway, Suite 310
Hurst, TX 76053
800-633-6233

NOVA (NATIONAL ORGANIZATION FOR VICTIM ASSISTANCE)

717 D Street NW
Washington, D.C. 20004
202-393-NOVA

NATIONAL SHERIFF'S ASSOCIATION VICTIM PROGRAM

1450 Duke Street
Alexandria, VA 22314
703-836-7837
800-424-7827

NATIONAL VICTIM CENTER

307 W 7th Street, Suite 1001
Fort Worth, TX 76102
817-877-3355

NATIONAL VICTIM'S RESOURCE CENTER

PO Box 6000 AIQ
Rockville, MD 20850
800-627-NVRC

OFFICE FOR VICTIMS OF CRIME

633 Indiana Avenue NW
Washington, D.C. 20531
202-724-5947

VICTIMS OF CRIME RESOURCE CENTER

McGeorge School of Law
University of the Pacific
3200 Fifth Ave.
Sacramento, CA 95817
800-VIC-TIMS

FOR GANGS

INSTITUTE FOR THE PREVENTION OF YOUTH VIOLENCE

c/o Neighborhood House of North
  Richmond
305 Chesley Ave.
Richmond, CA 94801

GANG RESISTANCE EDUCATION AND TRAINING (GREAT)

Tucson Police Department
Tucson, AZ
520-791-4177

FOR SUICIDE

AMERICAN ASSOCIATION OF SUICIDOLOGY

4201 Connecticut Ave., Suite 310
Washington, D.C. 20008
202-237-2280

SPEAK (SUICIDE PREVENTION EDUCATION AWARENESS FOR KIDS)

423 Dumbarton Road
Baltimore, MD 21212
410-377-4004

SUICIDE AWARENESS/VOICE OF EDUCATION SA/VE

PO Box 24507
Minneapolis, MN 55424-0507
612-946-7998

SUICIDE EDUCATION AND INFORMATION CENTER

723 Fourteenth Street NW #102
Calgary, AB
Canada T2N 2A4
403-283-3031

THE JASON FOUNDATION

A Promise for Tomorrow
PO Box 616
Hendersonville, TN 37077
888-881-2323

THE YELLOW RIBBON PROGRAM

Light for Life Foundation of America
PO Box 644
Westminster CO 80030-0644
303-429-3530

YOUTH SUICIDE NATIONAL CENTER

120 Wall St, 22nd floor
New York, NY 10005
888-333-AFSP

Support Groups

CENTER FOR GRIEF AND LOSS FOR CHILDREN

1010 N. Central Rd.
Glendale, CA 91202
818-245-1151

CHILDREN'S BEREAVEMENT CENTER

7610 South Red Rd., Suite 307
South Miamai, FL 33143
305-668-4902

COVE: A SUPPORT PROGRAM FOR GRIEVING CHILDREN AND FAMILIES

New England Center for Loss and
  Transition
PO Box 292
Guilford, CT 06437
203-456-1734

D'ESOPO RESOURCE CENTER

280 Main Street
Wethersfield, CT 06109
860-563-5677

DOUGY CENTER

PO Box 97286
Portland, OR
503-775-5683

FERNSIDE, A CENTER FOR GRIEVING CHILDREN

2303 Indian Mound Avenue
Cincinnati, OH 45212
513-841-1012

KID'S PLACE

PO Box 258
Edmund, OK 73083
405-844-5437

KINDER-MOURN

1320 Harding Place
Charlotte, NC 28204
704-376-2580

OPERATION RUNAWAY

Potomac Ridge Behavioral Health
  Center
14901 Broschart Rd.
Rockville, MD 20850
800-204-8600

PEACOCK FOUNDATION

PO Box 36187
Los Angeles, CA 90036
818-763-1072

RAINBOWS

2100 Golf Road, Suite 370
Rolling Meadows, Illinois 60008-4231
847-952-1770
http://www.rainbows.org
info@rainbows.org

SAFE HARBOR

Abington Memorial Health Center
Willow Building Suite 225
2510 Maryland Rd.
Willow Grove, PA 19090
215-481-5983
safeharbor@amh.org

SOLACE TREE

Center for Grieving Children, Teens,
    and Families
PO Box 2944
Reno, NV 89505
775-324-7725

HOTLINES

CHILD ABUSE HOTLINE

1-800-4ACHILD
1-800-2ACHILD (TDD for Hearing
    Impaired)
Covenant House "9-line"
1-800-999-9999
(24 hours/7 days a week)

A GENERAL HOTLINE FOR TEENS WITH ANY KIND OF PROBLEM

Girls and Boys Town Hotline
1-800-448-3000
(24 hours/7 days a week)
Trained counselors help with a variety
    of problems

GRIEF RECOVERY HOTLINE

1-800-445-4808
Kid Save
1-800-543-7283
Maryland Youth Crisis Hotline
1-800-422-0009

NATIONAL CENTER FOR MISSING & EXPLOITED CHILDREN

1-800-843-5678

NATIONAL COALITION AGAINST DOMESTIC VIOLENCE

1-800-333-7233

NATIONAL DOMESTIC VIOLENCE HOTLINE

1-800-799-7233

NATIONAL RUNAWAY AND SUICIDE HOTLINE

1-800-621-4000

PARENT'S ANONYMOUS

1-800-421-0352

CRISIS LINES

1-800-SUICIDE

(24 hours/7 days a week

NATIONAL MENTAL HEALTH ASSOCIATION CRISIS LINE

1-800-969-NMHA
(24 hours/7 days a week)

Internet Resources

ON DEATH AND TRAUMA FOR CHILDREN AND TEENS

ADEC: The Association for Death and Dying
www.adec.org

Children's Defense Fund
www.childrensdefense.org

The Child Trauma Academy
www.childtruama.org/

Compassionate Friends
www.compassionatefriends.org

Crisis, Grief, and Healing
www.webhealing.com

Death Education Resource
www.death.ed.com

D'Esopo Pratt Resource Center
www.safeplacetogrieve.com

Dougy Center for Grieving Children
www.dougy.org

Funeral Directory
www.thefuneraldirectory.com

Helping Children Deal with Grief
www.erols.com/lgold

Kids' Place
www.kidsplace.org

Kinder-Mourn
www.kindermourn.com

National Institute on Drug Abuse
www.drugabuse.gov

Stuyesant High School Spectator
www.stuyspectator.org

ON EDUCATION

Early Warning, Timely Response: A Guide to Safe Schools
www.ed.gov/offices/OSERS/OSEP

The National Education Association
www.nea.org/01crisis.html

National PTA
www.pta.org

Raising Children to Resist Violence: What You Can Do
www.//helping.apa.org

Trends and Issues: School Safety and Violence Prevention
www.nauticom.net/
www/cokids/School_Violence_and_Safety
.html

Zero to Three
www.zerotothree.org/coping

ON BULLYING

www.bullybeware.com and
www.bullying.org

ON GANGS

National Alliance of Gang Investigators Association
http://www.nagia.org

Tookie's Corner
http: www.tookie.com/aboutte.html

ON RESILIENCE

Appalachian Peace and Justice Network
www.frognet.net/«simil»apjn/

Connect for Kids: Guidance for Grown-ups
www.connectforkids.org

Family Education Network
www.family education.com

PBS Online: America Responds
www.pbs.org/americaresponds

Raising Resilient Children Foundation
www.raisingresilientkids.com/

Toward Resiliency: At-Risk Students Who Make It to College
www.ed.gov/pubs/Resiliency/index.html

Where You Are Not Alone
www.bullying.org/

ON GRIEF

Barklay and Eve
www.BarklayandEve.com/
Julie's Place www.juliesplace.com/

TAG Teenage Grief
www.smartlink.net/~tag

Teens Helping Teens
www.bigteens.com/links/survivors.html

The Waterbug Story
www.hospicecares.org/

ON SERVICE

FreeVibe
www.freevibe.com

In The Mix
www.inthemix.org

Tolerance.org
www.tolerance.org

Youth Action Net
www.youthactionnet.org

Book Services

Centering Corporation, Omaha, NE. This comprehensive grief resource center offers publications, workshops, and membership programs on all aspects of loss and grief. 402-553-1200.

Compassion Book Service, Burnsville, NC. This service offers a wealth of resources and trainings tools that include books, videos, and cassettes dealing with loss, death, dying, and bereavement. 704-675-9687.

Mental Health Resources, Saugerties, NY. This is an excellent and complete grief resource offering many publications and other tools for children and families. 845-247-0116.

Renew Center for Personal Recovery. This center provides needed books, journals, and curriculum guides on developing grief skills for all ages. 859-986-7878.

Western Psychological Services (WPS), Los Angeles, CA. This service is for therapists and counselors providing practical therapeutic tools to use with children. 800-251-8336.

CHAPTER 12

Topics, Trends, and Timely Information: Annotated Bibliography

RESOURCES FOR ADULTS • CHILDREN'S BOOKS • MANUALS • CURRICULA • VIDEOS • CD-ROMS

Resources for Adults

ON TRAUMA

Doka, K. (1996). *Living With Grief after Sudden Loss.* Bristol, PA: Taylor & Francis. This book discusses topics such as treatment implications for traumatic death, social psychological aspects of disaster death, and grief counseling for traumatic loss.

Doka, K., & Licht, M. (2003). *Living With Grief: Coping With Public Tragedy.* New York: Brunner Routledge. This book takes a comprehensive look at the many ways children and adults lived through and coped with the terrorist attack of September 11, 2001.

Goldman, L. (2001). *Breaking the Silence: A Guide to Help Children With Complicated Grief/Suicide, Homicide, AIDS, Violence, and Abuse.* 2nd Ed. New York: Taylor & Francis. This guide presents a comprehensive look at complicated grief and children and ways to work with them.

Janoff-Bulman, R. (1992). *Shattered Assumptions: Towards a New Psychology of Trauma.* New York: Free Press. This book is an excellent review of research and insights into the treatment of trauma.

Jenkins, B. (1999). *What to Do When the Police Leave.* Richmond, VA: WPJ Press. This book is a guide to the first days of traumatic loss after a homicide.

Jones, R. (1995). *Where was God at 9:02 A. M.?* Nashville, TN: Thomas Nelson. This book presents miraculous stories of faith and love from the Oklahoma City bombing.

Kauffman, J. (ed.) (2002). *Loss of the Assumptive World: A Theory of Traumatic Loss.* New York: Brunner Routledge. This book presents a diversity of perspectives and interpretations of the concept of the loss of the assumptive world facing many people.

Middelton-Moz, J. (1989). *Children of Trauma.* Deerfield Beach, FL: Health Communications, Inc. This book helps the reader discover his/her discarded self by coming face-to-face with emotional fears that may be the result of traumatic childhoods.

Stevenson, R. (1994) *What Will We Do?* Amityville, NY: Baywood Publishing Co. A book that prepares a school community to cope with crisis.

Taichung County Government. (2000). *Trauma of the Century*. Taichung County, Taiwan. The story of the Taiwan earthquake told through pictures and words.

Zero to Three. (2003). *Little Listeners in an Uncertain World*. Washington, D.C.: Zero to Three. This is a booklet to help adults with coping strategies for children after 9/11.

Zinner, E., & Williams, M. B. (1999). *When a Community Weeps*. Bristol, PA: Taylor & Francis. This book presents case studies in group survivorship in trauma and loss.

ON DEATH AND DYING

Callanan, M., & Kelley, P. (1992). *Final Gifts*. New York: Bantam Books. This book creates a sound understanding of the special issues and needs of communication with the dying.

Corr, C., Nabe, C., & Corr, D. (2003). *Death and Dying: Life and Meaning*. 4th Ed. : Thomson, Wadsworth: Belmont, CA. This book offers a comprehensive discussion of issues and insights into death, dying, and bereavement.

DeSpelder, L., & A. Strickland. (2005) *The Last Dance: Encountering Death and Dying*. 7th Ed. (2005). Boston: McGraw Hill. This thorough text combines theory and research on death and dying with practical application.

Doka, K. J. (2000). *Living With Grief: Children, Adolescents and Loss*. Washington, D.C.: The Hospice Foundation of America. This book offers many perspectives and interventions for living with grieving children and adolescents.

Dougy Center (1999a). *Helping Teens Cope with Death*. Portland, OR: The Dougy Center. This is a useful guide to help caring adults understand and work with grieving teens.

Dougy Center.(1999b). *What About the Kids? Understanding Their Needs in Funeral Planning and Services*. Portland, OR: The Dougy Center. This practical guide explain funerals and memorial services to children.

Fitzgerald, H. (1994). *The Mourning Handbook*. New York: Simon and Schuster. This is a comprehensive and compassionate resource to help families cope with death and dying. It explores complicated grief, murder, and suicide.

Fox, S. (1988). *Good Grief: Helping Groups of Children When a Friend Dies*. Boston: New England Association for the Education of Young Children. This excellent source of information helps adults working with children who have had a friend die.

Gilbert, D. (1999). *Finding Your Way after Your Parent Dies.* Notre Dame, IN: Ave Maria Press. This book provides inspiration and hope for grieving adults who have had a parent die.

Golden, T. (1994). *Swallowed by a Snake.* Gaithersburg, MD: Golden Healing. Tom Golden has written a valuable resource on men and grief. He defines grief for men, describes gender differences in grieving, and offers ways men can work with their grief.

Goldman, L. (2000). *Life and Loss: A Guide to Help Grieving Children.* 2nd Ed. New York: Taylor & Francis. A book that clearly and simply explains children's loss and grief issues and ways that caring adults can help.

Goldman, L. (2001). *Breaking the Silence: A Guide to Help Children with Complicated Grief.* 2nd Ed. New York: Taylor & Francis. This is a comprehensive guide that practically works with the many issues involving children and complicated grief.

Grollman, E. (1967). *Explaining Death to Children.* Boston: Beacon Press. A book geared to adults who want to ease a child's first confrontation with the death of a loved one.

Heavilin, M. (1986). *Roses in December.* San Bernardino, CA: Here's Life Publishers. The author expresses a deep understanding of the grieving process, having experienced the death of three children.

Huntley, T. (1991). *Helping Children Grieve When Someone They Love Dies.* Minneapolis, MN: Augsburg Fortress. This is an easy-to-read resource for caring adults that honestly addresses children's grief.

Kubler-Ross, E. (1975). *On Death and Dying.* Englewood, NJ: Prentice-Hall. This is a pioneering book on the subject of death and dying, using real-life situations to create true understanding.

Kushner, H. (1981). *When Bad Things Happen to Good People.* New York: Avon Books. Rabbi Kushner shares his thoughts and feelings on why we suffer. The book was written following his son's illness and subsequent death.

Levine, S. (1987). *Healing Into Life and Death.* New York: Anchor Press. Stephen Levine explores ways to open our hearts to healing.

Livingston, G. (1995). *Only Spring: On Mourning the Death of My Son.* New York: HarperCollins. An inspiring story of a father's love for his 6-year-old son, Lucas, and his deeply moving journey through his child's illness and death.

Nadeau, J. *Families Making Sense of Death.* (1998). Thousand Oaks, CA: Sage. This is an excellent resource for clinicians and families to understand the complexities of grieving families.

Parkes, C. M. (1996). *Bereavement*. 3rd Ed. New York: Routledge. Studies of grief in adult life are presented and explained.

Quackenbush, J. & Graveline, D. (1985). *When Your Pet Dies*. New York: Pocket Books. A book to help pet owners understand their feelings when a pet dies.

Rando, T. (1993). *Treatment of Complicated Mourning*. Champagne, IL: Research Press. This is a thorough and informative book presenting groundbreaking understandings on issues relating to complicated mourning.

Roberts, J., & Johnson, J. (1994). *Thank You for Coming to Say Good-bye*. Omaha, NE: Centering Corporation. This is for parents, funeral directors, and other caring professionals to help suggest ways to involve children in funeral services.

Sanders, C. (1992). *How to Survive the Loss of a Child*. Rocklin, CA: Prima Publishing. This book helps explain the phases of grief for the bereaved parent and offers help in understanding the process of healing through grief.

Schuurman, D. (2003). *Never the Same: Coming to Terms With the Death of a Parent*. New York: St. Martin's Press. This is an insightful book for those who have experienced the death of a parent as a child.

Silverman, P. (2000). *Never Too Young to Know*. New York: Oxford University Press. A book combining important research and historical data to broaden the understandings involved with grieving children.

Smilansky, S. (1987). *On Death (Helping Children Understand and Cope)*. New York: Peter Lang. The author bases her studies on children and their grief process in Tel Aviv.

Smith, H. I. (1994). *On Grievng the Death of a Father*. Minneapolis, MN: Augsburg. This is a comforting resource that addresses the special issues involved when a father dies.

Wolfelt, A. (1983). *Helping Children Cope with Grief*. Muncie, IN: Accelerated Development Inc. This is an informative resource for caring adults working with bereaved children that include ideas for creating discussions.

ON SUICIDE

Bolton, I. (1983). *My Son . . . My Son . . .* Atlanta, GA: Bolton Press. Iris Bolton's personal story of her son's suicide is deeply moving and revealing.

Gardner, S. (1990). *Teenage Suicide*. Englewood Cliffs: NJ. Julian Messner Publisher. This book examines some of the reasons and causes of teenage suicide and offers practical solutions.

MacLean, G. (1990). *Suicide in Children and Adolescents*. Lewiston, NY: Hogrefe & Huber Publishers. This is a practical and hands-on guide that helps working with children and young people at risk of killing themselves.

McEvoy, M., & McEvoy, A. (1994). *Preventing Youth Suicide*. Holmes Beach, FL: Learning Publications. This is a powerful handbook for educators and human service professionals to help prevent youth suicide.

Rickgarn, R. (1994). *Perspectives on College Student Suicide*. Amityville, NY: Baywood. This book offers a valuable perspective on working with challenging circumstances involving student suicide ideation.

Rubel, B. (1999). *But I Didn't Say Goodbye*. Kendall Park, NJ: Griefwork Center. This is a book for parents and professionals to help child suicide survivors.

Sandefer, K. (1990). *Mom, I'm All Right*. Garretson, SD: Sanders Printing. This is a book for parents and caring professionals addressing teen suicide. It's a mother's own story about her child's suicide that includes advice and helpful warnings.

Stillion, J., McDowell, E. (1996). *Suicide across the Lifespan—Premature Exits*. 2nd Ed. Washington, DC: Taylor & Francis. This book is designed for graduate and undergraduate college students to help them examine developmental principles applying to suicide.

ON HOMICIDE AND VIOLENT DEATH

Douglas, G. (1995). *Dead Opposite*. New York, NY: Henry Holt. A compelling account of the murder of a well-loved Yale student and the 16-year-old gang member accused of the murder.

Hendriks, J., Black, D., & Kaplan, T. (1993). *When Father Kills Mother*. New York: Routledge. The authors combine their knowledge of bereavement and posttraumatic stress disorder to help children who have witnessed extreme violence.

Kagan, H. (1998). *Gili's Book*. New York: Teacher's College Press. This excellent book tells of a mother's grief after the sudden death of her daughter, Gili.

Lord, J. (1993). *No Time for Goodbyes*. Ventura, CA: Pathfinder Publishing. This book provides important suggestions for survivors grieving a loved one who has been killed.

Redmond, L. (1990). *Surviving When Someone You Love was Murdered*. Clearwater, FL: Psychological Consultation and Educational Services. This is a professional's guide to group therapy for families and friends of murder victims.

Shamos, T., & Patros, P. (1990). *I Want To Kill Myself.* Lexington, MA: Lexington Books. This book talks frankly about children who are seriously depressed, signs to watch for, and ways to help.

ON BULLYING

Brohl, K., & Corder (1999), C. I*t Couldn't Happen Here.*. Washington, D.C.: Child Welfare League of America. This book recognizes and discusses the needs of many of today's desperate children.

Fried, S., and Fried, P.. (1996) *Bullies and Victims*. New York: M. Evans. This book describes today's schoolyard as a battlefield with practical solutions to help children.

Goldman, L. *Breaking the Silence: A Guide to Help Children With Complicated Grief / Suicide, Homicide, AIDS, Violence and Abuse.* 2nd Ed. (2002). New York: Taylor & Francis. This book provides a chapter on bullying with practical ideas and resources useful for parents and professionals.

Hazler, R. (1996). *Breaking the Cycle of Violence.* Bristol, PA: Taylor & Francis. This book offers good interventions for bullying and victimization.

Ross, D. (1996). *Bullying and Teasing.* Alexandria, VA: ACA Publishers. A book on childhood bullying and teasing and what educators and parents can do.

ON AGGRESSION

Goldstein, A. (1999). *Low-Level Aggression.* Champagne, IL: Research Press. This book presents a study of low-level aggresion in kids as the first step toward violence.

Goldstein, A., Glick, B., & Gibbs. J. (1998). *Aggression Replacement Training*. Champagne, IL: Research Press. This book presents a comprehensive intervention for aggressive youth.

ON RESILIENCE

Benard, B. (1991) *Fostering Resiliency in Kids: Protective Factors in the Family, School and Community*. Portland, OR: Northwest Regional Education Laboratory.

Brazelton, T. B., & Greenspan, S. I. (2000). *The Irreducible Needs of Children: What Every Child Must Have to Grow, Learn, and Flourish*. Cambridge, MA: Perseus Publishing,

Brooks, R., & Goldstein, S. (2001). *Raising Resilient Children: Fostering Strength, Hope, and Optimism in Your Child*. New York: Contemporary Books.

Brooks, R., & Goldstein, S. (2003). *Nurturing Resilience in Our Children: Answers to the Most Important Parenting Questions*. Chicago: Contemporary Books.

Frankl, V. (1984). *Man's Search for Meaning*. Boston: Washington Square Press. This book expresses a beautifully written philosophy about hope and optimism under difficult times.

Katz, M. (1997). *On Playing a Poor Hand Well: Insights from the Lives of Those Who have Overcome Childhood Risks and Adversities*. Chicago: W.W. Norton.

Levine, M.D. (1998). *Educational Care: A System for Understanding and Helping Children with Learning Problems at Home and in School*. Cambridge, MA: Educators Publishing Service.

Maston, A. S., Best, K. M., & Garmezy, N. "Resilience and Development: Contributions from the Study of Children who Overcome Adversity." *Development and Psychopathology* 2(1991): 425–555.

Werner, E., & Smith, S. (1992). Overcoming the Odds: High-risk Children from Birth to Adulthood. Ithaca, NY: Cornell University Press.

ON EDUCATION

Galinsky, E., & David, J. (1988). *The Preschool Years*. New York: Ballantine Books. This book contains a wealth of knowledge for parents and educators on children ages 2–5 to help them mentor resilient children.

Ginsberg, H., & Opper, S. (1976). *Piaget's Theory of Intellectual Development*. Englewood Cliffs, NJ: Prentice-Hall. This is a thorough presentation of Piaget's theory of cognitive development in children.

Goldman, L. (2000). *Helping the Grieving Child in the School*. Bloomington, IN: Phi Delta Kappa. This is a practical book for educators to help the grieving child in the schools.

ON PARENTING

Burt, S., & Perlis, L. (1999). *Parents as Mentors*. Prima Publishing. Rockling, CA. This effective book on parents as mentors creates practical ideas for instilling resilience in our children through adult role modeling.

Faber, A., & Mazlish, E. (1990). *Your Guide to a Happier Family*. New York: Avon Books. The authors present practical interventions with personal accounts of ways to create a peaceful family environment.

Fred, F. (1996). *Good Friends Are Hard to Find: Help Your Child Find, Make and Keep Friends*. Los Angeles: Perspective Publishing. This is a step-by-step parents' guide to help children make friends and solve problems.

Kohl, S. (2004). *The Best Things Parentes Do*. Boston: Conari Press. This book presents heartfelt ideas and insights into the real world of parenting.

Pipher, M. (1994). *Reviving Ophelia: Saving the Selves of Adolescent Girls*. New York: Ballentine Books. This book presents the daily danger of being a young female in today's world and how adults can help.

ON COUNSELING AND THERAPY

Bradshaw, J. (1988). *The Family: A Revolutionary Way of Self Discovery*. Deerfield Beach, FL: Health Communications. This book presents a unique view of family systems.

Furth, G. (1988). *The Secret World of Drawings*. Boston: Sigo Press. This comprehensive look at children's artwork and ways of understanding it provides valuable insights into art therapy with children.

Gil, E. (1991). *The Healing Power of Play*. New York: Guilford. This book gives a history of play therapy and specific considerations for working with abused and neglected children.

Johnson, S. (1987). *After a Child Dies: Counseling Bereaved*. New York: Springer. A comprehensive text that offers information on counseling bereaved families when a child dies.

Mills, G., Reisler R., Robinson, A., & Vermilye, G. (1976). *Discussing Death*. Palm Springs, CA: ETC Publication. This guide for death education gives practical suggestions and resources for many age levels.

Moustakas, C. (1992). *Psychotherapy with Children*. Greeley, CO: Carron. This is a classic text in understanding the therapeutic environment. This book creates guidelines and practical techniques to use when working with psychotherapy and children.

Oaklander, Violet. (1969). *Windows to our Children: Gestalt Therapy for Children*. New York: Center for Gestalt Development. This book presents a gestalt therapy approach to children's loss and grief work with stories and practical suggestions for play therapy.

Rosenthal. H. (1998) *Favorite Counseling and Therapy Techniques*. Bristol, PA: Taylor & Francis. Fifty-one therapists share their most creative strategies.

Rosenthal, H. (2001). *Favorite Counseling and Therapy Homework Assignments*. Bristol, PA: Taylor & Francis. Leading therapists share their therapeutic homework assignments.

Webb, N. (1993). *Helping Bereaved Children*. New York: Guilford Press. This text contains theory, illustrative cases, and practical examples that professionals can use when working with bereaved children.

Worden, J. W. (1991). *Grief Counseling and Grief Therapy*. New York: Springer. This is a comprehensive handbook for grief counseling.

ON PHILOSOPHY

Coles, R. (1991). *The Spiritual Life of Children*. Boston: Houghton Mifflin. A book sharing thoughts, drawings, and dreams that reflect the inner world of children.

Frankl, V. (1984). *Man's Search for Meaning*. New York: Simon and Schuster. A powerful account of the author's imprisonment in Nazi Germany and the love that helped him survive his losses.

Gibran, K. (1969). *The Prophet*. New York: Alfred A. Knoph. This beautiful book of poetry expresses timeless feelings of life and death, pleasure and pain, and joy and sorrow.

Siegel, B. (1986). *Love, Medicine and Miracles*. New York: Harper and Row. This book emphasizes recognizing how our mind influences our body and how to use that knowledge for healing.

CD-ROMS

Goldman, L. *A Look At Children's Grief by Linda Goldman.* (2002). Newark, DE: ADEC & University of Delaware. This is a comprehensive two-part module with available CEUs on children's grief.

Stillion, J. (2003a). *Adolescent Suicide: Premature Exit.* ADEC & University of Delaware. This is a comprehensive two-part module with available CEUs on adolescent suicide.

Stillion, J. (2003b). *Psychological Issues in Children and Adolescents with Terminal Illness.* Newark, DE: ADEC & University of Delaware. This is a comprehensive two-part module with available CEUs on psychological issues with terminal illness in children and adolescents

CURRICULA ON BULLYING

Beane, A. (1999). *The Bully Free Classroom.* Minneapolis, MN: Free Spirit Publishing. This is a book that contains many strategies for teachers.

Bitney, J. (1996). *No-Bullying Curriculum.* Minneapolis, MN: Johnson Institute. This is a manual for preventing bully-victim violence in schools.

Carlsson-Paige, N., & Levin, D. (1998). *Before Push Comes to Shove.* St. Paul, MN: Redleaf Press. This conflict-resolution curriculum is a guide to help young children use nonviolent behavior.

Garrity, C., Jens, K., Porter, N., & Short-Camilli, C. (2000). *Bully-Proofing Your School* 2nd Ed. Longmont, CO: Sopris West. This is a comprehensive guide for school interventions against bullying.

No-Bullying Curriculum. (1998). Chattanooga, TN: Star. This curriculum gives classroom teachers tools to deal with bullying.

No Putdowns Character Building Violence Prevention Curriculum. (1998). Chattanooga, TN: Star. A school-based curriculum for violence prevention.

ON VIOLENCE

Constans, Gabriel. (1997). *Picking Up the Pieces*. Warminster, PA: Mar-co Products. This is a program about violent death with interventions useful in working with middle-school students. Ages 10–13.

McDaniel, C. (2000). *Children Surviving in a World of Violence*. This curriculum includes 35 lessons for students in grades 5–9 to cope with a violent world. Ages 10–14.

ON SUICIDE

Celotta, B. (1991). *Generic Crisis Intervention Procedures*. Gaithersburg, MD: Celotta. This is a practical manual for youth suicide crisis intervention in the schools.

Leenaars, A., & Wenckstern, S. (1990). *Suicide Prevention in Schools*. New York: Hemisphere Publishing. The authors attempt to outline the state of the art of suicide prevention in schools.

Smith, J. (1989). *Suicide Prevention*. Homes Beach, FL: Learning Publications. A crisis intervention curriculum that provides a school-based program for teenagers on suicide prevention.

ON THERAPEUTIC TECHNIQUES

Allen, J., & Klein, R. (1996). *Ready . . . Set . . . R.E.L.A.X.* Watertown, WI: Inner Coaching. This is a research-based program of relaxation, learning and self-esteem for children.

Brett, D. (1986). *Annie Stories*. New York: Workman Publishing. This is a series of stories that can be read to children under 10 who are dealing with many childhood issues, such as death and divorce. The author provides advice for caring adults on how to use these stories.

Davis, N. (1990). *Once Upon a Time*. Oxon Hill, MD: Psychological Associates of Oxon Hill. Once of the best manuals I've seen, which provides therapeutic stories for children with a guide for each story. It covers a wide range of topics, including all abuses and death.

ON DIVORCE

Garon, R., DeLeonardis, G., & Mandell, B. (1993). Guidelines for Child Focused Decision Making. Columbia, MD: The Children of Separation and Divorce. This is an exceptional manual for judges, attorneys, mediators, and mental health professionals concerning children and divorce.

ON DEATH AND CRISIS IN THE SCHOOLS

Cassini, K., & Rogers, J. (1990). *Death and the Classroom.* Cincinnati, OH: Griefwork of Cinncinnati. This manual confronts death in the classroom in practical ways.

Gliko-Braden, M. (1992). *Grief Comes to Class.* Omaha, NE: Centering Corporation. This guide is meant to help teachers and parents assist bereaved children.

Kirsh, A., Cobb, S., & Curley. S. (1991). *Plan of Action for Helping Schools Deal With Death and Dying.* Center Line, MI: The Kids in Crisis Program. This excellent protocol provides help for schools working with kids in crisis when there is death or dying.

Klicker, R. (2000). *A Student Dies, A School Mourns.* Buffalo, NY: Thanos Institute. This manual guides the school community in reducing the effects of personal loss and suffering when death occurs.

Lagorio, J. (1991). *Life Cycle Education Manual.* Solana Beach, CA.: Empowerment in Action. A teacher's guide to help with loss issues, including specific lesson plans and guided book activities.

Miller, K. (1996). *The Crisis Manual for Early Childhood Teachers.* Beltsville, MD: Gryphon House. This guide shares information and ideas on how to handle really difficult problems in the classroom.

O'Toole, D. (1989). *Growing Through Grief.* Burnsville, NC: Compassion Books. This is a comprehensive K–12 curriculum to help children through loss.

ON PEACE IN THE CLASSROOM

Klein, N. (2001). *Healing Images for Children.* Watertown, WI: Inner Coaching. The activities in this book help children cope with stress and create positive outcomes.

Smith, C. (1993). *The Peaceful Classroom*. Beltsville, MD: Gryphon House. This book provides activities to teach preschoolers compassion and cooperation.

ON ANGER AND STRESS MANAGEMENT

Toner, P. Stress. (1993). *Management and Self-Esteem Activities*. West Nyack, NY: The Center for Applied Research in Education. This is a health curriculum sharing activities to help children feel better under stress.

Whitehouse, E., & Pudney, W. (1996). *A Volcano in My Tummy*. Gabriola Island, Canada: New Society Publishers. A curriculum for children in conflict that provides anger management plans.

ON RESILIENCE

Capacchione, L. (1989). *The Creative Journal for Children*. Boston: Shambhala. This is a creative journal that provides ways for caring adults to help children express their thoughts and feelings.

Goldstein, S., & Brooks R. (2003). *Raising Resilient Children*. Baltimore, MD: Paul H. Brookes. This is a curriculum to foster strength, hope, and optimism in children.

Guides for Grief Support Groups

Beckman, R. (2000). *Children Who Grieve*. Holmes Beach, FL: Learning Publications. This resource manual gives quidance for conducting support groups for grieving children.

Burrell, R., Coe, B., & Hamm, G. (1994). *Fernside: A Center for Grieving Children*. Cincinnati, OH: Fernside Publishers. This guidebook offers information for working with grief support group for facilitators.

Cunningham, L. (1990). *Teen Age Grief (TAG)*. Panarama City, CA. This excellent training manual is for initiating grief support groups for teens.

Haasl, B., & Marnocha, J. (2000). *Bereavement Support Group Program for Children*. 2nd Ed. This is an excellent children's workbook and leader's manual for children's grief support groups.

Harris, L., & Harris, E.S. (1999). *Death of the Forest Queen*. Wilmore, KY: Words on the Wind. This is a useful grief drama script for groups, camps, and counseling.

Perschy, M. (1997). *Helping Teens Work Through Grief*. Bristol, PA: Taylor & Francis. This guide contains ways to create a grief support group for teens and provides activities to use.

VIDEOS

For Adults

Braza, K. (1994). *To Touch a Grieving Heart*. Salt Lake City, UT: Panacom Video Publishing. This film has very sensitive and practical insights into helping families with grief.

Dougy Center. (1992). *Dougy's Place: A 20–20 Video*. Portland, OR: The Dougy Center. This is a candid look at the kids participating in the Dougy Center's Program.

Ebeling, C., & Ebeling, D. (1991). *When Grief Comes to School*. Bloomington, IN: Blooming Educational Enterprises. This is a film and manual showing families and school personnel discussing grief issues.

Kussman, L. (1992). *What Do I Tell My Children?* Wellesley: MA: Aquarian Productions. A film narrated by Joanne Woodward showing experts, adults, and children exploring their thoughts and feelings regarding death.

Research Press. (1989). *A Family In Grief: The Ameche Story*. Champagne, IL: A real family story of bereavement, with guide included.

Roberts, D. (2003). *You Can Do It*. Orange Villiage, Ohio: TEE Productions Foundation. This is an excellent video giving warning signs and preventative interventions for teenagers and the adults that work with them.

Wolfelt, A. (1991). *A Child's View of Grief*. Fort Collins, CO: Center for Loss and Life Transition. This is a 20-minute video with children and parents sharing stories and emotions.

For Children

Brown, M. W. (1979). *The Dead Bird.* New York: Dell. This video presents the story of four children who find a dead bird, bury it, and hold a funeral service. There is an accompanying book.

Brown, T. (1993). *Broken Toy: A Thomas Brown Film.* Zanesville, OH: Summerhills Production. This is a film for students that deals seriously with the danger of bullying for victims and bullies.

O'Toole, D. (1994). *Aarvy Aardvark Finds Hope.* Burnsville, NC: Compassion Books. The incredible journey of Aarvy Aardvark and the grief he experiences is presented through puppets and music for young children to relate to and learn from.

Rogers, F. (1993). *Mr. Rogers Talks about Living and Dying.* Pittsburgh, PA: Family Communications, Inc. This is a warm and comforting video that presents answers to questions about living and dying.

For Teens

Tee Productions. *Inside I ACHE: A Guide for Professionals Working with Teens Regarding Suicide. (2003)* Orange Village, OH: Tee Productions. This excellent video offers insights for professionals and students in dealing with suicide.

In the Mix, PBS Series. New York: Castleworks. (2001) This series includes 9/11: Looking Back . . . Moving Forward. These films made by teens for teens express meaningful information on adolescent responses to the terrorist attacks on the World Trade Center and the Pentagon.

TAPES

Cunningham, L. (1993). *Teen Age Grief.* Newhall, CA: Teen Age Grief. Teenagers give personal interviews about their grief and loss experiences. For teens.

Hoffman, J. (1985). *Children's Meditation Tape.* Shawnee Mission, KS: Rythmic Mission. This tape presents relaxation game and guided imagery to promote meditation and relaxation for children. Ages 2–11.

Resources for Children and Teens

ON DEATH FOR CHILDREN

Boritzer, E. (2000). *What is Death?* Santa Monica, CA: Veronica Lane Books. This book introduces concepts about death through presenting information on different cultures and religions. Ages 7–13.

Brown, L., & Brown M. (1996). *When Dinosaurs Die.* New York: Little, Brown & Co. This is a wonderful and practical guide for helping children to understand and deal with real concerns and feelings about death. Ages 5–11.

Brown, M. W. (1979). *The Dead Bird.* New York: Dell. A story of four children who find a dead bird, bury it, and hold a funeral service. Ages 4–8.

Campbell, J. A. (1992). *The Secret Places.* Omaha, NE: Centering Corporation. The story of Ryan and his journey through grief is for children and adults to gain an in-depth look at childhood grief. Ages 6–12.

Dodge, N. (1984). *Thumpy's Story: The Story of Grief and Loss Shared by Thumpy the Bunny.* Springfield, IL: Prairie Lark Press. This story of the death of Thumpy's sister, who was not strong enough to keep living, is a wonderful resource for children. Ages 5–12.

Ferguson, D. (1992). *A Bunch of Balloons.* Omaha, NE: Centering Corporation. A resource to help grieving children understand loss and remember what they have left after someone dies. Ages 5–8.

Harris, R. (2001). *Goodbye Mousie.* New York: Margaret K. McElderry Books. This is a wonderful book that shares the sadness of a little boy after the death of his pet mouse and the important ways the family comes together to grieve and commemorate. Ages 4–7.

McLaughlin, K. (2001). *The Memory Box.* Omaha, NE: The Centering Corporation. This is a delightful story about a grandson's transformation of his grandfather's fishing box into a memory box. Ages 5–9.

Oehler, J. (1978). *The Frog Family's Baby Dies*. Durham, NC: Duke University Medical Center. This coloring story book creates a space for very young children to discuss sibling loss. Ages 3–6.

O'Toole, D. (1988). *Aardy Ardvark Finds Hope*. (Adult manual available) Burnsville: NC: Compassion Books. This story of animals presents the pain, sadness, and eventual hope after death. Ages 5–8.

Scravani, M. *Love, Mark*. Syracuse, NY: Hope for Bereaved. This contains letters written by grieving children to help them express feelings. Ages 7–12.

Stein, S. (1974). *About Dying*. New York, NY: Walker and Company. This simple text and photographs helps young children understand death. It includes a discussion about children's feelings for adults. Ages 3–6.

Varley, S. (1984). *Badger's Parting Gifts*. New York: Morrow and Company. Badger was a special friend to all the animals. After his death, each friend recalls a special memory of Badger. All ages.

White, E.B. (1952). *Charlotte's Web*. New York: Harper and Row. Through the eyes of the farm animals, life and death are sweetly portrayed. Ages 8–13.

ON DEATH FOR TEENS

Bode, J. (1993). *Death is Hard to Live With*. New York: Bantam Doubleday Dell. Teenagers talk frankly about how they cope with loss.

Dorfman, E. (1994). *The C-Word*. Portland, OR: New Sage Press. This author battled her own cancer at 16 and her mother's death due to breast cancer. She interviews five teenagers and their families sharing their cancer experience.

Fitzgerald, H. (2000). *The Grieving Teen*. New York: Fireside Books. This guide for teens helps them through their experience of grief.

Gootman, M. (1994). *When a Friend Dies*. Minneapolis, MN: Free Spirit Publishing Inc. This book was inspired by a mom who watched her teenage children suffer over the loss of a friend. It helps teens recognize and validate their feelings and provides good suggestions for healing.

Kolf, J. (1990). *Teenagers Talk About Grief*. Grand Rapids, MI: Baker Book House. This book was written especially for and about teenage grief with accounts of firsthand experiences.

ON TRAUMA

Berry, J. (1990). *About Traumatic Experiences*. Chicago, IL: Children's Press. This book answers kid's questions about trauma and traumatic experiences. Ages 8–11.

Holmes, M. (2000). *A Terrible Thing Happened*. Washington, DC: Magination Press. Sherman is anxious and angry after he experiences something terrible and learns to talk about it.

Jordan, M. K. (1993). *The Weather Kids*. Omaha, NE: Centering Corporation. This is a book for children who have experienced devastation caused by weather and earthquakes.

Mills, J. (1993). *Little Tree*. Washington, D.C.: Magination Press. This is a story for children with serious medical problems.

Salloum, A. (1998). *Reactions*. Omaha, NE: Centering Corporation. This workbook helps young people who are experiencing trauma and grief.

Sheppard, C. (1998). *Brave Bart*. Grosse Pointe Woods, MI: TLC. This is an excellent story for traumatized and grieving children.

ON A PARENT DYING

Levine, J. (1992). *Forever in My Heart*. Burnsville, NC: Compassion Books. A story to help children participate in life as a parent dies.

Jonah, S. (1999). *Transitions Along the Way*. Fairfield, CA: Visions. This is a guide to the dying process for children and young adults.

McNamara, J. (1994). *My Mom Is Dying*. Minneapolis, MN: Augsburg Fortress. This book is a diary by Kristine, a young girl who learns her mom is dying. It includes a discussion section for parents. Ages 5–9.

ON HOSPICE

Carney, K. (1999). *Everything changes, But Love Endures*. Wethersfield, CT: Dragonfly Publishing. This book gives excellent explanations of hospice for young children. Ages 3–7.

Flynn, J. (1996). *Hospice Hugs*. Louisville, KY: Accord Aftercare Services. This book speaks to young children about hospice. Ages 3–7.

ON THE DEATH OF A PARENT

Blume, J. (1981). *Tiger Eyes*. New York, NY: Macmillan Children's Group. Fifteen-year-old Davey works through the feelings of his father's murder in a store hold-up. Ages 11 and up.

Brisson, P. (1999). *Sky Memories*. New York: Delacorte Press. Emily is 10 years old when her mother is diagnosed with cancer and eleven when her mother dies. Ages 9–13.

Clifton, L. (1983). *Everett Anderson's Goodbye*. New York: Henry Holt & Company. Everett struggles with his sadness after his father's death. Ages 5–9.

Douglas, E. (1990). *Rachel and the Upside Down Heart*. Los Angeles: Price Stern Sloan. This is a true story of 4-year-old Rachel, and how her father's death affects her life. Ages 5–9.

Frost, D. (1991). *DAD! Why'd You Leave Me?* Scottdale, PA: Herald Press. This is a story about 10-year-old Ronnie who can't understand why his dad died. Ages 8–12.

Greenfield, E. (1993). *Nathanial Talking*. New York: Black Butterfly Children's Group. Nathanial, an energetic 9-year-old, helps children and adults understand Nathaniel's world after his mom dies. He uses rap and rhyme to express his feelings. Ages 7–11.

Klein, L. (1995). *The Best Gift for Mom*. Mahwah, NJ: Paulist Press. This story is about a boy and his feelings for his dad, who had died when the boy was a baby. Ages 7–12.

Krementz, J. (1996). *How it Feels When a Parent Dies*. New York: Knopf Publishing Co. Eighteen children (ages 7–16) speak openly about their feelings and experiences after the death of a parent.

Lanton, S. (1991). *Daddy's Chair*. Rockville, MD: Kar-Ben Copies. Michael's dad died. The book follows the shivah, the Jewish week of mourning, when Michael doesn't want anyone to sit in Daddy's chair. Ages 5–10.

LeShan, E. (1975). *Learning to Say Goodbye When a Parent Dies*. New York, NY: Macmillan. Written directly to children about problems to be recognized and overcome when a parent dies. Ages 8 and up.

Lowden, S. (1993). *Emily's Sadhappy Season*. Omaha, NE: Centering Corporation. The story of a young girl's feelings after her father dies. Ages 6–10.

Powell, E. S. (1990). *Geranium Morning*. Minneapolis, MN: Carol Rhoda Books. A boy's dad is killed in a car accident and a girl's mom is dying. The children share their feelings. Ages 6 and up.

Robinson, A. (1994). *Sophie*. New York: Voyager Books. Sophie's grandfather dies and she feels very alone. Ages 3–7.

Thaut, P. (1991). *Spike and Ben*. Deerfield Beach: FL: Health Communications. The story of a boy whose friend's mom dies and how he helps. Ages 5–8.

Tiffault, B. (1992). *A Quilt for Elizabeth*. Omaha, NE: Centering Corporation. Elizabeth's grandmother helps her understand her feelings after her father dies. This is a good story to initiate an open dialogue with children. Ages 7 and up.

Vigna, J. (1991). *Saying Goodbye to Daddy*. Niles, IL: Albert Whitman and Company. A sensitive story about a dad's death and the healing that takes place in the weeks that follow. Ages 5–8.

Whelan, G. (1998). *Forgive the River, Forgive the Sky*. Grand Rapids, MI: Eerdmans Books. Twelve-year-old Lilly struggles with her dad's death in the river. Ages 9–13.

ON SIBLING DEATH

Alexander, S. (1983). *Nadia the Willful*. New York: Pantheon Books. Nadia's older brother dies, and she helps her father heal his grief by willfully talking about her brother. Ages 6–10.

Erling, J., & Erling, S. (1986). *Our Baby Died. Why?* Maple Plain, MN: Pregnancy and Infant Loss Center. A little boy shares his feelings about the death of his stillborn brother and eventual birth of sibling twins. Children can read, draw, and color with this book. Ages 4–10.

Gryte, M. (1991). *No New Baby*. Omaha, NE: Centering Corporation. Siblings express their feelings about their mom's miscarriage. Ages 5–8.

Johnson, J., & Johnson M. (1982). *Where's Jess?* Omaha, NE: Centering Corporation. This book for young children addresses the questions and feelings kids have when a sibling dies. Ages 4–7.

Linn, E. (1982). *Children Are Not Paperdolls*. Springfield, IL: Human Services Press. Kids who have had brothers and sisters die draw and comment on their experiences. Ages 8–12.

Richter, E. (1986). *Losing Someone You Love: When A Brother or Sister Dies*. New York: Putnam. Adolescents share feelings and experiences about the death of a sibling. Ages 11 and up.

Romond. J. (1989). *Children Facing Grief*. St. Meinrad, IN: Abbey Press. Letters from bereaved brothers and sisters are presented in this book, telling of children's experiences and offering hope. Ages 6–14.

Sims, A. (1986). *Am I Still A Sister?* Slidell, LA: Big A and Company. This story was written by an eleven-year-old who experienced her baby brother's death. Ages 8–12.

Temes, R. (1992). *The Empty Place*. Far Hills, NJ: Small Horizons. The story of a third-grade boy whose older sister dies. Ages 5–9.

ON A FRIEND'S DEATH

Blackburn, L. (1987). *Timothy Duck*. Omaha, NE: Centering Corporation. Timothy Duck's friend John gets sick and dies. He shares his feelings. Ages 5–8.

Blackburn, L. (1991). *The Class in Room 44*. Omaha, NE: Centering Corporation. The children in Room 44 share their feelings of grief when their classmate Tony dies. Ages 6–10.

Cohen, J. (1987). *I Had A Friend Named Peter*. New York: William Morrow. Betsy's friend Peter dies suddenly. She learns through parents and teachers that Peter's memory can live on. Ages 5–10.

Gootman, M. (1994). *When a Friend Dies*. Minneapolis, MN: Free Spirit Press. This is a book about grieving and healing when a friend dies. For teens.

Kaldhol, M., & Wenche, O. (1987). *Goodbye Rune*. New York: Kane-Miller. This story is about the drowning death of a girl's best friend and how parents can help. Ages 5–12.

Kubler-Ross, E. (1987). *Remember the Secret*. Berkeley, CA: Celestial Arts. This is the imaginative story of love and faith of two children, and their experience with death. Ages 5–10.

Park, B. (1995). *Mike Harte Was Here*. New York: Random House. Mike Harte dies in an accident when he wasn't wearing his bike helmet. His friends grieve. Ages 10–14.

ON THE DEATH OF A GRANDPARENT

Fassler, J. (1983). *My Grandpa Died Today.* Springfield, IL: Human Sciences Press. David did not fear death as much because Grandpa knew that David would have the courage to live. Ages preschool to 7.

Holden, L. D. (1989). *Gran-Gran's Best Trick.* New York: Magination Press. This book deals directly with cancer. It follows the treatment, sickness, and death of a grandparent. Ages 6–12.

Liss-Levinson, N. (1995). *When a Grandparent Dies.* Woodstock, VT: Jewish Lights Publishing. This is a children's memory workbook dealing with shivah and the year beyond. Ages 8–12.

Pomerantz, B. (1983). *Bubby, Me, and Memories.* New York: Union of American Hebrew Congregations. A child's grandmother dies. His feelings are addressed and his questions answered. Good source to explain Jewish rituals. Ages 5–8.

Thomas, J. (1988). *Saying Goodbye to Grandma.* New York: Clarion Books. A sensitively written book about a family's joining together for grandma's funeral. Ages 5–10.

Thornton, T. (1987). *Grandpa's Chair.* Portland, OR: Mulnomah Press. This story tells of a small boy's love for his grandfather, his last visit to see him, and his grandfather's eventual death. Ages 4–8.

Yolen, J. (1994). *Grandad Bill's Song.* New York: Philomel Books. A little boy asks "What do you do on the day your grandfather dies?" and family and friends talk about memories. Then he discovers his own feelings. Ages 5–9.

ON PET DEATH

Heegaard, M. (2001). *Saying Goodbye to Your Pet.* Minneapolis, MN. Fairview Press. This workbook allows children a safe space to work through feelings after the death of a pet.

ON CREMATION

Carney, K. (1997). *Our Special Garden: Understanding Cremation.* (Barklay and Eve Series, Book 4). Wethersfield, CT: Dragonfly Publishing. This book is an excellent resource to explain cremation to young children. Ages 3–7.

Flynn, J. (1994). *What is Cremation?* Louisville, KY: Accord Aftercare Services. This book helps young children understand cremation. Ages 3–7.

ON FUNERALS AND MEMORIAL SERVICES

Ancona, G. (1993). *Pablo Remembers*. New York: Lothrop, Lee & Shepard Books. This beautifully illustrated book explains the Mexican festival of the Day of the Dead, which celebrates the life of loved ones each year. Ages 6–11.

Balter, L. (1991). *A Funeral for Whiskers*. Hauppauge, NY: Barron's Educational Series, Inc. Sandy's cat dies, and she finds useful ways to express her feelings and commemorate. Ages 5–9.

Carney, K. (1997). *Barklay and Eve: Sitting Shiva* (Barklay and Eve, Book 3). Wethersfield, CT: Dragonfly Publishing. This book explains the Jewish ritual of sitting shivah after a funeral. Ages 3–7.

Carson, J. (1992). *You Hold Me and I'll Hold You*. New York: Orchard Books. This is a soft story for young children about a little girl's feelings of wanting to hold and be held at a memorial service. Ages 5–9.

Grollman, E., & Johnson, J. (2001). *A Child's Book about Funerals and Cemeteries*. Omaha, NE: Centering Corporation. This is a helpful, interactive guide for children to understand and express feelings about cemeteries and funerals. Ages 4–9.

Johnson, J., & Johnson M. (1990). *Tell Me, Papa*. Omaha, NE: Centering Corporation. This book simply and clearly explains how kids feel about death, burial, and funerals. Ages 6–10.

Jukes, M. (1993). *I'll See You In My Dreams*. New York: Knopf. A little girl prepares to visit a seriously ill uncle and imagines writing a farewell message across the sky. Ages 5–10.

Kloeppel, D. (1981). *Sam's Grandma*. College Park, GA: Darlene Kloeppel. A 7-year-old boy tells the story of his grandma's death and subsequent funeral. Kids can color in this book. Ages 4–8.

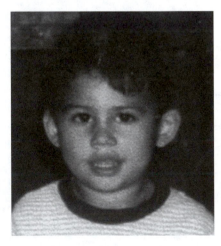

Techner, D., & Hirt-Manheimer, J. (1993). *A Candle for Grandpa: A Guide to the Jewish Funeral for Children and Parents*. New York: UAHC Press. This simply written book for children explains a Jewish funeral and burial practices. Ages 7–12.

WORKBOOKS ABOUT DEATH

Boulden, J., and Boulden, J. (1991). *Saying Goodbye.* Santa Rosa, CA: Boulden Publishing. A bereavement workbook for young children. Ages 5–8.

Carney, K. (1997). *Together, We'll Get Through This! Learning to Cope with Loss and Transition.* Wethersfield, CT: Dragonfly. This is an excellent resource for young children on death. Ages 3–7.

Haasl, B., & Marnocha, J. (2000). *Bereavement Support Group Program for Children.* 2nd Ed. Muncie, IN: Accelerated Development. This step-by-step children's workbook and leader's manual offers practical steps to facilitate children's bereavement groups. Ages 8–13.

Hammond, J. (1980). *When My Mommy Died* or *When My Daddy Died.* Flint, MI: Cranbrook Publishing. Both workbooks are geared to young children's bereavement work and parent death. Ages 4–8.

Heegaard, M. (1988). *When Someone Very Special Dies.* Minneapolis, MN: Woodland Press. This excellent workbook allows expression for children's grief. Ages 5–12.

O'Toole, D. (1995). *Facing Change.* Burnsville, NC: Compassion Books. This is an excellent resource for pre-teens and teens. Ages 11 and up.

Rogers, F. (1991). *So Much To Think About.* Pittsburgh, PA: Family Communications, Inc. This is an activity book for young children when someone they love has died. Ages 5–8.

Traisman, E. S. (1992). *Fire in My Heart; Ice in My Veins.* Omaha, NE: Centering Corporation. This is a wonderful workbook for teenagers to explore grief memories.

ON LIFE CYCLES AND SPIRITUALITY FOR TEENS

Buscaglia, L. (1982). *The Fall of Freddie the Leaf.* Thorofare, NJ: Charles B. Slack Company. This story of the changing seasons presented as a metaphor for children of life and death. Ages 4–8.

Gerstein, M. (1987). *The Mountains of Tibet.* New York: Harper and Row. This story tells of a woodcutter's journey from the mountains of Tibet through the universe of endless choices and back home again to provide a basic understanding of reincarnation. Ages 7 and up.

Glowatsky, P. (2003). *The Light of Stars*. Summerville, SC. Coastal Publishing. This beautifully illustrated book tells the story of life and death and the cycle of life. Ages 5–10.

Mellonie, B., & Ingpen, R. (1983*). Lifetimes: The Beautiful Way to Explain Death to Children.* New York: Bantam Books. This book explains the ongoing life cycle of plants, animals, and people. Ages 3–10.

Munsch, R. (1983). *Love You Forever.* Willowdale, Ontario, Canada: A Firefly Book. This beautiful book for adults and children tells about the continuance of love throughout life. All ages.

ON DEPRESSED PARENTS

Hamilton, D. (1995). *Sad Days, Glad Days*. Morton Grove, IL: Albert Whitman & Co. This story tells how a child feels living with a parent suffering from depression. Ages 6–11.

Sanford, D. (1993). *It Won't Last Forever*. Sisters, OR: Questar Publishers. This is the story of Kristen, a little girl who worries over her mom's ongoing sadness, explaining depression to children. Ages 6–10.

ON SUICIDE

Cammarata, D. (2000). *Someone I Love Died By Suicide.* Palm Beach Gardens, FL: Grief Guidance, Inc. This is a story for child survivors and those who care for them. Ages 5–9.

Garland, S. (1994). *I Never Knew Your Name*. New York: Ticknor & Fields. A young boy tells the story of a teenage boy's suicide, whose name he did not know. Ages 5–11.

Goldman, L. ((1998). *Bart Speaks Out on Suicide*. This is an interactive storybook for children on suicide. It serves as a memory book for their person who died and also gives words for the way the person died. Ages 5–10.

Grollman, E., & Malikow, M. (1999). *Living When a Young Friend Commits Suicide.* Boston: Beacon Press. This book discusses why people may die of suicide, and how we can talk about it. Teens and young adults.

Harper, J. (1993). *Hurting Yourself*. Omaha, NE: Centering Corporation. This is a pamphlet for teenagers and young adults who have intentionally injured themselves. For teenagers.

Kuklin, S. (1994). *After a Suicide: Young People Speak Up*. New York: G.P. Putnam's Sons. This book addresses young people who are survivors after a parent suicide. For teens.

McDaniel, L. (1992). *When Happily Ever After Ends*. New York: Bantam Books. Shannon is a teen who struggles with living with her father's violent death by suicide.

Nelson, R., & Galas, J. (1994). *The Power to Prevent Suicide*. Minneapolis, MN: Free Spirit Publishing. This book is useful in involving teenagers with suicide prevention. It provides practical suggestions and examples with which teenagers can identify.

Norton, Y. (1993). *Dear Uncle Dave*. Hanover, NH: Shirley Baldwin Waring. This story is written by a fourth-grade girl sharing memories about Uncle Dave and his death by suicide. Ages 5–10.

Rubel. B. (1999). *But I Didn't Say Goodbye*. Kendall Park, NJ: Griefwork Center, Inc. This is a practical approach for parents and professionals to help children discuss suicide. Ages 9–13.

ON VIOLENCE AND MURDER

Aub, K. (1995). *Children Are Survivors Too*. Boca Raton, FL: Grief Education Enterprises. This book presents many stories by young children to teenagers on their journey as homicide survivors. Ages 6 through teens.

Cohen, J, (1994). *Why Did It Happen?* New York: Morrow Junior Books. This is a story about a boy who witnesses a violent crime in his neighborhood. The author provides ways to cope. Ages 6–11.

Dougy Center. (2001). *After a Murder: A Workbook for Grieving Children*. Portland, OR: The Dougy Center. This is an interactive workbook for children experiencing a murder and the many issues that surround it. Ages 8–12.

Henry-Jenkins, W. (1999). *Hard Work Journal*. Omaha, NE: Centering Corporation. This is a book for teenagers and young adults to help them understand and overcome homicidal loss and grief.

Loftis, C. (1997). *The Boy Who Sat by the Window*. Far Hills, NJ: New Horizon Press. This is an excellent book for young children about a boy who gets murdered and the cycle of violence that surrounds him. Ages 6–12.

Lorbiecki, M. (1996). *Just One Flick of the Finger*. New York: Dial Books. This is the story of a young boy who brings a gun to school and accidentally shoots a friend. Ages 5–10.

Mahon, K.L. (1992). *Just One Tear*. New York: Lothrop, Lee, and Shepard. This book is an honest account written by a 14-year-old of the overwhelming emotions after a boy witnesses his father being shot and fatally wounded. It includes accounts of the trial and its outcome. Ages 8–14.

Schleifer, J. (1998). *When Someone You Know Has Been Killed*. New York: Rosen Publishing Group. This book discusses the emotions felt when someone experiences a murder and strategies to cope. Ages 10 to teens.

Schulson, R. (1997). *Guns*. Morton Grove, IL. Albert Whitman & Company. This is a story for young children that presents the facts they need to know about guns.

ON BULLYING

Boatwright, B., Mathis, T., & Smith, S. (1998). *Getting Equipped to Stop Bullying: A Kid's Survival Kit for Understanding and Coping with Violence in the Schools*. Minneapolis, MN: Educational Media Corporation. This book provides understandings of the dynamics of bullying and empowers children to recognize and deal with bullies. Ages 10 and up.

Bosch, C. (1988). *Bully on the Bus*. Seattle, WA: Parenting Press. The book allows readers to make the choice about how they would resolve a bullying situation. Ages 8–12.

Cohen-Posey, K. (1995). *How to Handle Bullies, Teasers and Other Meanies*. Highland City, FL: Rainbow Books. This resource helps children with complex issues of bullying. Ages 8–13.

Johnston, M. (1996). *Dealing with Bullying*. New York: Rosen Publishers. A book that defines bullying, explains why bullies act as they so, and ways to change. Ages 4–8.

McCain, R. (2001). *Nobody Knew What to Do*. Morton Grove, IL. Albert Whitman & Co. This is a true story about bullying with meaningful drawings that stresses the power of onlookers. Ages 4–8.

Romain, T. (1997). *Bullies are a Pain in the Brain*. Minneapolis, MN: Free Spirit Publishing. This practical guide helps children cope with bullying problems. Ages 7–11.

Romain, T. (1998). *Cliques, Phonies, and Other Baloney*. Minneapolis, MN: Free Spirit Publishing. This is a story for middle school children that deals directly with issues involving cliques and insincerity. Ages 10 and up.

ON WAR

Bunting, E. (1990). *The Wall*. New York: Clarion Books. These Illustrations and stories are about a father and son who visit the Vietnam Veterans Memorial and the impact of three generations of war. Ages 5–8.

Coerr, E. (1993). *Sadako and the Thousand Paper Cranes*. New York: Putnam. This is a true story about a Japanese girl who is dying from her exposure to radiation from the bomb at Hiroshima. Her hope for peace and life is symbolized in her paper cranes. Ages 8–13.

Corder, B., & Haizlip, T. (1990). *Feelings About War*. Chapel Hill, NC: University of North Carolina School of Medicine. This is a coloring book for young children that addresses questions and concerns they may have about war. Ages 5–10.

Hilbrecht, K., & Hilbrecht, S. (2002). *My Daddy Is a Soldier*. New Canaan, CT: New Canaan Publishing Co. This story for young children speaks to the many losses children face when their parent is a part of the military. Ages 4–7.

ON 9/11

Kalman, M. (2002). *Fireboat: The Heroic Adventures of the John J. Harvey*. New York: G. P. Putnam. This is the story of a large fireboat that was not needed after 1995 until 9/11. Then it was called upon to battle roaring fires and became a hero. Ages 5–10.

Poffenberger, N. (2001). *September 11th, 2001*. Cincinnati, OH: Lotspeich School. This book was made by children to share their experience of 9/11. Ages 5–8.

Roth, S. (2001). *It's Still a Dog's New York*. Washington, DC: National Geographic. This is a story of two dogs after 9/11, expressing their feelings and recognizing the heroics that took place and the hope of rebuilding and going on. Ages 5–10.

ON THE HOLOCAUST

Finkelstein, N. (1985). *Remember Not to Forget*. New York: Mulberry Book. This book clearly describes for young children the history and origins of the Holocaust in Nazi Germany. Ages 6–10.

Levine, K. (2003). *Hana's Suitcase*. This is a touching story about Hana, a young girl, her empty suitcase and those that try to trace her life from it. She was taken to a Nazi concentration camp when she was a young girl. Ages 10 and up.

ON DRUGS

Sanford, D. (1987). *I Can Say No*. Portland, OR: Multnomah Press. David's story is about his feelings concerning his older brother's involvement with drugs. Ages 6–10.

Taylor, C. (1992). *The House That Crack Built*. San Francisco, CA: Chronicle Books. This is a poetic story for young children that explores today's drug problems. Ages 7–12.

Vigna, J. (1990). *My Big Sister Takes Drugs*. Morton Gove, IL: Albert Whitman & Co. This is a story about a young sister who tells about her sister taking drugs in order to help her. Ages 5–9.

ON MEDIA INPUT

Gellman, M., & Hartman, T. (2002). *Bad Stuff in the News: A Guide to Handling the Headlines*. New York: SeaStar Books. This book offers advice for young people in handling headlines about timely issues such as terrorism, drugs, violent crime, disasters, and more. Ages 12 and up.

ON PREJUDICE

Heegaurd, M. (2003). *Drawing Together to Accept & Respect Differences*. Minneapolis, MN: Fairview Press. This workbook helps children to communicate and learn to respect one another. Ages 6–12.

Simon, N. (1976). *Why Am I Different?* Morton Grove, IL: Albert Whitman & Co. This is a book that emphasizes the special and unique qualities of each person and explores differences. Ages 5–9.

Thomas, P. (2003). *The Skin I'm In*. New York: Barron. This is a first look at racial discrimination for very young children. Ages 4–7.

ON WEIGHT DISORDERS AND EATING PROBLEMS

Berry, J. (1990). *About Weight Problems and Eating Disorders*. Chicago, IL: Children's Press. This is an informative book that explains the realities of eating disorders and weight problems. Ages 7–13.

ON FOSTER HOMES AND ABANDONMENT

Lowery, L. (1995). *Somebody Somewhere Knows My Name*. Minneapolis, MN: Carolrhoda Books. Grace describes what happened when she and her brother are abandoned by their mom.

Nasta, P. (1991). *Aaron Goes to the Shelter*. Tucson, AZ: Whole Child. This story and workbook are about children who have experienced family chaos and may be placed in a shelter or foster care. Ages 6–12.

Sanford, D. (1993). *For Your Own Good*. Sisters, OR: Questar Publishers. This book is for children involved with foster care and ways that caregivers can help them. Ages 6–10.

Simon, N. *I Wish I Had my Father*. Morton Grove, IL: Albert Whitman & Co. A boy tells his feelings about a dad who left a long time ago and never communicates. Ages 6–10.

Wilgocki, J., & Wright, M. (2002). *Maybe Days*. Washington, DC: Magination Press. This is a story for children in the foster care system that speaks to their experience and ways they can cope. Ages 4–8.

ON HOMELESSNESS

Kroll, V. (1995). *Shelter Folks*. Grand Rapids, MI: Eerdmans. Nine-year-old Joelle tells about her life in a shelter. Ages 6–10.

Powell, S. (1992). *A Chance to Grow*. Minneapolis, MN: Carolrhoda Books. Joe, his mom, and his sister Gracey are evicted from their apartment. They are left homeless and live on the streets and in shelters, seeking a permanent home. Ages 6–11.

Trottier, M. (1997). *A Safe Place*. Morton Grove, IL: Albert Whitman & Co. Emily and her mother come to a shelter to escape her father's abuse. Ages 5–9.

ON SEXUAL ABUSE

Girard, L. (1984). *My Body Is Private*. Morton Grove, IL: Albert Whitman and Co. This book presents a direct approach to help children distinguish between good touching and bad touching, including help for parents. Ages 5–10.

Heegaurd, M. (2004). *When Adults Hurt Children*. Minneapolis: MN. Fairview Press. This is an excellent resource to help children when an adult hurts them. Ages 5–10.

Lowery, L. (1994). *Laurie Tells*. Minneaplois, MN: Carolrhoda Books. Twelve-year-old Laura tells a supportive aunt that her father is sexually abusing her. Ages 10–14.

Russell, P., & Stone, S. (1986). *Do You Have a Secret?* Minneapolis, MN: CompCare Publishers. This book helps adults talk to children about sexual abuse and explains how they can seek help. Ages 4–8.

Sanford, D. (1986). *I Can't Talk About It*. Portland, OR: Multinomah Press. Annie talks to an abstract form, Love, about her sexual abuse and begins to heal and trust. Ages 8–13.

Sanford, D. (1993). *Something Must be Wrong with Me*. Portland. OR: Multinomah Press. This is the story of Dino, a boy who is sexually abused. He finds the courage to talk about it. Ages 7–12.

ON SEXUAL ISSUES

Marcus, E. (2000). *What If Someone I Knew Was Gay?* New York: Penguin Putnam Readers. This is a book that addresses questions about gay and lesbian people. Ages 12 and up.

Newman, L. (2000). *Heather Has Two Mommies*. 10th Ed. Los Angeles, CA: Alyson Pub. This book addresses the issue of families with two moms and gives a voice to lesbian issues for young children. Ages 5–10.

Willhoite, M. (1990). *Daddy's Roommate*. Los Angeles, CA: Alyson Pub. This book provides words to use to explain a gay relationship to young children. Ages 5–8.

ON VIOLENCE IN THE HOME

Bernstein, S. (1991). *A Family That Fights.* Morton Grove, IL: Albert Whitman & Co. This is a story about a family's domestic violence and ways children and adults can get help. Ages 5–9.

Davis, D. (1984). *Something Is Wrong In My House.* Seattle, WA: Parenting Press. This book is about parents fighting, ways to cope, and how to break the cycle. Ages 8–12.

Hochban, T,. & Krykorka, V. (1994). *Hear My Roar: A Story of Family Violence.* New York: Annick Press Ltd. This book is the story of Lungin, a boy bear whose dad is violently abusive. He and his mom choose to take action and go to a shelter as a first step. Ages 7–12.

Paris, S. (1986). *Mommy and Daddy are Fighting.* Seattle, WA: Seals Press. This is an honest discussion of parental fighting, with a guide for parents. Ages 5–8.

Sanford, D. (1989). *Lisa's Parents Fight.* Portland, OR: Multnomah. This a story of 10-year-old Lisa, her siblings, and parents who interact with angry outbursts and occasional physical abuse. Ages 8–12.

Winston-Hiller, R. (1986). *Some Secrets Are for Sharing.* Denver, CO: MAC Publishing. This is a story of a family secret about a boy being beaten by his mom. He finally tells and gets help for him and his mom. Ages 6–11.

ON GANGS

Myers, W. D. (1994). *Bad Boy.* New York: Harper Tempest. This is a story about a boy who lives in a foster care situation and becomes involved with gangs and drugs. He finally graduates school, joins the army, and then begins to write books for children. Ages 11 and up.

Williams, S. (1996a). *Gangs and Self-Esteem.* New York: PowerKids Press. The author, "Tookie," a founder of the Crips in Los Angeles, talks about the benefits of not joining a gang. Ages 7–11.

Williams, S. (1996b). *Gangs and the Abuse of Power.* New York: PowerKids Press. The author, "Tookie," a founder of the Crips in Los Angeles, explains to kids the way gangs members abuse the power they have to hurt others and eventually hurt themselves. Ages 7–11.

Williams, S. (1996c). *Gangs and Your Friends*. New York: PowerKids Press. The author, "Tookie," a founder of the Crips in Los Angeles, introduces kids to the way gangs operate focusing on the powerful influence of "bad" friends. Ages 7–11.

Williams, S. (1996d). *Gangs and Violence*. New York: PowerKids Press. The author, "Tookie," a founder of the Crips in Los Angeles, tells kids to the dangers of belonging to a gang. Ages 7–11.

Williams, S. (1998). *Life In Prison*. New York: Seastar. Te author wwries true stories about prison life and encourages children to make better choices than the author did when he was young. Ages middles school and up.

ON IMMIGRATION

Fassler, D., & Danforth K. (1993). *Coming To America: The Kid's Book about Immigration*. New York: Waterfront Books. This book presents an excellent discussion of the many issues, questions, and concerns of immigrant children coming to America. Ages 5–10.

ON MOVING

Blume, J. (1986). *Are You There God? It's Me Margaret*. New York: Dell Publishing. Margaret has to face moving and a new life. Ages 9–12.

McKend, H. (1988). *Moving Gives Me a Stomachache*. Ontario, Canada: Black Moss Press. This is a story of a child's anxiety and fear of moving. Ages 5–8.

Viorst, J. (1998). *Alexander, Who's Not (Do you hear me? I mean it!) Going to Move*. New York: Aladdin Paperbacks. This story is about Alexander's overwhelming feelings on moving. Ages 4–10.

ON DIVORCE

Boulden, J., & Boulden J. (1991). *Let's Talk*. Santa Rosa, CA: Boulden Publishing. This is a kid's activity book for separation and divorce. Ages 5–8.

Evans, M.D. (1989). *This is Me and My Single Parent*. New York: Magination Press. This is a discovery workbook for children and single parents. Ages 8–13.

Fassler, D., Lash, M., & Ives, S. (1988). *Changing Families*. Burlington, VT: Waterfront Books. This book offers advice for kids in coping with divorce and remarriage. Ages 4–12.

Heegaard, M. (1990). *When Mom and Dad Separate*. Minneapolis, MN: Woodland Press. This workbook for children explores thoughts and feelings about separation and divorce. Ages 6–12.

Krementz, J. (1988). *How it Feels When Parents Divorce*. New York: Knoph. Many children describe how divorce has affected them. Ages 8–13.

Sanford D. (1985). *Please Come Home*. Portland, OR: Multnomah Press. Jenny's thoughts and feelings are expressed to her teddy bear about her parents divorce. Ages 7–12.

Stern, E. S. (1997). *Divorce is Not the End of the World*. Singapore, China: Tricycle Press. A teenage brother and sister discuss topics related to divorce. Teens.

Swan-Jackson, A. (1997). *When Your Parents Split Up . . .* New York: Price Stern Sloan, Inc. This book focuses on various aspects of divorce and provides practical advice. Teens.

ON NATURAL DISASTER

American Red Cross. (1993). *Disaster Preparedness*.Washington, DC: FEMA. This is a coloring book for young children to prepare them for a disaster. Ages 4–7.

Harrington, H. (2001). *The Disaster Twins*. FEMA. This story talks about what to do during a disaster and how to plan for one. Ages 5–10.

Jordon, M. (1993) *The Weather Kids*. Omaha, NE: Centering Corporation. Stories in this book tell about kids who have experienced devastation through tornadoes, earthquakes, and floods. Ages 8–11.

Williams, V. (1992). *A Chair for My Mother*. New York: Mulberry Books. After a fire destroys their home, Rosa, her mom, and grandmother save their money for a big chair to share. Ages 5–10.

ON MAGICAL THINKING

Blackburn, L. (1991). *I Know I Made It Happen*. Omaha, NE: Centering Corporation. This book presents different circumstances where children find themselves feeling guilty and responsible for making things happen. Ages 5–8.

Hazen, B. (1992). *Even If I Did Something Awful*. New York: Aladdin Books. The reassuring story of a little girl who realizes Mom will love her no matter what she does. Ages 5–8.

Rappaport, D. (1995). *The New King*. New York: Penguin Books. A boy becomes king after his father dies and commands his court to bring his father back from the dead. Ages 6–11.

ON FEELINGS

Crary, E. (1992). *I'm Mad*. Seattle, WA: Parenting Press. This children's book is part of a series that identifies feelings and gives options on how to work with them. Ages 3–8.

Crary, E., & Steelsmith, S. (1996). *When You're Mad and You Know It*. Singapore: Parenting Press. This book helps young children learn to identify and express feelings. Ages 2–5.

Doleski, T. (1983). *The Hurt*. Mahwah, NJ: Paulest Press. The wonderful story about a little boy who keeps all of his hurts inside, until the hurt grows so big it fills his room. When he shares his feelings, the hurt begins to go away. All ages.

Freymann, S., & Elfers, J. (1999). *How Are You Feeling?* New York: Arthur A. Levine Books. This book for young children uses wonderful illustrations of fruits and vegetables to illustrate feelings in a most delightful way. Ages 4–8.

Munsch, R., & Martchenko, M. (1985). *Thomas's Snowsuit*. Ontario, Canada: Annick Press Ltd. In this story a child refuses to wear his snowsuit and will not be manipulated by adults. Ages 5–8.

Oram, H. (1982). *Angry Arthur*. New York: E.P. Dutton. Arthur becomes enraged with his mom and creates havoc on the planet. Ages 5–8.

Sanford, D. (1986). *Don't Look at Me*. Portland, OR: Multnomah Press. This is a story of Patrick who feels very stupid and learns to feel special about him. Ages 7–11.

Simon, N. (1989). *I Am Not a Crybaby*. New York: Puffin Books. This book shows how children of different races and cultures share the commonality of feelings. Ages 5–8.

Steig, W. (1988). *Spinky Sulks*. Singapore: Sunburst Books. Spinky is angry and begins to sulk. No one can make him stop until he is ready. Ages 5–8.

Viorst, J. (1972). *Alexander and the Terrible Horrible No Good Very Bad Day*. New York: Aladdin Books. Alexander has a day where everything goes wrong. Everyone can relate to this. Ages 5 and up.

Viorst, J. (1981). *If I Were in Charge of the World and Other Worries.* New York: Alladdin Books. This book of poems for children shares kids feelings about different issues. Ages 5 and up.

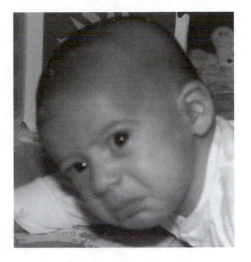

ON PERFECTIONISM

Adderholdt, M. & Goldberg, J. (1999). *Perfectionism: What's Bad About Being Too Good?* Minneapolis, MN: Free Spirit Press. This book for high achieving students explains the differences between perfectionism and a healthy pursuit of excellence. Ages 12 and up.

ON STRESS

Moser, A. (1988). *Don't Pop Your Cork on Monday.* Kansas City, MO: Landmark Editions. This handbook for children explores the causes of stress and techniques to deal with it. Ages 5–8.

Moser, A. (1991). *Don't Feed the Monster on Tuesday.* Kansas City, MO: Landmark Editions. Dr. Moser offers children information on the importance of knowing their own self-worth and ways to improve self-esteem. Ages 5–8.

ON NIGHTMARES

Devlin, W., & Devlin H. (1994). *Maggie Has A Nightmare.* New York: Macmillan Publishing Company. Maggie's daytime fears appear in her dreams. Sharing them helped her fears disappear. Ages 4–7.

Lobby, T. (1990). *Jessica and the Wolf.* New York: Magination Press. Jessica's parents help her solve the problem of her recurring nightmare. Ages 4–8.

Marcus, I., & Marcus P. (1990). *Scary Night Visitors.* New York: Magination Press. Davey has fears at night and learns to feel safe through experiencing his feelings directly. Ages 4–7.

McGuire, L. (1994). *Nightmares in the Mist.* Palo Alto, CA: Enchante Publishing. Alicia has many fears since her mom went into the hospital. Magical paint helps her overcome them. Ages 5–9.

ON FAMILY

Cart, M. (Ed.). (2003). *Necessary Noise*. New York: Joanna Cotler Books. This is a compilation of stories that speak of many situations in today's families including a sibling's overdose, life with two mothers, and a dad visiting his son on death row. Ages 10 and up.

ON RESILIENCE

Morrison, T. (1999). *The Big Box*. New York: Hyperion Books for Children. This is a story about children put in a box by adults and their strong desire to gain personal freedom. Ages 5–10.

Seuss, Dr. (1990). *Oh, the Places You'll Go*. New York: Random House. Dr. Seuss uses his magical creativity to inspire young and old to succeed in life, despite the many ups and downs they face. Ages 5 and up.

Stepanek, M. (2001a). *Heartsongs*. Alexandria, VA: VSP Books. This is a compilation of poems written by a young boy expressing hope and optimism for the future. Ages 6 and up.

Stepanek, M. (2001b). *Journey Through Heartsongs*. Alexandria, VA: VSP Books. Another volume of Mattie's poems stressing peace and faith in mankind. Ages 6 and up.

ON SERVICE

Jampolsky, G., & Cirincione, D. (1991). *"Me First" and the Gimme Gimmes*. Deerfield Beach, FL: Health Communication, Inc. This story shows the transformation of selfishness into love. All ages.

Lewis, B. (1995). *The Kid's Guide to Service Projects*. Minneapolsi, MN:Free Spirit Publishing. This book provides over 500 service ideas for young people who want to make a difference. Ages 10 and up.

Silverstein, S. (1964). *The Giving Tree*. New York: HarperCollins. This is a sensitive story for children about the gift of giving and getting love in return.

ON AFFIRMATIONS AND MEDITATIONS

Garth, M. (1991). *Starbright*. New York: HarperCollins Publisher. This is a book of meditations for children, with simple visualizations to help create peaceful images. Ages 7–12.

Payne, L. (1994). *Just Because I Am*. Minneapolis, MN: Free Spirit Press. This is a children's book of affirmations and positive self-talk.

ON EMPOWERMENT

Aboff, M. (1996). *Uncle Willy Tickles: A Child's Right to Say NO*. 2nd Ed. Washington, D.C.: Magination Press. This book creates words to use for children to feel they have the right own their body and say "no" to what doesn't feel good. Ages 5–9.

Browne, A. (1985). *Willy the Champ*. New York: Knopf.. The story of Willy, a mild-mannered hero who stands up to a bully and shows he is a champion. Ages 5–10.

Heegaard, M. (2001). *Drawing Together to Develop Self-Control*. Minneapolis: MN. Fairview Press. This is a useful tool to help children develop self-control and achievement. Ages 5–10.

Kaufman, G., & Raphael, L. (1990). *Stick Up for Yourself*. Minneapolis: MN Free Spirit Publishing. This guide for children helps them develop techniques to feel personal power and self-esteem in many life situations. Ages 8–12.

Lalli, J. (1997). *I Like Being Me*. New York: Free Spirit Publishing. This is a series of poems for children about feeling special. Ages 5–10.

O'Neal. (2003). *When Bad Things Happen: A Guide to Help Kids Cope*. St. Meinrad, IN: Abbey Place. This storybook shares about a traumatic event and ways that children can live with it and grow.
Ages 5–9.

ON HOPE AND OPTIMISM

Agee, J. (1985). *Ludlow Laughs*. Toronto: A Sunburst Book. Ludlow, a boy who never smiles, learns how laughter can be life changing. Ages 5–10.

Lewis, B. (1992). *Kids with Courage*. Minneapolis, MN. Free Spirit Publishing. This book contains a series of stories about young people making a difference by taking a stand. Ages 11 and up.

Piper, W. (1954). *The Little Engine That Could*. New York: Platt & Munk. This story provides children an insight into the value of positive thinking and perseverance. Ages 5–10.

Seuss, Dr. (1990). *Oh, the Places You'll Go!* New York: Random House. Dr. Suess encourages all of us to find the successes that lie within us. Ages 5 and up.

Waber, B. (2002). *Courage*. New York: Houghton Mifflin. This is a beautiful book for young children that describes the levels of courage that take place every day. Ages 4–8.

ON PEACE

Thomas, S. (1998). *Somewhere Today: A Book of Peace*. Morton Grove: IL. Albert Whitman. This book shares beautiful words and illustrations that help children see they can make a difference in the world to create peace. Ages 5 and up.

Wood, D. (1992). *Old Turtle*. Duluth, MN: Pfeifer-Hamilton. This fable for children and adults captures the message of peace on earth and oneness with nature. The illustrations are beautiful. Ages 5 and up.

References

Arce, R. (March 8, 2001). Study: Kids rate bullying and teasing as 'big problem' :http//www.cnn.com/2001/us/03/08/violence.survey/index.html.

APA. (2004)Fostering resilience in response to terrorism: For psychologists working with children/fact sheet and appendix A.www://apa.org/psychologist/pdfs/children/pdf.

Arizona Attorney General Website for Teens. Gangs. *Hot Topics, Kids 9–12*. Teens. http://www.ag.state.az.us/ChildrensPage/gangs.html.

Auger, R., Seymour, J., & Roberts, W. (2004). Responding to terror: The impact of September 11 on K–12 schools and schools' responses. *American School Counseling Association* 7(4): 222–230.

Brown.T. (1993). *Broken Toy*. A Thomas Brown Film. Zanesville, Ohio: Summerhill Productions.

Burrell, J. (2004). Bay area teens cultivate their global citizenship. *The Times*. 1 and A23.

Celotta, B., Jacobs, G., & Keys, S. (1987). Searching for suicidal precursors in the elementary school child. *American Mental Health Counselors Association Journal,* January, 38–47.

Dickinson, A. (2001, March 19). To Tattle vs. to Tell. *Time Magazine* 82.

Doka, K. (1996). *Living with grief after sudden loss*. New York: Taylor & Francis.

Doka, K. J. (2000). *Living with grief: Children, adolescents and loss*. Washington, D.C.: The Hospice Foundation of America.

Doka, K., & Licht, M. L. (Ed.) (2003). Foreward J. Gordon. *Living with grief: Coping with public tragedy*. Washington. D.C. Hospice Foundation of America.

Fassler, D., & Danforth K. (1993). *Coming to America: The kid's book about immigration*. New York: Waterfront Books.

Fein, R., et al. (May, 2002). Threat assessment in schools: A guide to managing threatening situations and to creating safe school climates, Washington, DC: US Secret Service and US Department of Education, 1–99. http://www.treas.gov/usss/ntaac/ssi_guide.pdf.

Fox, S. (1988). *Good grief: Helping groups of children when a friend dies*. Boston, MA: The New England Association for the Education of Young Children.

Frankl, V. (1984). *Man's search for meaning*. Boston: Washington Square Press.

Fried, S, & Fried, P. (1996). *Bullies and victims*. NY: Evans and Co.

Gaensbauer, T. (1996). Developmental and therapeutic aspects of treating infants and toddlers who have witnessed violence. *Zero to Three* 16(5): 96.

Garrity, C., Jens, K., Porter, W., Sager, N., & Short-Camilli, C. (2000). *Bully proofing your school: A comprehensive approach for elementary schools* 2nd ed. Longmont, CO: Sopris West.

Ginsberg, H., & Opper, S. (1969). *Piaget's theory of intellectual development*. Englewood, NJ: Prentice Hall.

Goldman, L. (1998, October). How to make yourself bully-proof. *Current Health Magazine*, 22(2).

Goldman, L. (2000). *Life and loss: A guide to help grieving children*. New York: Taylor & Francis.

Goldman, L. (2001). *Breaking the silence: A guide to help children with complicated grief*. New York: Taylor & Francis.

Goldman, L. (2002). Terrorism, trauma, and children: What can we do? *Healing Magazine* 7, 10–13.

Goldstein, S., & R. Brooks. (2002). *Raising resilient children: A curriculum to foster strength, hope, and optimism in children*. Harvard Medical School, Boston MA: Paul. H. Brookes Publishing Co.

Goodman, S. (2001). No bullies allowed. *The Herald*. 1L, 6L.

Greenwald & Rubin (1999). Assessment of posttraumatic symptoms in children: Development and preliminary validation of parent and child scales. *Research on Social Work Practice* 9:61–75.

Hamblen, J. PTSD in children and adolescents. National Center for PTSD. Retrieved August 10, 2002 from http://www.ncptsd.org/facts/specific/fs_children.html.

Hockstader, L. (January 12, 2004). War shadows school near Fort Hood. *The Washington Post*.

Hogan, N., & Graham, M., (Winter, 2001). Helping children cope with disaster. *Focus on Pre-K & K A Quarterly Newsletter for the Education Community*, 14(2): 1–8.

Hunter, S., Boyle, J., & Warden, D. (2004). Help seeking amongst child and adolescent victims of peer-aggression and bullying: The influence of school-stage, gender, victimization, appraisal, and emotion. *British Journal of Educational Psychology*.

In The Mix, Show #445.(2001) *9-11 Looking Back . . .Moving Forward*. NY: Castleworks Inc.

James, H. (2001). Our children are particularly vulnerable at this time. *Monitor on Psychology APA* 32: 64.

Janoff-Bulman, R. (1992). *Shattered assumptions: Towards a new psychology of trauma*. New York: The Free Press 175.

Johnson Institute. (1999). *No-bullying program*. Johnson Institute, 17.

Johnson, K. (1998). Trauma in the lives of children. Alameda, CA: Hunter House.

Kastenbaum, R. (1972, December 23). The kingdom where nobody dies. *The Saturday Review of Literature* 33–38.

Kaufman, J. (2002). *Loss of the assumptive world: A theory of traumatic loss*. New York: Taylor & Francis.

Kelly, J. & Rivera, E. (2003, November 3). A challenging question of remote control. *Washington Post*, B1 & B7.

LaGreca, M., Silverman, W.K., & Wasserman, S.B. (1998). Children's disaster functioning as a predictor of posttraumatic stress following hurricane Andrew. *Journal of Consulting and Clinical Psycholog,* 66: 883–892.

Lefevre, G. (Dec. 4, 2000) CNN.com.U.S.News/ Death row inmate nominated for Nobel peace prize. http://archives.CNN.com/2000/US/12/O2/death.row.nobel/.

Lutzke, J. R. et al. (1997). "Risk and interventions for the parentally bereaved child." In N. Sandler and S. Wolchik (Eds.), *Handbook of Children's Coping: Linking theory and intervention*. New York: Plenum Press, 214–242.

Maine Project against Bullying (2000). Brave enough to be kind. Lincoln.midwest. com%ewps/againstbullying.html (Edited 2004).

Masten, A.S. (2001). Ordinary magic: Resilience processes in development. *American Psychologist 56*: 227–238.

McLellan, W. & Peplar, D. (October 22, 2000). "Expert on bullying tells how it can be stopped." *The Province News*, A12.

Mishara, B. (1999). Conceptions of death and suicide in children ages 6–12 and their implications for suicide prevention. *Suicide and Life-Threatening Behavior*, 29: 105–118.

Moyers, B. (1995). *What can we do about violence? Solutions for children, Part 4*. Princeton, NJ: Films For the Humanities & Sciences.

Mundy, L. (November 16, 2003). Do you know where your children are? *The Washington Post Magazine* 12–16.

National Association of Mental Health (NASP). Memorials/activities/rituals/ following traumatic events. Retrieved August 10, 2002, from http://www.nasponline.org/ NEAT/memorials-general.html.

Neuman-Carlson, D. & Horne, A. (2004). Bully Busters: A psychoeducational intervention for reducing bully behavior in middle school. *Journal of Counseling and Development*. 82: 259–267.

Noppe, I.C. et al. (April, 2004). A Qualititative Study: adolescents' and teachers' experiences with September 11th. *Paper to be presented to the 27th Annual Conference of the Association for Death Education and Counseling*, Pittsburgh, PA.

Olweus, D. (2000). *Bullying at school*. Oxford, UK: Blackwell Publishing.

Peplar, D. (October 22, 2000). "Expert on bullying tells how it can be stopped." *The Province News*, A22.

Pfefferbaum, B. et al. (2001). Television exposure after a terrorist event. *Psychiatry*, 64: 202–211.

Rak, C.F., & Patterson, L.E. (1996). Promoting resilience in at-risk children. *Journal of Counseling and Development*, 74(4): 368–373.

Reddy, M., Borum, R., Berglund, J., Vossekuil, B., Fein, R., & Modzeleski, W. (2001). Evaluating risk for targeted violence in schools: Comparing risk assessment, threat assessment, and other approaches. *Psychology in the Schools*, 38(2): 1–16.

Rigby, K., & Slee, P. (1999). Suicidal ideation among adolescent school children, involvement in bully-victim problems, and perceived social support. *Suicide and Life Threatening Behaviors*, 29 (2): 119–130.

Rogers, F., & Bluestone Sharapan, H. Helping parents, teachers and caregivers deal with concerns about violence in the news. Retrieved September 18, 2001, from http://pbskids.org/rogers/paretns/sept11.htm.

Rogers, F., & Head, B. (1983). *Mr. Rogers talks with parents*. Pittsburgh: Family Communications, 256.

Rosenfeld, L. (2001). Children's responses to terrorism, *NASW Online*, 1–9. Retrieved December 17, 2001, from http://www.naswdc.org/terror/rosenfield.htm.

Sawyer, D. (March 8, 2001). Fatal Attraction. Prime Time Thursday. (Original air date 05/21/99).

Seith, R. Teens and War. CWK. http://www.connectingwithkids.com/tipsheet/2003/117 mar 26/war.html.

Shen, F. (April 10, 2003). Watching, Waiting, Wondering. *KidsPost*. *Washington Post*, C15.

Shen, F. (July 24, 2004). Just teasing. Sometimes the kidding goes too far. *KidsPost*. *Washington Post*, C14.

Sheppard, C. (1998). *Brave Bart*. Grosse Pointe Woods, MI: TLC.

Silverman, P., Nickman, S., & Worden, J.W. (1992). Detachment revisited: The child's reconstruction of a dead parent. *American Journal of Orthopsychiatry*, 62, 494–503.

Simon H., Boyle, J., & Warden, D. (in press, 2004). Help seeking amongst child and adolescent victims of peer-aggression and bullying: The influence of school-stage, gender, victimization, appraisal, and emotion. *British Journal of Educational Psychology*.

Sloan, C. (2002) *Bury the Dead*. Washington, DC: National Geographic.

Snyder, C. R. (1995). Conceptualizing, measuring, and nurturing hope. "Current Trends" Focus Article in *Journal of Counseling and Development*, 73: 355–360.

Steele, W., & Raider, M. (2001). *Structured sensory intervention for traumatized children, adolescents and parents*. New York: Edward Mellon.

Steele, W. (2002). Trauma's impact on learning and behavior: A case for interventions in schools. Trauma and Loss: Research and Interventions. *TLC Journal*, 2(2): 35–57.

Stepp, L.S. (June 19, 2001). A lesson in cruelty: Anti-gay slurs common at school. *The Washington Post*, A1 and A7.

Stepp, L.S. (November 2, 2001). Children's worries take new shape. *The Washington Post*, C1.

Stevenson, R. (1994) *What will we do?* (1994). New York: Baywood Publishers.

Svoboda, E. (March/April, 2004). Everybody loves a bully. *Psychology Today*, 20.

Thormachien, D, & Bass-Feld, E. (1994, April). Children: The secondary victims of domestic violence. *Maryland Medical Journal*, 43(4): 355–359.

U.S. Secret Service. (2002). Preventing school shootings: A summary of U.S. Secret Service Safety School Initiative. *National Institute for Justice (NIJ) Journal*, 248: 10–15.

Vedantam, S. (2004, April 18). Antidepressant use in children soars despite efficacy doubts. *The Washington Post*, 1 and 10.

Wallis, C. (Ed.) (2003, April 4). Life for the Troops, *Time for Kids: News Scoop Edition*, 8(22): 1–2.

Walls, S. L. (2004). Bullying and Sexual Harassment in Schools, Committee for Children, 1. http://www.cfchildren.org/PUbully.shtml.

Wall Street Journal, NBC News. Washington Wire (1998, April 24).

Webb, N.B. (Ed.) (2002). *Helping bereaved children: A handbook for practitioners* (2nd Ed). New York: Guilford Press.

Williams, S. (1996). *Gangs and the abuse of power*. NY: PowerKids Press. 22.

Williams, S. (2001). *My letter to incarcerated youth*, no. 1. Tookie's Corner. http://www.tookie.com/abouttc.html.

Worden, J. W. (1991). *Grief counseling & grief therapy: A handbook for the mental health practitioner*. New York: Springer.

Zimmerman, C. (April, 1998). *Weekly Reader Survey*. Stamford, CT: Weekly Reader.

About the Author

Linda Goldman is certified in thanatology, death, dying, and bereavement (CT), with an MS degree in counseling and master's equivalency in early childhood education. Linda is a Licensed Clinical Professional Counselor (LCPC) and a National Board Certified Counselor (NBCC). She worked as a teacher and counselor in the Baltimore County School System for almost twenty years. Currently she has a private grief therapy practice in Chevy Chase, Maryland. She works with children, teenagers, families with prenatal loss, and grieving adults. Linda shares workshops, courses, and trainings on children and grief and teaches as an adjunct member on the faculty of the graduate program of counseling at Johns Hopkins University. She has also taught on the faculty at the University of Maryland School of Social Work/advanced certification program for children and adolescents, and she has lectured at many other universities including Pennsylvania State University, University of North Carolina, and The National Changhua University of Education in Taiwan, as well as numerous school systems throughout the country. She has shared many of her articles, translated into Chinese, with the Suicide Prevention Program of Beijing.

Linda has worked as a consultant for the National Head Start Program, National Geographic, and was a panelist in the national teleconference, *When A Parent Dies: How to Help the Child.* She has appeared on the Diane Rehms show to discuss children and grief. She was named by the *Washingtonian Magazine* as one of the top therapists in the MD, VA, DC area (1998) and again named by *Washingtonian Magazine* as a therapist to go to after the terrorist attacks in 2001. She has served on the board of The Association for Death Education and Counseling (ADEC) and is presently on the advisory board of Suicide Prevention Education Awareness for Kids (SPEAK), the advisory board of RAINBOWS, and the advisory board of TAPS (The Tragedy Assistance Program for Survivors) as their children's bereavement advisor. Linda is the recipient of the ADEC Clinical Practice Award for 2003.

Linda Goldman is the author of *Life and Loss: a Guide to Help Grieving Children* (First edition, 1994/Second edition 2000), Taylor & Francis Publishers. Her second book is *Breaking the Silence: A Guide to Help Children With Complicated Grief* (First edition, 1996/Second edition 2002), published by Brunner-Rutledge. Her other books include *Bart Speaks Out: An Interactive Storybook for Young Children On Suicide* (1998), a Phi Delta Kappan International fastback, *Helping the Grieving Child in the School* (2000), a Chinese edition of *Breaking the Silence: A Guide to Help Children With Complicated Grief* (2001), and the Japanese edition of *Life and Loss: A Guide to Help Grieving Children* (in press 2003). The Chinese translation of *Children Also Grieve* is in press for 2004. Linda also created a CD-ROM, *A Look at Children's Grief* (2001), published by ADEC, The Association for Death Education and Counseling. Her op/ed "Cut Out Guns, Bullying" appeared in the *Baltimore Sun*, March 2001.

Linda contributed in many ways after the attacks of September 11. She authored the chapter about children, "Talking to Children about Terrorism" in *Living With Grief: Coping With Public Tragedy*, published by the Hospice Foundation of America (2003). She contributed an article to the *Journal for Mental Health Counseling* in their special issue on grief, "Grief Counseling With Children in Contemporary Society" (2004). She was a strong part of the TAPS (Tragedy Assistance Program for Survivors) response team at the Pentagon Family Assistance Center, conducted a workshop about children and grief at the 2002 TAPS National Military Survivor Seminar, and authored an article, "Helping Children With Grief and Trauma" for the fall 2002 and spring 2003 *TAPS Journal*.

Index

A

Acceptance of child's reactions, 34–36, 249
Adolescent Social Action Program (ASAP), 282
Adult involvement, bullying and, 55–56
Adult modeling, bullying and, 51–52
Adults as models, 243
Advocacy, 262–263
Advocates for Children and Youth, Inc., 279
Aesop, 50
"After Disaster at World Trade Center," poem, 173
Age, responses related with, 19–21
Aggressive acts, as sign of trauma, 94
"All on This Beautiful Day," poem, 197
American Academy of Child and Adolescent Psychiatry, 89
American Association for Protecting Children, 279
American Association of Suicidology, 284
American flag, display of, 143
American Psychological Association, 90
American Red Cross, 280
American School Counselor Association, 280
American Trauma Society, 282
Anger, 17
Anger contract, with bullying, 72
Anorexia, 59
Anthrax, child's definition of, 31
Anticipatory grief, 37–38
Anxiety
    providing expressive vehicle, 206
    as sign of trauma, 94
Appreciation, offers of, 261
Appreciation of self, 247–248
Artifacts, after terrorism, archiving of, 234–236
Asking children questions, 36–37
Association for Care of Children's Health, 279
Association for Death Education and Counseling (ADEC), 278
At-risk children
    identifying, 209–210

B

Balloon release, as symbolic action, 225
Baton Rouge Crisis Intervention Center, 278
Befriending victim of bullying, 71
Big Brothers Big Sisters of America, 281
Biological warfare, child's definition of, 31
Black Elk, 181
Bomb, child's definition of, 31
Book services, 289
Boys, bullying by, 59
Brainstorming, ways to stay safe, 99
Bravery, class discussions on, 197–198
Bullying, 49–86, 88–89, 109
    adult guidelines, 67–77
    adult involvement, 55–56, 64
    adult modeling, 51–52
    adult strategies, 82–83
    anger contract, 72
    befriending victim, 71
    behaviors of, 66–67
    channels of communication, 79
    control, 54
    curricula, 83
    curricula for educators, 85
    defense of classmates from, 77
    defined, 65–66
    democratic values, modeling, 69
    dialogue about, 78
    documentation, 68
    essays, composition of, 80
    exclusion, 61
    family violence, 52
    gender, 66
    gender and, 59

girls, 57–62, 59
giving guidelines, 71
group play, creation of, 80
groups, children's increased effectiveness in, 77
guidelines, creation of, 68
harassment as, 69
harassment by group, 60
helping bully, strategies for, 71–75
humor, 60
interventions, 70, 71, 77–81
intimidation, 58, 67
inventory, 81
inventory of, 80–81
jokes, 59
journal about, 58–62
kids helping themselves, 76–77
letter writing, 79
listening, 68
myths of, 73–75
onlooker, power of, emphasizing, 70–71
onlookers's voices, 63–64
onlooker strategies, 70–71
physical aggression, 67
popularity, 55
power, 54
power of bully, identification of, 72
prevention program in school, 77
racial taunting, 59
relationship to terrorism, 51
reporting, 76
research on, 83
resources, 83, 84–85
    for adults, 85
    for students, 84–85
ridicule, 59
role plays, creation of, 78
rumors, 60
in schools, 56–57
school support, 56
    classroom interventions, 56
    individual-level interventions, 56
    school wide interventions, 56
secretive act, 66
self-examination for signs of, 76
sexual harassment, 60
sharing experiences of, 78–79
social alienation, 67
story writing, 80
taking action against, 54–56

teaching positive conflict resolution, 69–70
telling, tattling, distinguished, 77, 82–83
unresolved grief, 51–54
verbal aggression, 67
verbal attacks, 58
victim's feelings, identification of, 72
victims' voices, 62
violence policies for schools, 69
voices of bullys, 63
ways to help children with, 64–66
"Butterflies," poem, 204

C

Camp, grief support, 219–220
Center for Grief and Loss for Children, 285
Channels of communication, with bullying, 79
Child Abuse Hotline, 286
Children's Bereavement Center, 285
Children's Defense Fund, 280, 282
Children's Hospice International, 278
Children's voices, 41–45
    middle school children, 42–44
    teenagers, 44–45
    young children, 41
Child Welfare League of America, 280
Choice, importance of, 244
Class meeting surrounding trauma, model for, 97–102
Collage, 138
Comfort, 249
    parents providing, 177
Community action, 215–238
    artifacts, after terrorism, archiving of, 234–236
    balloon release, 225
    children's outreach, 219
    family community outreach, 229–230
    grief support camp, 219–220
    letters, 225–228
    memory activities, 222–223
    mentors, honor guards as, 220–221
    military, tragedy assistance program for, 219–230
    outreach program, 217–218
    participation in world events, 231–234
    peer mentors, 221–222
    resources, 237
    umbrella project, 223–225
Community rituals, impact on youth, 232
Community support, 259–260

Compassionate Friends, Inc., 278
Complex events, talking to children about, 27–28
Concerns of Police Survivors (COPS), 283
Concrete operations stage, children's understanding of death, 7
Conflict, as part of evolution, 163
Conflict resolution, teaching, 69–70
Contagious disease, 29–30. *See also* SARS
Counseling sessions, daily, 192
Courage, 245
COVE: A support Program for Grieving Children and Families, 285
Creative writing, for trauma resolution, 137
Creativity, 251–252
Crime Victims Litigation Project, 283
Criminal, child's definition of, 31
Crisis lines, 286
Culture, influence of, 54
Cultures of past, studying, 163

D

Daily events, re-triggering of trauma through, 40–41
"The Daily Gift," poem, 248
Dalai Lama, 4
Death, children's developmental understanding of, 6–8
  concrete operations stage, 7
  logic stage, 8
  pre-operational stage, 6–7
Deceased, children's connection with, 9
Defense of classmates from bullying, 77
Definitions, children, about traumatic events, 31–32
Democratic values, modeling, 69
Deployment, 156–158
  school changes, 157
  school system accommodation of, 156–158
  student reactions, 157
D'Esopo Resource Center, 285
Development, child's definition of, 31
Developmental understanding of death, children's, 6–8
  concrete operations stage, 7
  logic stage, 8
  pre-operational stage, 6–7
Dialoging about everyday risks, 46
Dialogue, preparing children for, 34–36
Dialogue about bullying, 78

The Diary of Anne Frank, 264
Disaster information, overloading with, 206
Distorted perceptions, trauma and, 17
Doctors Without Borders USA, Inc., 280
Documentation of bullying, 68
Dougy Center, 285
Drawing
  about school violence, 100–102
  telling stories through, for trauma resolution, 120
  for trauma resolution, 129–131
Dream work, for trauma resolution, 124–125

E

Early intervention, research, 22–23
Education for Social Responsibility, 281
Egocentricity, 6
Einstein, Albert, 150
Emergency, telephone numbers, 202
Emergency planning, 140, 202, 207–208
Empathy, 259
  modeling, 261
Empowerment, 162
Encouragement, 261
Essays about bullying, composition of, 80
Everyday risks, dialoging about, 46
Exclusion, as bullying, 61
Expression of feelings, 33–34

F

Factual information, determination of, 193–194
"Fallen Towers-Risen Powers," poem, 144
Family activities, 172–173
Family collage, 138
Family community outreach, 229–230
Family disaster plan, 181–182
Family pets, 140
Family violence, bullying and, 52
Fear box, 142
Fears, 12–13
  providing expressive vehicle, 206
  repetitive, with trauma, 131–135
Federal Emergency Management Agency (FEMA), 280
Federation of Families for Children's Mental Health, 281
Feelings
  expression of, 33–34
  sharing of, 192–193
Fernside, A Center for Grieving Children, 285

"The Fire of Love Is Burning," poem, 197
Flag, display of, 143
Flexibility, 263
    importance of, 206
Food, comfort from, parents providing, 177
Ford, Henry, 181
Frank, Anne, 240
Frankl, Victor, 264
Friends, role of, school violence and, 88–89
Fundraising, 143, 199–201

G

Gandhi, Mahatma, 87, 159
Gangmember's story, 107–108
Gang Resistance Education and Training
    (GREAT), 282, 283
Gangs, 104–110
    children's books, 107
    joining, 105–107
    power of, 105–106
    resources on, 112
    signs of membership, 106
General Hotline for Teens with any Kind of
    Problem, 286
Generational family role models, 265–266
Girls, bullying and, 57–62
Good Grief Program, 278
Grief. *See also* Greiving
    anticipatory, 37–38
    children's, nature of, 8–10
    deceased, children's connection with, 9
    defined, 5–6
    magical thinking, 10
    process, factors, 14
    responses, overriding, 17
    signs of, in children, 11–12
    tasks of, 10
    unresolved, bullying and, 51–54
Grief Recovery Hotline, 286
Grief support camp, 219–220
Grief support groups, guides for, 304–306
Griefwork Center, Inc., 278
Grieving classmates, children helping, 160–161
    peer groups, 162–163
    peer mentors, 161–162
Group
    children's increased effectiveness in, 77
    physical harassment, as bullying, 60
Guest speakers, 268
Guidance group, with school violence, 103

Guilt
    creation of, 17
    survivor, 125
Guns in school, 88–89, 92, 95–103, 108–109. *See also* Shootings in school

H

Harassment policies for schools, 69. *See also* Bullying
Healthy choices, encouraging children to make, 206
Hidden rage, within schools, 88–89
Home as safe places for expression of feelings, 174
Homeland, child's definition of, 31
Homework assignments, emergency planning, 202
Honor, discussions on, 197–198
Hope for Grieving Heart, 278
Hospice Education Institute, 278
Hospice Foundation of America, 278
Hotlines, 286
Hugs, by parents, importance of, 177
Human development, effect of witnessing trauma, 94–95
Humor, 246
    in bullying, 60
    sense of, in parental environment, 176–177
Hypervigilance, as sign of trauma, 94

I

Identifying at-risk children, 209–210
Images, impact of, 192
Immigrant children, parenting of, 185
Information appropriateness, developmental level of child and, 206
Insightfulness, 257–259
Institute for Advancement of Service, 278
Institute for Prevention of Youth Violence, 283
Integrity, child's definition of, 31
Interagency on Child Abuse and Neglect (ICAN), 281
Internet resources, 287–289
Intervention research, 22–23
Intimidation, in bullying, 58, 67
Intrusive thoughts, as sign of trauma, 94
Inventory of bullying behavior, 80–81

J

Janoff-Bulman, Ronnie, 26

Jason Foundation, 284
Jokes, as bullying, 59
Journal about bullying, 58–62
"Julia," poem, 193

K

Kid's Place, 285
Kinder-Mourn, 285
King, Martin Luther, Jr., 181

L

Lamb, Matt, 223
Letter writing
    with bullying, 79
    for trauma resolution, 136
Lincoln, Abraham, 159
The Little Engine That Could, 264
Logic stage, children's understanding of death, 8

M

Magazine for kids, 152
Magical thinking, 10
Man's Search for Meaning, 264–265
Media
    monitoring of, 46–47, 178–179
    re-triggering of trauma through, 39–40
Membership in gang, signs of, 106
Memorializing, impact on youth, 232
Memorials
    creation of, 143
    projects, 204–205
Memory boxes, for trauma resolution, 126–127
Memory work, 195
    for trauma resolution, 125
Mentor: National Mentoring Partnership, 282
Mentors
    parents as, 184
    peer, 161–162
Military, tragedy assistance program for,
        219–230. *See also* Deployment; War
    balloon release, 225
    children's outreach, 219
    family community outreach, 229–230
    grief support camp, 219–220
    letters, 225–228
    memory activities, 222–223
    mentors, honor guards as, 220–221
    peer mentors, 221–222
    umbrella project, 223–225

Minnesota Coalition for Death Education and
        Support, 279
Misconceptions, clarification of, 206
Modeling, by parents, 177–178
Models, promoting, 261–266
Money, raising for victims of tragedy, 199
Monitoring media, 46–47, 178–179
Moody, Roy, 159
Mothers Against Drunk Driving, 283
Mother Theresa, 159
Music, for trauma resolution, 124–125
"My Hero" contest, 269
Myths of bullying, 73–75

N

National Alliance for Safe Schools, 281
National Center for Missing & Exploited
        Children, 286
National Coalition Against Domestic Violence,
        286
National Domestic Violence Hotline, 286
National Education Association, 281
National Family Resiliency Center, Inc. (NFRC),
        282
National Hospice Organization, 279
National Mental Health Association, 279
National Mental Health Association Crisis Line,
        286
National Military Survivor Seminar, TAPS
        Good Grief Camp, 223–230
National Runaway and Suicide Hotline, 286
National School Safety Center, 281
National Sheriff's Association Victim Program,
        283
National Victim Center, 283
National Victim's Resource Center, 283
Nature of trauma, overview, 13
New England Center for Loss and Transition,
        279
Newman's Own Awards for Military
        Community Excellence, 224
Newspapers, kids' sections, 233
Nightly prayer, for world peace, 143
Nightmares, creation of, 17
Normalizing feelings, 137
NOVA (National Organization for Victim
        Assistance), 283
Nuclear bomb, child's definition of, 31
Nuclear war, child's definition of, 31

O

Obsessive thoughts, as sign of trauma, 94
Office for Victims of Crime, 283
Office of National Preparedness in Federal
    Emergency Management Agency,
    208
Older children, vulnerability of, 19–20
Onlookers to bullying, 63–64, 70–71
Operation Runaway, 285
Opportunities to become responsible, support-
    ing, 263–264
Optimism, 245, 256
Order, sense of, parents establishing, 171–172
Outreach program, 217–218

P

Paine, Thomas, 159
Panic, controlling, 206
Parental care, for child surviving trauma,
    168–188
    comfort, 177
    daily risks, discussion of, 179–180
    family activities, 172–173
    family disaster plan, 181–182
    feelings, expression of, safe places for, 174
    food, 177
    foundation, providing, 171
    hugs, 177
    humor, 176–177
    immigrant children, 185
    mentors, parents as, 184
    modeling, practicing of, 177–178
    outreach, 187
    patriotism, 183
    resources, 188
        for adults, 188
        for children, 188
    safe places for feeling, 174
    sense of order, establishing, 171–172
    solutions, involving children in, 185–186
    teachable moments, creation of, 180–181
    television monitoring, 178–179
    values, reinforcement of, 175–176
Parent Encouragement Center (PEP), 281
Parent involvement with trauma, 194–195
Parent modeling, 257
Parents Anonymous, 281, 286
Past cultures, studying, 163
Past experience, learning from, 263
Patriotism, 183

child's definition of, 31
    displaying, 157
Peace, prayer for, 143
Peaceful box, 138
    construction of, 141
"Peacemaker of Century" contest, 231
Peacemakers' Clubs, 57
Peacock Foundation, 285
Peer mentors, 161–162
Perceptions, distortion of, with trauma, 17
Perseverance, 256–257
Pets, 140
Physical aggression, in bullying, 67
Physical proximity to disaster, vulnerability and,
    18
Play about bullying, creation of, by group, 80
Poetry, for trauma resolution, 137
Popularity, bullying and, 55
Positive conflict resolution, teaching, 69–70
Poster contest, 198–199
Posttraumatic play
    projective play, difference between, 123
    for trauma resolution, 123
Posttraumatic stress, symptoms of, 210
Power, bullying and, 54
Power of bully, identification of, 72
Prayer for world peace, 143
Predictors of vulnerability, 18
Prejudice, discussions on, 197–198
Pre-operational stage, children's understanding
    of death, 6–7
Productive action, processing life through,
    249–251
Projective play, for trauma resolution, 121–123
Projective techniques for anger management,
    81–92
Psychological proximity to disaster, vulnerabil-
    ity and, 18–19
Puppets, use of, for trauma resolution, 124–125

Q

Quilts, made by children in appreciation, 236

R

Racial taunting, as bullying, 59
Raising money, for victims of tragedy, 199
Random acts of violence, 95–103
Random violence, 25–48
Realistic goals, 245–246
Reassuring children, 45–46

Repetitive thoughts, with trauma, 131–135
Reporting of bullying, 76
Rescue workers, letter to, 198
Resilience in children, 239–274
    acceptance, 249
    activities to promote, 266–269
    adults as models, 243
    advocacy, 262–263
    appreciation, offer of, 261
    appreciation of self, 247–248
    choice, 244
    comfort, 249
    community support, 259–260
    courage, 245
    creativity, 251–252
    dialogue, creation of, 266
    empathy, 259
        modeling, 261
    encouragement, 261
    flexibility, 263
    generational family role models, 265–266
    guest speakers, 269
    humor, 246
    insightfulness, 257–259
    keys to, 243–255
    models promoting, 261–266
    "My Hero" contest, 269
    opportunities to become responsible, sup-
        porting, 263–264
    optimism, 245, 256
    parent modeling, 257
    past experience, learning from, 263
    perseverance, 256–257
    productive action, processing life through,
        249–251
    questionnaire, 268
    realistic goals, 245–246
    resilience awards, 269
    resources, 264–265, 274
    role models, 266
    self-confidence, 246–247
    self-discipline, promotion of, 263
    service/giving to others, 255
    sociability, 259
    social action, 268
    spirituality, 252–254
    survive/thrive chart, 268
    volunteerism, 268
Resilient Youth Program and Curriculum, 282
Resolution of trauma, techniques for, 117–148

activities, 137–144
Retelling of story, for trauma resolution,
    119–137
Re-triggering of trauma, 38–41
    through daily events, 40–41
    through media exposure, 39–40
Revenge, child's definition of, 31
Reviving Ophelia novel, 57
Ridicule, as bullying, 59
Risks, dialoging about, 46
Rituals, impact on youth, 232
Rogers, Fred, 170
Role models, 47, 55, 266
Role plays about bullying, creation of, 78
Roosevelt, Eleanor, 181
Rumors, as bullying, 60

S
Safe Alternatives and Violence Education
    (SAFE), 281
Safe box, 138, 141
Safe Harbor, 286
Safe place, scary place, contrast between, 139
SARS, 25–48
    child's definition of, 31
Save Children, 280
School, bullying prevention program, 77
School book, 203–204
School counselor, consultation with, 206
School involvement with trauma, 189–214
    anxiety, providing expressive vehicle, 206
    at-risk children, 208–210
        identifying, 209–210
    bravery, class discussions on, 197–198
    counseling sessions, daily, 192
    disaster information, overloading with, 206
    emergency planning, 207–208
    facts, determination of, 193–194
    fears, providing expressive vehicle, 206
    feelings, sharing of, 192–193
    flexibility, 206
    fundraising, 199–201
    healthy choices, encouraging children to
        make, 206
    homework assignments, emergency plan-
        ning, 202
    honor, discussions on, 197–198
    images, impact of, 192
    information appropriateness, developmental
        level of child and, 206

involvement of students, 202–203
memorial projects, 204–205
memory work, 195
misconceptions, clarification of, 206
panic, controlling, 206
poster contest, 198–199
prejudice, discussions on, 197–198
resources, 212–213
    for children on terrorism, 212
    for educators, 213
school book, 203–204
school counselor, consultation with, 206
taunting, 206
terrorism, responding to student grief, 191
trauma information, school providing to
        community, 205–208
tributes, 202
uncertainty, acknowledge of, 206
wall of thoughts, 196–197
war, discussions on, 197–198
School response to war, 151–155
Schools, harassment policies for, 69
School support with bullying, 56
    classroom interventions, 56
    individual-level interventions, 56
    school wide interventions, 56
School system, accommodation of deployment,
        156–158
School violence, 86–113
    bullying, 88–89, 109
    friends, role of, 88–89
    gangs
        joining, 105–107
        power of, 105–106
        resources on, 112
        signs of membership, 106
    guidance group, 103
    guns, 92
    rage, hidden, 88–89
    shootings, 88–89, 92, 95–103, 108
    trauma, class meeting surrounding, model
        for, 98–102
Secret Service Safe Schools Initiative Report,
        108
Security, child's definition of, 31
Self, appreciation of, 247–248
Self-confidence, 246–247
Self-destructive behaviors, as sign of trauma, 94
Self-discipline, promotion of, 263
Self-examination for signs of bullying, 76

Sense of order, establishing, 171–172
Separation anxiety, as sign of trauma, 94
September 11. *See* Terrorism
Service/giving to others, 255
Sexual harassment, as bullying, 60
Shared family trauma patterns, 95
Shared memorializing, impact on youth, 232
Sharing experiences of bullying, 78–79
Shootings in school, 88–89, 92, 95–103
        school, 108
Sleep disturbance, as sign of trauma, 94
Sniper attacks, 95, 98–102
        child's definition of, 31
Sociability, 259
Social action, 268
Social alienation, bullying and, 67
Solace Tree, 286
SPEAK (Suicide Prevention Education
        Awareness for Kids), 284
Spirituality, 252–254
Story telling, for trauma resolution, 121,
        127–128
Stress, posttraumatic, symptoms of, 209
Suicidal ideation, as sign of trauma, 95
Suicide, of child, 257
Suicide Awareness/Voice of Education SA/VE,
        284
Suicide Education and Information Center, 284
Survive/thrive chart, 268
Survivor guilt, 125

T
TAPS. *See also* Military, tragedy assistance pro-
        gram for
    Good Grief Camp, 2002 National Military
        Survivor Seminar, 223–230
    Tragedy Assistance Program for Survivors,
        Inc., 282
Tattling, telling, distinguished, 77, 82–83
Taunting, 206
    as bullying, 59
"Tears Flow," poem, 137
Teen Age Grief, Inc., 279
Teenagers, vulnerability of, 20–21
Telephone numbers, emergency, 202
Television monitoring, by parents, 178–179
Telling, tattling, distinguished, 77, 82–83
Telling own story, for trauma resolution, 121,
        127–128
Terror, 17. *See also* Fear

child's definition of, 31
Terrorism, 12–13, 25–48, 126
    children's misconceptions about, 27–28
    child's definition of, 31
    responding to student grief, 191
"Thoughts and Memories," poem, 258
Time for Kids, magazine, 152
"The Tortoise and Hare," 264
Trauma
    children's reactions to, 27
    child's definition of, 32
    class meeting surrounding, model for,
        97–102
    nature of, 13
    reactions to, 17
    re-triggering of, 38–41
        through daily events, 40–41
        through media exposure, 39–40
    school involvement with, 189–214
    signs of, 15–17
    studying, 163
Trauma information, school providing to community, 205–208
Trauma resolution techniques, 117–148
    activities for, 137–144
    boxes, memory, 126–127
    creative writing, 137
    drawing, telling stories through, 120
    drawing pictures, 129–131
    dream work, 124–125
    fears, repetitive, 131–135
    letter writing, 136
    memory work, 125
    music, 124–125
    poetry, 137
    posttraumatic play, 123
    projective play, 121–123
    puppets, 124–125
    repetitive thoughts, 131–135
    resources, 146–147
    retelling of story, activities for, 119–137
    teens, telling stories, 121
    telling story, 127–128
    wishes, 135
Traumatic loss, 14–15
    helplessness with, 15
    hopelessness with, 15
    powerlessness with, 15
Traumatized classmates, children helping children, 160–161

Tribute, writing, 143
Tributes, 202

U
Umbrella project, 223–225
Uncertainty, acknowledge of, 206
UNICEF House, 280
Unresolved grief, bullying and, 51–54
U.S. Secret Service Safe Schools Initiative
        Report, 108
    rage, hidden, 88–89
    shootings, 95–103
    victimization, 89–92

V
Values, reinforcement of, by parents, 175–176
Van Gogh, Vincent, 181
Verbal aggression, as bullying, 58, 67
Verbalizing thoughts, 193
Victims of Crime Resource Center, 283
Violence. *See also under* specific type of violence
    random, 25–48, 95–103
    within school, 86–113
Voices of children, 41–45
    middle school children, 42–44
    teenagers, 44–45
    young children, 41
A Volcano in My Tummy book, 92
Volunteerism, 268
Vulnerability of children, 17–21
    age, responses related with, 19–21
    older children, 19–20
    physical proximity to disaster, 18
    predictors of vulnerability, 18
    previous life circumstances, 21
    psychological proximity to disaster, 18–19
    teenagers, 20–21
    young children, 19

W
Wall of thoughts, 196–197
War, 25–48, 151
    children's voices about, 151–153
    child's definition of, 32
    class discussions, 154–155
    deployment, 156–158
    discussions on, 197–198
    feelings about, 154–155
    as part of evolution, 163
    school response, 151–155

Washington, Booker T., 216
Weapons in school, 88–89, 92, 95–103
    school, 108
*What Can We Do About Violence: Solutions for
    Children,* film, 52
"Why Did This Happen," poem, 44
Williams, Stanley "Tookie," 104
William Wendt Center, 279
Wishes, discussion of, for trauma resolution,
    135
Witnessing trauma
    effect on development, 94–95
World events, children's participation in,
    231–234
World Pastoral Care Center, 279

World War II, studying, 163
Worry list, 141
Writing about school violence, 100–102
Writing bullying story, 80
Writing tribute, 143

Y
Yellow Ribbon Program, 284
Young children, vulnerability of, 19
Youth Suicide National Center, 284

Z
Zero tolerance policy, 55
Zero to Three, 281